The Cost-Benefit Revolution

The Cost-Benefit Revolution

Cass R. Sunstein

The MIT Press
Cambridge, Massachusetts
London, England

This book was set in ITC Stone Sans Std and ITC Stone Serif Std by Toppan Best-set Premedia Limited. Printed and bound in the United States of America.

Library of Congress Cataloging-in-Publication Data

Names: Sunstein, Cass R., author.
Title: The cost-benefit revolution / Cass R. Sunstein.
Description: Cambridge, MA : MIT Press, [2018] | Includes bibliographical
    references and index.
Identifiers: LCCN 2017052759 | ISBN 9780262038140 (hardcover : alk. paper)
Subjects: LCSH: Administrative law--United States--Cost effectiveness. |
    Trade regulation--United States--Cost effectiveness. | Cost
    effectiveness--Political aspects--United States. | Public
    administration--United States--Decision making.
Classification: LCC KF5407 .S86 2018 | DDC 361.60973--dc23 LC record available
    at https://lccn.loc.gov/2017052759

10 9 8 7 6 5 4 3 2 1

I must again repeat, what the assailants of utilitarianism seldom have the justice to acknowledge, that the happiness which forms the utilitarian standard of what is right in conduct, is not the agent's own happiness, but that of all concerned. As between his own happiness and that of others, utilitarianism requires him to be as strictly impartial as a disinterested and benevolent spectator. In the golden rule of Jesus of Nazareth, we read the complete spirit of the ethics of utility. To do as you would be done by, and to love your neighbour as yourself, constitute the ideal perfection of utilitarian morality.

—John Stuart Mill

If there won't be dancing at the revolution, I'm not coming.

—Emma Goldman

Contents

Preface: Against Expressivism

People often have clear intuitions about social problems. Perhaps you are alarmed about pesticides, illegal immigration, unsafe drinking water, highway safety, genetically modified organisms, sugary drinks, terrorism, or climate change. You might favor some measure that will reduce the associated risks.

You may or may not feel strongly. Or perhaps one or more of these issues does not concern you at all, and you are puzzled about why other people are so worried. You might think that they are way off the mark, even nuts.

Arguments about public policy are often *expressive*. People focus on what they see as the underlying values. They use simple cues. They favor initiatives that reflect the values that they embrace or even their conception of their identity. If the issue involves the environment, many people are automatically drawn to aggressive regulation, and many others are automatically opposed to it. When you think about regulation in general, you might ask: What side are you on? That question might incline you to enthusiastic support of, for example, greater controls on banks or polluters—or it might incline you to fierce opposition toward those who seek to strengthen government's hand.

In this light, it is tempting to think that the issues that divide people are fundamentally about values rather than facts. If so, it is no wonder that we have a hard time overcoming those divisions. If people's deepest values are at stake, and if they really differ, then reaching agreement or finding productive solutions will be difficult or perhaps impossible. Skepticism about experts and expertise—about science and economics—is often founded, I suggest, on *expressivism*.

I aim in this book to combat expressive approaches to policy issues. I contend that contrary to appearances, the issues that most divide us are fundamentally about facts rather than values. (Not all the time, of course, but often enough.) In my view, expressive approaches are a great obstacle to progress. Take the question of highway safety. In 2016, nearly forty thousand Americans died in motor vehicle crashes. That number is far too high, and some imaginable approaches would help. If we can agree on the facts, we should be able to agree on what to do—or at least our disagreements should be narrowed greatly.

Climate change is far more sharply contested, of course, but even on that issue, agreement on the facts would help us identify reasonable paths forward. On climate change, people's judgments about the facts may be *motivated* in one way or another; people believe what they want to believe. It is partly for that reason that in the domain of climate change, judgments about the facts might not be based on knowledge. But if we all *knew* that climate change would cause devastation, or that it really would not, then we would find it much easier to agree on how to proceed.

As an alternative to expressive approaches, I will explore and celebrate the cost-benefit revolution, which focuses on actual consequences—on what policies would achieve—and which places a premium on two things: science and economics. Above all, I will suggest that diverse people should be able to enter into an *incompletely theorized agreement* in favor of cost-benefit analysis, in the form of an agreement about what to do and how to proceed, amid uncertainty or disagreement about the deepest theoretical issues.

A Celebration

Cost-benefit analysis asks: What are the bad and good effects of imaginable policies? Will we save one life, ten lives, or one thousand lives? Will we impose costs on consumers? What will those costs be, exactly? Will policies hurt workers and small businesses? If so, precisely how much?

Suppose that an effort to increase safety on the highways is expected to save five hundred lives annually and to cost very little. If so, it's probably a good idea (whatever our theoretical commitments). But if it is expected to save two lives annually and to cost hundreds of millions of dollars, we might not want to go forward with it (whatever our theoretical commitments).

Cost-benefit analysis reflects a firm (and proud) commitment to a *technocratic conception of democracy*. The public is ultimately sovereign, but, for good reasons, technocrats are given a lot of authority—by the public itself. Most citizens know that they do not have the background or the time to answer hard questions about food safety, about air pollution, and about carcinogens in the workplace. Cost-benefit analysis insists that difficult questions of fact should be answered by those who are in a good position to answer them correctly. The reason is that consequences matter, and scientists and economists can help us get a handle on consequences.

These claims raise many questions: Who are those experts? Can we trust them? What about their own ignorance and their own biases? Aren't they vulnerable to powerful interest groups? Don't they seek to expand their own authority? Mightn't they be foolish or ignorant, too?

These are fair questions. For now, let me offer two suggestions. First, the cost-benefit revolution requires regulators to demonstrate a genuine need for government action. They must always identify some kind of market failure, warranting intervention. Second, the cost-benefit revolution has the advantage of forcing officials to ask the right questions in the domains in which it has been on the ascendency, including environmental protection, highway safety, energy policy, occupational safety, obesity, and food safety. Whether or not an analysis of costs and benefits tells us everything we need to know, at least it tells us a great deal that we need to know. We cannot safely proceed without that knowledge.

As we shall see, an understanding of costs and benefits enables us to figure out how to lengthen lives; improve health, security, and education; save money; improve the delivery of essential goods and services; and promote economic growth. Even in the most controversial areas—immigration, national security, climate change, heath care reform—some form of cost-benefit analysis is indispensable to arriving at sensible outcomes.

Consider a question that attracted a great deal of attention in the United States after the election of President Donald Trump: Should the United States build a wall between itself and Mexico? One issue is the cost of building that wall. Another issue is the benefit. We might not be able to obtain full answers to these questions, but how can we make an assessment without asking them? (By the way, we should not build that wall: The benefits do not justify the costs.)

Three Concerns

Celebrations are backward-looking, and we will do plenty of looking back. From 2009 to 2012, I was privileged to serve as Administrator of the Office of Information and Regulatory Affairs, and I will draw on that experience here. One of the advantages of that period of service is that I was able to learn a great deal about what my predecessors had done and hence about the operation of the American regulatory state over a period of decades. I also have had occasional, informal interactions with national regulators since that time, and I will draw on that experience as well.

But it is even more important to look forward. The cost-benefit state is in its early adolescence, and in the next decades it will probably get much better. (I am bracketing the possibility that because of politics, a Republican or Democratic administration might pay less attention to costs and benefits than it should.) Like some kind of chrysalis, it might even be transformed into something else. While celebrating the revolution, I hope also to place a bright spotlight—perhaps uncomfortably bright—on three important concerns.

Distribution

The first concern involves questions of distribution and distributive justice. Suppose that we knew, for a fact, about the effects of occupational safety regulations on every member of society. Suppose that we knew that a particular regulation would reduce the well-being of five million people—mostly consumers, who would have to pay more for certain goods—and do so by two well-being units per person. (I am just making up the idea of well-being units; please bear with me.) Suppose that the regulation would also increase the well-being of one million people—mostly workers, who would be safer—and do so by three well-being units per person.

In terms of overall well-being, the regulation is not a good idea: Society loses well-being on balance. But maybe the consumers start quite well-off, and maybe the workers do not; maybe they are struggling in many ways. If a regulation would hurt those who are doing well and help those who are doing poorly, perhaps it is justified on distributive grounds even if it decreases overall welfare.

Cost-benefit analysis runs into precisely this difficulty whenever the costs are incurred by the well-off and the benefits are enjoyed by those at the bottom. In such cases, there is an argument that a regulation is an excellent idea even if its costs exceed its benefits. The larger question is this: *Don't we always have to know who bears the costs and who obtains the benefits?*

In some cases, that is an important point—but in my view, it is not a fundamental objection to cost-benefit analysis. True, it suggests that the outcome of cost-benefit balancing may not be decisive if those who gain have a strong claim to public support and when those who lose do not—but for now, consider a practical point. In my years as Administrator of the Office of Information and Regulatory Affairs, when about four thousand regulations were under discussion, I saw very few that failed cost-benefit analysis but looked good on distributional grounds. The claim that distributional considerations matter has a great deal of theoretical interest, and I will have a fair bit to say about it—but it is much less significant in practice than one might think.

A qualification: Some regulations are characterized as "transfers." The clearest illustrations are regulations implementing a progressive income tax, which (to simplify) takes money from the wealthiest and gives it to the poorest. Or consider regulations that set payment levels for reimbursing hospitals that provide emergency services to poor people, or the Affordable Care Act's ban on annual or lifetime limits for insurance payments. Such regulations are not subject to the cost-benefit framework at all. They are not designed to maximize net benefits. They do not even have significant social costs or benefits. They are analyzed as transfers. They take from some people and give to others, and that is that. Transfers are not my topic here, though I shall have something to say about the relationship between cost-benefit analysis and distributional concerns.

Welfare

The second concern is, I think, more fundamental. It involves *the possible disconnect between the focus on welfare and the focus on costs and benefits*. Welfare, understood as well-being, is what most matters, and the claim for use of cost-benefit analysis is that it helps focus us on what matters. But if we care about welfare, cost-benefit analysis sometimes leads us in the wrong directions. If we have a reliable welfare meter, we should use it. We should not use cost-benefit analysis.

Unfortunately, none of us has a welfare meter. If officials make the air a bit cleaner or reduce the risks of highway accidents, they lack tools to measure, directly, the effects on human welfare. That's a problem. A signal advantage of cost-benefit analysis is that we can actually engage in it. For over three decades, many questions have been resolved with the help of monetary figures, capturing the anticipated effects of reforms. Those figures are a proxy for welfare. Proxies are helpful, but they can produce serious errors.

Let's look at a real-world example. If the government requires all motor vehicles to come with rearview cameras, to reduce the risk of accidents, the monetized costs might well exceed the monetized benefits. The US government so concluded. It is also possible, however, that the regulation is a terrific idea on welfare grounds. As we shall see in chapter 4, the US government so concluded. (My new car, a Toyota RAV4, has a rearview camera, perhaps because regulators required it. I did not particularly want it, but I love it. I had no idea that it would be so useful.) Another example: Whenever a regulation causes job losses, it produces significant adverse effects on people's welfare. Cost-benefit analysis does not now consider those effects, and some people believe that it should not. If they are right, so much the worse for cost-benefit analysis. Those losses matter.

The good news is that even if we lack a welfare meter, we are learning more, every day, about the welfare effects of regulations and reforms. Behavioral research in psychology and economics is telling us a great deal. A welfare revolution would be even better than a cost-benefit revolution, and the latter is best understood as a way of moving us toward the former. I shall offer some suggestions about how those who endorse cost-benefit balancing can incorporate what we are learning about welfare. On this count, a great deal of progress should be expected in the next generation.

Knowledge

The third concern, to which I will devote considerable attention, involves what is sometimes called *the knowledge problem*, which means an absence of necessary information. It can be extremely difficult for anyone, including the most well-motivated and the most expert, to catalog the costs and benefits of many imaginable policies. Try, if you would, to specify and monetize the benefits of improving security at airports; reducing exposure to an air pollutant by two parts per billion; cutting greenhouse gas emissions from trucks; requiring copilots to have fifteen hundred hours of flying time; increasing capital and liquidity requirements at large financial institutions; reducing the incidence of prison rape; and making it easier for people who use wheelchairs to have access to bathrooms where they work.

These are real problems, not hypothetical ones. For some and perhaps most of them, specialists and scientists may not be able to give us the information that would be necessary to get us started—for example, about the number of lives likely to be saved each year by improved security or cleaner air. If so, cost-benefit analysis is not feasible. Even if specialists can give us some clear answers, it may be challenging to turn beneficial effects into monetary equivalents. There is a risk that we will be engaging in a lot of guesswork, and our guesses might turn out to be entirely wrong. In addition, unintended consequences are inevitable, and they might be terrible (or great).

The knowledge problem should not be taken as an objection to cost-benefit analysis as such. In some cases, the problem is not terribly severe. Even when it is hard to specify the costs and benefits of a regulation, we might be able to come up with ranges (lower and upper bounds), which can give us enough information to decide if that regulation is worth pursuing. But the problem can be serious, and we need to know how to deal with it. New methods are becoming available, and they will get better. Governments should use them.

Some companies "measure and react," which means that they measure, in real time, the effects of what they do, and they react very quickly to make those effects better. If effects can be measured in real time, then it is not necessary to place such reliance on ex ante estimates by public officials.

The triumph of cost-benefit analysis deserves a celebration, and this book can certainly be counted as that. But we also need to find ways to come to terms with the concerns.

The Plan

This book comes in two parts. The first discusses the cost-benefit revolution in general. The second explores particular issues, with emphasis on those that are on the frontiers and likely to receive considerable attention in the future.

Part I defends the revolution and casts it in a particular light. Chapter 1 offers a tour of the horizon, with particular emphasis on actual practice. It provides an account of what has been done and, with reference to actual political choices, explains why. Chapter 2 provides an initial justification for the cost-benefit revolution, emphasizing certain features of human cognition. It suggests that cost-benefit analysis distances us from our intuitions, which can badly mislead us, especially on issues of risk. Cost-benefit analysis is, in a sense, a foreign language, and it is helpful for that very reason.

Chapter 3—in some ways the heart of the book—contends that cost-benefit analysis is justified as a way of both increasing welfare and respecting individual autonomy. It does so with special reference to the "value of a statistical life"—a controversial idea that plays a large role in cost-benefit analysis as it is practiced. I try to show why we need some such value and when its use is a terrific idea. At the same time, I explore potential problems with it—and why and when the outcome of cost-benefit analysis, based on the use of the value of a statistical life, should not be decisive.

Chapter 4 explores the possible disconnect between social welfare and cost-benefit analysis. Emphasizing new findings in behavioral science, including efforts to study happiness and well-being, it shows that cost-benefit analysis can lead us astray. The central inspirations are a series of behavioral findings on how people's choices may not promote their welfare and continuing research on the sources of well-being (including pleasure and purpose). As of this writing, we do not have enough information to substitute welfare analysis for cost-benefit analysis, but welfare analysis can supplement the outcome of cost-benefit balancing in concrete ways.

Chapter 5 turns to the knowledge problem. The central inspiration here is Friedrich Hayek's work on the challenges faced by even the most well-motivated planners, who cannot know what individuals (as a whole) know and whose plans often go awry. Hayek objected to socialist planning for that reason. In important cases, cost-benefit analysis is susceptible to Hayek's objection. Chapter 5 explores how cost-benefit analysts can learn what they need to know, with particular reference to public comments, randomized controlled trials, retrospective analysis, and strategies of "measure-and-react."

Part II begins with a discussion, in chapter 6, of the role of moral commitments in cost-benefit analysis. As we shall see, many people do not merely care deeply about moral issues; they are also willing to pay something to ensure that their moral commitments are respected. Chapter 6 makes the admittedly adventurous claim that their willingness to pay should be part of cost-benefit analysis.

Mandatory labels have become a crucial tool that regulators use to inform consumers, to save money, and to reduce risks. Chapter 7 explores the best, and the worst, ways of calculating the benefits of disclosure. A central point is that receiving information can be a cost as well as a benefit. It can even be a kind of tax, because it takes away people's time and attention and because it can make them either sad or upset. At the same time, many people want information—perhaps to improve their health, perhaps for moral reasons. *Breakeven analysis* can be a valuable way to make progress in deciding whether the benefits of disclosure justify the costs. As we shall see, breakeven analysis is an important way to deal with the knowledge problem, even if we cannot solve it.

Chapter 8 turns to the role of courts. Judges are increasingly being asked to invalidate official decisions on the ground that their benefits do not justify their costs. In some cases, officials have not even bothered to assess benefits or costs—and that is the problem as a matter of law. The central rubric, for judicial intervention, is that officials have acted "arbitrarily," which is unlawful. I argue that *in general*, federal agencies indeed are obligated to attempt to assess both costs and benefits and to show that the former outweigh the latter. The words *in general* are crucial. In courts, as well as in the executive branch, there are good-faith justifications for failing to do what generally must be done—as, for example, when information about costs and benefits is lacking or when the real point is redistributive.

Chapter 9 explores the trade-off between national security and personal privacy, suggesting that some form of cost-benefit balancing is essential and that, for that reason, two opposing camps—familiar in modern politics—are off the mark. Chapter 10 explores the question of freedom of speech, an area of law in which courts have generally refused to engage in cost-benefit thinking, at least in recent decades. It offers a qualified defense of that refusal, in the process spelling out some circumstances in which it might make sense to say that "rights" take precedence over cost-benefit analysis. But it also suggests that in light of current terrorist threats that threaten to produce significant numbers of deaths, some form of cost-benefit thinking might eventually be mandatory.

The conclusion explores what happens to the best-laid plans, even of cost-benefit analysts. It offers a glimpse of what might happen if the cost-benefit revolution fully flowers and turns into something even better than itself.

I Where We Are

1   The Triumph of the Technocrats

Over the last fifty years, the United States experienced a revolution. No gun was fired. No lives were lost. Nobody marched. Most people didn't notice. Nonetheless, it happened.

The revolution focused public officials on the human consequences of their actions. It weakened the hold of interest groups, popular opinion, anecdotes, and intuitions. It gave new authority to experts, above all in science, statistics, and economics. Much of the time, it defied the wishes of the left and the right.

In terms of actual government practice, the revolution was genuinely new, but it hardly came out of the blue. On the contrary, it accomplished what many political thinkers have wanted. Its foundations can be traced directly to the work of such diverse figures as Alexander Hamilton, Adam Smith, Jeremy Bentham, John Stuart Mill, Friedrich Hayek, Walter Lippmann, and Amartya Sen. In important ways, it can be connected to Aristotle as well.

As a result of the revolution, many public officials work under a simple principle. It operates a little like a constitutional amendment. Its text, in full:

No action may be taken unless the benefits justify the costs.

Here, as in so many other places, the most important leadership has come from the president of the United States—not Congress, and certainly not courts. For this amendment, Ronald Reagan is the principal architect, and Barack Obama is an especially significant figure. But the two were hardly alone. If anyone is responsible for the cost-benefit revolution, it is a diverse assortment of presidents: Reagan, George H. W. Bush, Bill Clinton, George W. Bush, Obama, and Donald Trump.

For all their disagreements, they share enthusiasm for this particular revolution.

The issue might involve safety on the roads, clean air, occupational health, food safety, or even homeland security and immigration. In those areas, and many more, American presidents have been loath to allow federal officials to proceed unless the benefits justify the costs. And if the benefits do justify the costs, they have often insisted on going forward, whatever the political price. This last point is worth underlining. The cost-benefit revolution bans some actions, but it compels others—and they often save lives.

What about federal courts? In general, they do not make policy, and they have played a subordinate role. But increasingly, judges have shown keen interest in the cost-benefit revolution, and they are very much on the train. If the Environmental Protection Agency issues an air-quality regulation without considering the costs and the benefits and making some effort to compare them, it might well lose in court. The cost–benefit principle is not quite judicially enforceable law, but it is getting there. Whatever the issue, agencies should be forewarned: they violate the principle at their peril. It would not be easy to defend a decision of the Food and Drug Administration that imposes big costs on farmers without showing that it would confer comparably big benefits in terms of health.

In Congress, the story is more complicated. Everyone knows that in the United States, the national legislature has often been blocked. That is one reason that the cost-benefit revolution has not been enacted into law. Despite some serious attempts, Congress, as such, has not embraced the cost-benefit revolution, except in the context of specific statutes involving, for example, safe drinking water and toxic substances. But if any principle unifies efforts at legislative reform over the past two decades, it is probably the cost-benefit principle. It would not be at all surprising to see Congress formally enacting that principle into law in the coming years. Democrats and Republicans alike embrace cost-benefit analysis, and many of them support legislation that requires it.

Questions

I am well aware that these claims raise many questions. The most obvious involves *domain*. The quick answer is that the cost-benefit revolution mostly involves regulators working within executive agencies, which means that three important areas are now excluded.

First, the revolution does not involve the actions of the national legislature. When Congress enacts food-safety legislation or revises laws involving the financial sector or health care, it may or may not pay attention to costs and benefits. Often it does not. (Sad but true.) Second, some regulators are "independent," in the sense that they are free from the policy control of the president; examples include the Federal Communications Commission, the Federal Trade Commission, and the Federal Reserve Board. Such agencies often use cost-benefit analysis, but often they do not. Third, executive agencies make policy through enforcement activity and public pronouncements of various sorts. When they do, cost-benefit analysis is often absent.

We are speaking, then, of a revolution whose major domain, at least to date, involves regulations issued by executive agencies. Among other things, regulations specify air and water quality, increase food and drug safety, reduce exposure to carcinogens in the workplace, make motor vehicles and railroads safer, and reduce risks of terrorism at airports. (Enforcement activity is undertaken by reference to regulations.) That's a large domain, but it's certainly not everything.

In terms of *substance*, the most important questions are these: Isn't the cost-benefit principle hopelessly open-ended? Couldn't it mean anything at all? How can we decide how to quantify costs and benefits? How do you put a value on a human life? What is a cost, and what is a benefit?

For the moment, let me deflect these questions by emphasizing that many constitutional provisions, some of which come from revolutions of their own, have something important in common with the cost-benefit principle: They consist of generalities, which other officials have to fill in. They consist of *incompletely specified abstractions*. The first amendment, for example, protects "the freedom of speech." What is that? Does it include perjury, bribery, and commercial advertising? The fourteenth amendment bans states from denying people "the equal protection of the laws." Do those words forbid sex discrimination and discrimination on the basis of sexual orientation? By itself, the text of the equal protection clause cannot answer that question. In the same way, we have to do a lot of work to quantify costs and benefits—and even to figure out what they are.

There are also *institutional* questions. Who, exactly, does that work, and can we trust them? In 2016 and 2017, I was privileged to speak to high-level advisers in three different European nations. All of them were reform-minded, and all of them were drawn to cost-benefit balancing. But all of them were puzzled and a bit skeptical. Does the United States hire economists? How many? Can we trust what they say? Are economists going to make policy for our nation with respect to consumer protection, labor-management relations, and clean air? What exactly are they going to do when they tell us about costs and benefits?

Of these questions, the most interesting is how to specify what it means to require the benefits to justify the costs. When people embrace the general idea of cost-benefit balancing, they disagree intensely about the best specification. The question of climate change is only one obvious example. (What is the cost of a ton of carbon emissions?) Another is how to handle efforts to reduce the likelihood of a financial crisis; yet another involves regulations that would reduce discrimination on the basis of disability.

For the moment, notice that even when a principle has to be specified, it does not lack force. The cost-benefit principle has a lot of force. It requires people to ask excellent questions. It disciplines how they can answer. This is a meaningful revolution—even if it has yet to flower fully, even if it does not operate in every domain, and even if crucial work remains to be done.

Three Defining Moments

To date, the cost-benefit revolution has had three defining moments. They stem from the work of presidents Ronald Reagan, Bill Clinton, and Barack Obama.

Reagan's Innovation

The first moment, and by far the most important, came from Ronald Reagan in 1981, when he signed Executive Order 12291, with the most boring imaginable title: Federal Regulation. (Executive orders bind federal agencies; they create the formal law of the executive branch, though they are not enforceable in court and though they can be instantly repealed by later presidents.) Reagan's order imposed five general requirements. They do not read like poetry or even like a campaign speech, but each of them is massively important and thus worth pausing over:

(1) Administrative decisions shall be based on adequate information concerning the need for and consequences of proposed government action.

(2) Regulatory action shall not be undertaken unless the potential benefits to society for the regulation outweigh the potential costs to society.

(3) Regulatory objectives shall be chosen to maximize the net benefits to society.

(4) Among alternative approaches to any given regulatory objective, the alternative involving the least net cost to society shall be chosen.

(5) Agencies shall set regulatory priorities with the aim of maximizing the aggregate net benefits to society, taking into account the condition of the particular industries affected by regulations, the condition of the national economy, and other regulatory actions contemplated for the future.[1]

It is logical to start with requirement (1), which draws direct attention to the consequences and to the importance of obtaining "adequate information" about them. That requirement gives real authority to scientists and science; it does the same for other sources of knowledge (including statisticians and economists). The requirement might seem obvious, but in even in democratic governments it is anything but that. Much of the time, officials are under pressure to act because a well-organized private group wants it to do so, because a political party is all charged up, because important people have a clear sense that some problem needs to be fixed (right now!), because a recent event has triggered public concern, or because a newspaper or cable television show or even a tweet suggests that something must or must not be done. Simple though it is, requirement (1) empowers the technocrats; it calls for evidence. It puts technocrats in charge.

For present purposes, however, the most important requirement is (2), which says that the benefits must "outweigh" the costs. That requirement is naturally preceded by (1), which provides the foundations of the accounting for both costs and benefits. Neither can be made up; both must be grounded in the best available evidence. With requirement (2), we have a clear statement of the cost-benefit principle, with the operative verb "outweigh" suggesting that the simple question is which is larger.

In the long history of democratic thought, many people have given pride of place to the judgments of We the People. But others have sounded a cautionary note, emphasizing the need for careful analysis from officials who are, by training and experience, able to engage in it. Requirement (2) reflects that cautionary note and more.

Requirement (5), which requires maximizing "aggregate net benefits," is also exceptionally important. It embodies an independent idea, because it directs agencies to prioritize, among the approaches that have benefits in excess of costs, the one that has the highest net benefits. We could imagine a highway safety regulation that would have benefits of $300 million and costs of $200 million—and hence would have benefits in excess of costs (by $100 million). So far, so good—great, even.

But perhaps a different and slightly less aggressive approach would have benefits of $275 million and costs of $100 million—and hence have higher net benefits ($175 million). That's better. In the last decades, the requirement of maximizing net benefits has had great significance, because it has moved government in the right direction. Unfortunately, it has not been adequately enforced, so it has had less impact than it should have and much less than it might in the future. We could easily imagine an administration that would take the idea very seriously, sometimes producing less regulation and sometimes more than it would otherwise do.

Principles are one thing; action is another. Reagan's order also required executive agencies to produce, for every regulation, a Regulatory Impact Analysis (RIA), which is a written document with four central elements:

(1) A description of the potential benefits of the rule, including any beneficial effects that cannot be quantified in monetary terms and identification of those likely to receive the benefits

(2) A description of the potential costs of the rule, including any adverse effects that cannot be quantified in monetary terms and the identification of those likely to bear the costs

(3) A determination of the potential net benefits of the rule, including an evaluation of effects that cannot be quantified in monetary terms

(4) A description of alternative approaches that could substantially achieve the same regulatory goal at lower cost, together with an analysis of this potential benefit and its costs and a brief explanation of the legal reasons why such alternatives, if proposed, could not be adopted[2]

In the scheme of things, these provisions are quite remarkable. They are action-forcing. They are plainly designed to implement the general requirements with which Reagan's order begins. They acknowledge that some benefits and some costs cannot be quantified. They draw attention to issues of distribution: Who is likely to obtain the benefits and to bear the costs? The requirement that regulations come with an RIA has turned out to matter—a lot. The central reason is that Reagan directed federal agencies to submit every regulation, and every accompanying RIA, to the Office of Information and Regulatory Affairs (OIRA) within the Office of Management and Budget. If OIRA concluded that the regulation or the analysis was shoddy or that the agency had not complied with Reagan's requirements, it would not approve of the regulation.

As James Miller, the first administrator of OIRA, liked to say, "If you're the toughest kid on the block, most kids won't pick a fight with you. The executive order establishes things quite clearly."[3]

What Miller meant was that Reagan put OIRA in charge of the regulatory state, with close reference to cost-benefit analysis. If the benefits did not outweigh the costs, there would be no rule (unless Congress explicitly required it). The reason is that OIRA could say that the RIA was lousy, that the agency had not used the best available information, that the benefits were too low, that the costs was too high, or that the rule was generally a terrible idea. That's a lot of authority, and a lot of the time, it placed the technocrats squarely in charge. They could say to heads of Cabinet departments who emphasized political considerations: "The President told us to tell you no."

To be sure, and importantly, OIRA was not (and is not) working on its own. It is part of the Executive Office of the President—the White House and its extended operations. On important matters, OIRA will consult carefully with many other officials, including (for example) those who work with the National Economic Council, the Domestic Policy Council, and the Office of the Chief of Staff. And of course, the head of a Cabinet department can always appeal to the president—and ask him to overrule any OIRA administrator.

But as Reagan designed the system, that would be highly unusual. If the OIRA administrator thought that a regulation was not a good idea, and if other White House officials agreed, the regulation be unlikely to see the light of day. Cost-benefit analysis would often play a central and even critical role in the decision, with important officials constantly asking: Do the benefits outweigh the costs? Of course, that was not the only question they would ask, but it had pride of place.

Note that the question is both a red light for many regulations and a bright green light for others. Under Reagan's approach, a regulation with high costs and low benefits would famously be blocked at OIRA— but a regulation with low costs and high benefits would have the wind at its back, even if many political officials were skeptical about it. Sometimes high benefits and low costs lead to regulatory action, whether or not political forces favor it.

An instructive book on cost-benefit analysis, published in 2017, proclaims that "one would be hard pressed to find any significant case of policy making in representative government in which CBA [cost-benefit analysis] is a decisive decision rule rather than an input to the policy making process."[4] Not so hard-pressed! From 1981 to the present, cost-benefit analysis has often been a decisive decision rule in significant cases.

Fast Track   At the time of Reagan's executive order, I was lucky enough to be working as a young lawyer in the Office of Legal Counsel in the Department of Justice. Keenly interested in regulation, I was directed to advise the White House on the legality of Reagan's order. At the time, there was a lot of drama, because we were in the very first weeks of a new presidency, and everyone knew that this executive order would be transformative. We also knew that it had to comply with the law, not least because the stakes were so high. No one wanted the president to issue an order that would be struck down in court—or that would violate his oath of office. As is standard, the lawyers went back and forth with policymakers within the White House, scrubbing every word, until we had obtained a product that fulfilled the president's objectives while also surviving legal scrutiny.

In view of my lowly position, I did not know it at the time, but I was later told that this particular executive order was put on a uniquely fast track. Whether the president is a Democrat or a Republican, executive orders usually have to run a kind of marathon. The formal *clearance process*, as it is called, is often time-consuming and frustrating, and the president usually does not intervene personally unless he believes that time is of the essence.

Executive orders are almost always circulated in draft and subject to intense scrutiny by relevant agencies within the federal government, which get to weigh in before they are finalized and which often press their own distinctive concerns. When multiple agencies object, draft executive orders usually bite the dust—or at least are radically changed. After a few months in the White House, I remarked, to more than a few people: "Isn't it amazing that the word *clearance* has exactly the same letters as the word *excrement*?" Everyone knew what I meant.

Reagan's team was acutely aware that his order on federal regulation would be subject to fierce objections from executive agencies, They would vigorously resist OIRA control and they would not exactly love cost-benefit analysis, which could well be an obstacle to their plans. To be sure, those agencies were or would soon be headed by Reagan appointees, but no secretary of state, agriculture, or transportation loves the idea of having to face new constraints, procedural or substantive, from the White House. If the normal process had been followed, there is a good chance that Reagan's order would never have been issued—at least not unless the president or his chief of staff absolutely insisted on it.

As it happened, this executive order escaped the normal painstaking process of internal scrutiny. After the Department of Justice approved of the text, I am told, a high-level official in the Executive Office of the President called a meeting of top agency officials, in which he circulated the text of the order. (I am not sure who it was; it might have been the director of the Office of Management and Budget.) As agency officials read the text, they started to state their objections, loudly and passionately, with the confident expectation that the text was (as usual) a mere draft and that it would eventually be scrapped or at least significantly changed.

After they finished, the White House official calmly said, "Turn to the last page." There it was: Reagan's signature. The executive order had already been finalized.

Urgency That signature signaled a sense of urgency, which was a product of four independent judgments within the Reagan administration. First, and in my view most importantly, some influential White House officials were passionate technocrats—or at least they wanted to empower technocrats. They firmly believed that a requirement of cost-benefit analysis would make public officials focus on what matters: the human consequences. By requiring an accounting of both costs and benefits, White House officials meant to increase the probability that regulations would increase social welfare. They wanted to minimize the role of interest groups, anecdotes, intuitions, and symbols. They did not like expressive regulation. They wanted officials to ask: How much are people being helped? How much are they being hurt?

Second, some White House officials simply wanted to reduce the flow of new regulations. They were skeptical about regulation. They wanted less of it. They believed that the executive order would proliferate veto points on regulatory activity—and so weaken the ability of federal agencies to go forward simply because they wanted to do so. In their view, weakening that ability was a terrific idea, because regulation was an obstacle to economic growth and job creation.

From this point of view, Reagan's order was a political document, though with a substantive commitment behind it. It was important not because it would empower technocrats, but because it would scale back the regulatory state, which was good for both prosperity and freedom. Decades later, one of President Trump's former senior advisers, Steve Bannon, argued for "the deconstruction of the administrative state"; on that count, he had precursors in the Reagan administration.

Third, all White House officials agreed that the federal bureaucracy was sprawling, massive, and uncoordinated, and that different agencies had overlapping missions. For example, the Department of Agriculture and the Food and Drug Administration are concerned with food safety, and some companies have to worry whether they have to comply with requirements from both agencies. Shouldn't their efforts be brought together? Many agencies are concerned about environmental protection; what if they produce inconsistent or redundant requirements? Reagan's order would increase coherence and coordination, if only because OIRA would be able to have a centralizing role, ensuring that different agencies talk to each other and work to produce coherent requirements.

This is a point about consistency—but taken more broadly, it is also a point about sound management of the federal government. Reagan's executive order could increase the ability of the White House to ensure that agencies within the federal government focused on the particular issues that it wanted to prioritize, and that agencies did not march off with their own agendas. This point might sound boring, but it really isn't. Any president wants and needs to set priorities. The OIRA process is extremely helpful on that count.

A tale: During the Obama administration, I was asked in my capacity as OIRA administrator to speak at a Cabinet meeting, emphasizing that the president was focused on some very specific issues and not so much on others. Everyone got the message. Their own efforts had to be consistent with the president's personal focus.

Fourth, some of Reagan's top advisers thought that the real issue was democratic self-government. They believed that for emphatically democratic reasons, the regulatory process should be overseen by the president and his closest advisers (including OIRA, because it was, and remains, part of the White House apparatus). After all, the president was the only executive branch official who had been elected. (Well, the vice president too—but for whom does he work?) On this view, the executive order was necessary to concentrate ultimate authority in the boss, who had the only real electoral pedigree. Insofar as the executive order would reduce the power of agency heads and increase the power of the White House, it would be essential on democratic grounds.

At this point, a skeptic might emphasize that agency heads work for the president, too—indeed, they are chosen by him—and then ask: What makes White House officials so special? If democratic self-government is the goal, why favor some presidential advisers over others? One answer, and it is important, involves sheer *proximity*. If you work in the White House or in the Eisenhower Executive Office Building (next door), you are likely to have a keen sense of what the president is actually thinking. You might be talking to him personally, at least on occasion; even if you aren't, you are probably in daily contact with his top advisers. As OIRA administrator, I found myself in the West Wing at least once every day, and often four times or more. Another answer involves *mission*: agency heads are focused on something specific (terrorism, transportation, immigration, agriculture, the environment), whereas the White House has a general overview and is in the best position to decide what matters most.

During the Reagan administration, the four goals could usually work together, certainly to support the executive order itself. But there was potential tension among several of them and, in particular, between the technocratic goal and the democratic one. Suppose that the technocrats, investigating the costs and benefits, supported some environmental initiative—but that the president really didn't like it. At first glance, of course, the president would prevail; famously, he is the Decider. But shouldn't there be a meeting? In the Oval Office? Shouldn't the president see the actual numbers? At the very least, shouldn't he have a sense that the costs are low and that the benefits are high?

In a way, these questions seem fantastic. When things are working well, the president does not simply "like" or "dislike" an initiative. In most administrations, his conclusions usually follow an extensive briefing process, in which he sees detailed arguments and counterarguments, sometimes including the numbers (at least in broad outline). In addition, his time is very scarce, and he cannot be expected to resolve all or most of the many disputes that occur within a large staff. They have to work it out themselves, with the help of numbers. That is what Reagan's executive order contemplates. In other words, the process of analyzing draft regulations and of deciding whether to go forward with them rarely requires the personal participation of the president.

It is certainly true that the order requires close attention to costs and benefits. In one famous case, involving depletion of the ozone layer, Reagan himself was moved by a demonstration, from his advisers, that aggressive regulation, phasing out ozone-depleting chemicals, would have high benefits and low costs. One of the most important environmental treaties in world history, the Montreal Protocol, was embraced and promoted by Reagan and the United States. That probably would not have happened without cost-benefit analysis, which showed that the economic costs would be pretty low, and that the benefits (in terms of skin cancers and cataracts avoided) would be very high. Whatever their political affiliation, anyone who saw those numbers would think that the United States and the world would do very well to phase out ozone-depleting chemicals.

The example is worth underlining, because it confirms that cost-benefit analysis often turns out to require rather than to prohibit regulatory action. In both Republican and Democratic administrations, that happens a fair bit, at least when things are working well. The example also shows that cost-benefit analysis can quiet political disagreement. A Republican president, often skeptical about environmental regulation, became an enthusiastic defender of aggressive action to address the depletion of the ozone layer. So too, Democratic presidents, generally receptive to environmental regulation, have become skeptical in the face of a demonstration that a step to protect the environment would have high costs and low benefits.

Reagan's executive order continued in force under the presidency of George H. W. Bush and for a full twelve years, it provided the essential framework for the executive branch of the federal government. Although Bush and Reagan were both Republicans, they did not agree on everything. It is a tribute to Reagan's original design that Bush did not see fit to change a single word.

Clinton's Consolidation

With the election of Bill Clinton, many progressives hoped that Reagan's framework would be jettisoned. There was reason for their hope: cost-benefit analysis was hardly a rallying cry for the Clinton campaign, and in view of the many regulatory initiatives that the new administration promised to undertake, perhaps the executive agencies and the regulatory state would be unshackled. Perhaps cost-benefit analysis would be rejected.

Nothing like that happened. On the contrary, Clinton is responsible for the second defining moment, which came in 1993. Executive Order 12866, called Regulatory Planning and Review, affirmed the essentials of Reagan's own. True, it was a lot longer, and it has many more details. But its "regulatory philosophy" was close to what Reagan had embraced. Indeed, it could have been written by Reagan's White House:

Federal agencies should promulgate only such regulations as are required by law, are necessary to interpret the law, or are made necessary by compelling public need, such as material failures of private markets to protect or improve the health and safety of the public, the environment, or the well-being of the American people. In deciding whether and how to regulate, agencies should assess all costs and benefits of available regulatory alternatives, including the alternative of not regulating. Costs and benefits shall be understood to include both quantifiable measures (to the fullest extent that these can be usefully estimated) and qualitative measures of costs and benefits that are difficult to quantify, but nevertheless essential to consider. Further, in choosing among alternative regulatory approaches, agencies should select those approaches that maximize net benefits (including potential economic, environmental, public health and safety, and other advantages; distributive impacts; and equity), unless a statute requires another regulatory approach.[5]

Let's focus on the initial sentence, which is exceedingly important. Before we even get to cost-benefit analysis, agencies are sharply constrained in what they may do. Where the law does not require them to act, agencies need to show that regulations "are made necessary by compelling public need, such as material failures of private markets to protect or improve the health and safety of the public, the environment, or the well-being of the American people." True, a compelling public need is not limited to market failures in the strict economic sense. But agencies have to show that markets have failed in some way. They cannot act simply because they think action is a good idea. When the process of regulatory oversight is working well, agencies often decline to regulate at all, because they cannot identify a "compelling public need." The presumption is against regulation, at least in the sense that some strong justification has to be specified on its behalf.

With respect to cost-benefit analysis, Clinton's order goes beyond Reagan's. Note in particular the emphasis on assessing "all costs and benefits of available regulatory alternatives, including the alternative of not regulating," as well as the clear direction to "maximize net benefits."

True, Clinton emphasized the difficulty of quantifying some costs and benefits. And, true, Clinton's order refers to "distributive impacts" and "equity," which broadened the focus. But all this was written in a way that complemented and did not reject the cost-benefit framework. Indeed, Clinton's executive order offered "principles of regulation" that were quite clear and quite Reaganite, including these three in particular:

- Each agency shall assess both the costs and the benefits of the intended regulation and, recognizing that some costs and benefits are difficult to quantify, propose or adopt a regulation only upon a reasoned determination that the benefits of the intended regulation justify its costs.
- When an agency determines that a regulation is the best available method of achieving the regulatory objective, it shall design its regulations in the most cost-effective manner to achieve the regulatory objective. In doing so, each agency shall consider incentives for innovation, consistency, predictability, the costs of enforcement and compliance (to the government, regulated entities, and the public), flexibility, distributive impacts, and equity.
- Each agency shall base its decisions on the best reasonably obtainable scientific, technical, economic, and other information concerning the need for, and consequences of, the intended regulation.[6]

Under Clinton's approach, the cost-benefit principle thus remained intact. With technical qualifications that need not detain us here, the same is true for the process that Reagan established, including the requirement that agencies prepare and submit to OIRA an RIA, with an accounting of both costs and benefits.

Clinton's order stayed in place for his two-term presidency, establishing a bipartisan consensus in favor of the cost-benefit principle. After the election of George W. Bush in 2000, no one doubted that the principle would remain intact, but many people expected a new executive order, perhaps eliminating the reference to "distributive impacts" and "equity," perhaps intensifying the emphasis on quantifying costs and benefits. In its first term, however, the Bush administration did nothing to the Clinton order—and in its second, it merely tinkered with it and did not alter anything of much importance. This was a big surprise to many observers, including me.

As it happened, several friends of mine worked on regulatory issues in the Bush administration, and at a certain point, I expressed my astonishment to one of them. The response was very simple, and it suggested that I didn't know a thing: "Cass, the Clinton order gives us *everything we need.*" My friend was saying that the regulatory philosophy, quoted earlier, was embraced by Bush and his advisers, and so were Clinton's regulatory principles. If the Bush White House wanted to block some proposals and to spur others, the Clinton order was just fine. There was no need to change it.

Obama's Cement

For many years, Barack Obama taught at the University of Chicago Law School, where I also taught. I greatly admired him, and he became a friend. When he ran for president, I was a part-time adviser on his campaign. When he was elected, I had the opportunity to work for him. In terms of jobs, my first choice was easy: I hoped to be administrator of OIRA.

True, that's not exactly the most conspicuous position in the federal government, and it isn't even a little bit glamorous. But in view of its range and importance, I thought that I could do more good for the American people in that position than I could do in any other position. I was lucky enough to work in the Executive Office of the President for nearly four years—from early 2009 to late 2012—and after I left, I continued to have an occasional, informal role as an adviser to White House officials.

As early as the presidential transition, in December 2008, I thought that Obama should issue his own executive order, firmly embracing cost-benefit analysis while also making an assortment of changes and clarifications. I even wrote a draft of such an order. In January 2009, the new president indicated, through a presidential memorandum, that he would indeed produce his own order, and the Obama administration asked for public comments on its content.

Within the White House, however, there was no consensus in favor of any such executive order. On the contrary, most people opposed the idea. They didn't like my draft. Many officials had the same view as my friend in the Bush administration: the Clinton executive order gave us everything we needed. To the extent that cost-benefit analysis was important (and people disagreed about whether it was), the Clinton order already gave us that. Some of the president's highest advisers emphasized that we were struggling to avert a depression, to enact health care reform, and to reform the financial system. Was an executive order really required?

Their advice to me was straightforward: do your job, and don't worry about any big, splashy announcement. There was also an intensely political concern. If the Obama administration publicly embraced cost-benefit analysis, progressive groups, including environmental, labor, and consumer organizations, would be quite unhappy, even angry. Conservatives and business organizations would give us no credit. What was the point? Some of the president's high-level economic advisers, playing political analysts, raised that question. Within the White House, most people thought that this was a low-priority item and that it probably should not be done at all.

In 2009, I attended endless, frustrating meetings on the subject, in which I urged the importance of an executive order embracing cost-benefit analysis, but no one seemed to agree with me. I wrote many new drafts of such an order, some long, others short. No one liked any of them. With so many issues to resolve, I gave up fighting.

But in 2010, the president called for a general meeting on regulatory reform. Because there was no support within the White House for an executive order—again, I was the only one who wanted it—the written materials to the president made no reference to the idea. But my friend Larry Summers, director of the National Economic Council, authorized me to mention the idea in my oral presentation to the president. (That was a generous act, because Summers did not favor it.) President Obama immediately seized on the idea. He liked it. He emphasized that he wanted to issue his own order, with his own defining principles. He also said that he wanted to endorse cost-benefit analysis. He said, "That's what the American people want, and that's what they deserve." As I recall, almost all of his advisers were unhappy, but he was firm.

Executive Order 13563 was issued in early 2011, under the title of "Improving Regulation and Regulatory Review." It began:

Our regulatory system must protect public health, welfare, safety, and our environment while promoting economic growth, innovation, competitiveness, and job creation. It must be based on the best available science. It must allow for public participation and an open exchange of ideas. It must promote predictability and reduce uncertainty. It must identify and use the best, most innovative, and least burdensome tools for achieving regulatory ends. It must take into account benefits and costs, both quantitative and qualitative. It must ensure that regulations are accessible, consistent, written in plain language, and easy to understand. It must measure, and seek to improve, the actual results of regulatory requirements.[7]

It explicitly incorporated the Clinton order, emphasizing and explicitly quoting the requirement that the benefits must justify the costs. In a ringing endorsement of cost-benefit analysis, it added that "each agency is directed to use the best available techniques to quantify anticipated present and future benefits and costs as accurately as possible." It added that "each agency may consider (and discuss qualitatively) values that are difficult or impossible to quantify, including equity, human dignity, fairness, and distributive impacts." The term *human dignity* appeared for the first time in Obama's order.

Crucially, the order included a requirement of "retrospective analysis" of existing rules, stating: "To facilitate the periodic review of existing significant regulations, agencies shall consider how best to promote retrospective analysis of rules that may be outmoded, ineffective, insufficient, or excessively burdensome, and to modify, streamline, expand, or repeal them in accordance with what has been learned. Such retrospective analyses, including supporting data, should be released online whenever possible."

With these provisions—and the president was personally involved in their development—the Obama administration cemented the cost-benefit revolution. Executive Order 13563 organized the regulatory work of the federal government between 2011 and 2017. It has something like the status of a constitution.

President Trump did not jettison Executive Order 13563. On the contrary, he retained it. But more than any president in the modern era, he sought to reduce regulatory activity. He seemed to oppose it on principle and essentially across the board. He wanted to stem the flow and to reduce the stock. To entrench his opposition, he supplemented the work of his predecessors in various ways, above all by directing that in 2017, the net costs of regulations must be *zero*, and that for every regulation issued, two regulations must be removed.

The first requirement is a kind of regulatory budget: no net costs! The second requirement creates a strong disincentive to issue any regulations at all. If an agency issues one, it has to eliminate two. That means that if any agency wants to engage in regulatory activity, it cannot add to current total costs, and it must take away double the number of regulations that it adds.

We can see these requirements as adding additional filters to the issuance of regulations. From the standpoint of the cost-benefit revolution, Trump's initiatives are hard to defend. Suppose that an agency wants to issue three regulations, each with benefits of $500 million and each with costs of $200 million. Shouldn't the agency proceed, even if it is adding $600 million in costs? After all, it is also producing $1.5 billion in benefits, which means that the net benefits are very high ($900 million). What matters is not whether the agency has added to the total amount of costs, or whether it has added more regulations than it has taken away, but whether it has produced benefits on balance.

That is a serious and in my view decisive objection both to the regulatory budget of zero (focusing solely on costs, and disregarding benefits) and to the rule of "one in, two out." Importantly, however, Trump meant his filters to supplement the cost-benefit principle: he embraced the idea that regulations may not be issued unless the benefits justify the costs.

Mill's Triumph

Why has Reagan's initiative proved so enduring? How has a once-controversial idea become a core part of the shared values of both Republicans and Democrats?

We could approach these questions by asking about institutional incentives, interest groups, and political economy. Presidents need tools with which to manage the regulatory state, and cost-benefit analysis is a capacious organizing idea, one that operates as such a tool. You could even consider it as a kind of placeholder, saying: "All important regulations must be submitted to the White House for clearance. They will be approved if the White House likes them." From that point of view, cost-benefit analysis is not what most matters. We are speaking of a political check, putting the White House in charge.

We could also disaggregate the concerns, substantive and political, of various presidents. The cost-benefit revolution was part of the Reagan revolution, because Reagan sought to discipline the flow of new regulations and because the principle that benefits must outweigh costs proved attractive to him and his advisers. At the time, many powerful interests—above all, in the business community—embraced the idea of cost-benefit balancing. They saw cost-benefit analysis as a way of reducing the flow of new requirements.

For their own reasons, latter presidents found that the principle worked well, or well enough. President Obama thought that the cost-benefit requirement was attractive in principle, an excellent way of testing whether a regulation was in the public interest. But I am more interested here in evaluating the revolution than in specifying its origins. Is this a good revolution? What good does it do?

The simplest point, and the most important, was emphasized by some of Reagan's own advisers: Policies should make people's lives better. Officials should not rely on intuitions, interest groups, polls, or dogmas. In a nutshell: *quantitative cost-benefit analysis is the best available method for assessing the effects of regulation on social welfare.*[8] It is fair to see the insistence on that form of analysis as a vindication of the utilitarian project, pioneered by Jeremy Bentham, John Stuart Mill, and Henry Sidgwick. Utilitarians famously argue against relying on ad hoc judgments, intuitions, and beliefs about what rights people have. They ask instead: What effect would different alternatives have on overall utility?

Of course, utilitarianism is highly controversial, and many people, including many philosophers, reject it. There are pervasive questions about the meaning of the idea of *utility*. In ordinary language, the term seems to refer to usefulness, which is not exactly an attractive foundational commitment. Utilitarians do not understand it that way. In Bentham's own words: "By utility is meant that property in any object, whereby it tends to produce benefit, advantage, pleasure, good, or happiness, (all this in the present case comes to the same thing) or (what comes again to the same thing) to prevent the happening of mischief, pain, evil, or unhappiness to the party whose interest is considered."[9]

But that might seem too narrow: Are we speaking only of maximizing pleasure and minimizing pain? Doesn't that seem to be a constricted account of what people do and should care about? When people live their lives, they value much more than pleasure and pain. A satisfying day or week might not have a whole lot of pleasure, and it might have plenty of pain, but it might still have been extraordinarily satisfying. Perhaps you did something wonderful for others or for your children; perhaps your work went really well.

The very idea of happiness itself needs to be defined, but it is too narrow as well. People care about other things, including a sense of meaning or purpose. A good life is not merely "happy." The ingredients of happiness are varied, and there are qualitative differences among them.

A good day can be "happy" in a thousand disparate ways. Unhappy days take radically different forms: you might be in physical pain; you might be lonely; you might be tired; you might be hungry; you might be bored; you might be anxious; you might not be treated with respect; you might not have enough money; your romantic partner might treat you unkindly; your child might be suffering; you might be grieving; you might feel stress.

Perhaps Bentham's references to "benefit," "good," "mischief," and "evil" are capacious enough to capture the full range of people's concerns. But from Bentham's voluminous writings on utilitarianism, it is not clear that his own approach sufficiently recognizes the wide range of those concerns or the qualitative differences among them.

There are also questions about whether people have rights that can override the utilitarian calculus. Suppose that social utility would increase if certain points of view were suppressed (because people hate hearing those points of view) or if certain religions were banned (because they did not have many adherents and because people despise them). Suppose that racial segregation could be justified on utilitarian grounds. Suppose that torture of suspected rapists or suspected terrorists would increase overall utility. Might people's rights operate as trump cards, and deserve to be vindicated, even so?

These questions deserve answers, and I will spend some time on them. But as it usually operates in most domains, cost-benefit analysis can be understood to avoid these various objections and hence to be the foundation of an incompletely theorized agreement. The reason is that it is a capacious variation on the Benthamite creed, associated with John Stuart Mill's thinking, and especially his emphasis on the qualitative distinctions among goods and his objections to the narrowness of Bentham's approach. Cost-benefit analysis is an effort to implement the broader idea of *welfarism*, not of Benthamite utilitarianism. It does not focus solely on pleasures and pains, important though they are.

Cost-benefit analysis includes everything that matters to people's welfare, including such qualitatively diverse goods as physical and mental health, freedom from pain, a sense of meaning, culture, clean air and water, animal welfare, safe food, pristine areas, and access to public buildings. (This statement requires some qualifications, and I will turn to them in due course; but it is mostly true.) At least in most cases, there is no conflict between what emerges from cost-benefit analysis and the best thinking about human rights (see chapter 3 for details). True, some such conflicts exist, but for cost-benefit analysts in government, they are rare.

It is for this reason that the cost-benefit revolution is welfarist rather than narrowly utilitarian. Above all, it insistently focuses attention on the actual consequences of regulatory initiatives. When President Obama said, "It is what the American people want, and it is what they deserve," he was not speaking of surveys or opinion polls. He was not making an empirical claim. He was saying that after a period of reflection, the American people—like the people of the United Kingdom, Canada, Germany, France, Denmark, Sweden, Finland, Ireland, Australia, Brazil, South Africa, Italy, and countless other nations—would want their government to make its decisions on the basis of what regulations and policies would actually achieve. Cost-benefit analysis is a way of finding out.

To make this claim more concrete, imagine that a regulation designed to make automobiles safer would cost consumers $700 million per year, because it would require cars to come with safety equipment that would increase their price. Suppose that twenty million cars are sold in the United States each year, and each one would cost forty dollars more. Whenever people buy a car, they would have to pay that cost. Imagine too that the regulation would save three hundred lives per year, prevent one thousand serious injuries, and avoid $650 million in property damage.

To turn those prevented deaths and injuries into monetary equivalents, we would have to do some work, but on any reasonable assumptions, the regulation should go forward. Its benefits justify its costs. In cases of this kind, cost-benefit analysis mandates regulation, even if intuitions, or well-organized private groups, suggest that it is not a good idea. Indeed, numbers of this kind have led high-level officials to approve of regulations even in the face of strong political headwinds against them.

Now imagine that a food safety regulation would cost $1.5 billion per year. Suppose that it would prevent four deaths annually and prevent seventy illnesses. On any reasonable assumptions, the regulation should not go forward. Every death matters, but $1.5 billion is not worth spending for those relatively meager gains.

Of course we would have to investigate the details to earn this conclusion. And we could imagine harder cases, in which the ultimate conclusion is not obvious and much work has to be done on questions of valuation. But even when that is so, cost-benefit analysis has the great virtue of explaining why some decisions are difficult—and of forcing officials and others to ask the right questions. It directs them to ask: Are people's lives being improved, or not, by the relevant initiative?

To these points, it might be added that cost-benefit analysis can operate as a valuable check on the operation of misleading intuitions or behavioral biases within the national government—and on the role of powerful private groups trying to move federal policy in their favor. Daniel Kahneman is widely known for his pioneering work with Amos Tversky, but his earliest book, published in 1973, had a revealing and, in its way, magnificent title: *Attention and Effort*. The title points to the fact that focusing attention requires effort, which people try to minimize. Whether they work for government or not, they are often attentive to some aspects of a problem, but far from all of them. Intuitions go wrong for that reason; they produce behavioral biases. I shall have more to say about that problem in chapter 2.

Numbers

Of course, cost-benefit analysis runs into a host of other concerns and objections, which I will explore in due course. For now, return to the knowledge problem: How is it possible to quantify the various goods that are at stake in public policy? In some cases, doing that is not all that hard. An automobile safety regulation might require the installation of equipment that costs fifty dollars per car. The total cost can be calculated with a little arithmetic. But quantification of the benefits might be more challenging.

The first questions are whether the regulation will reduce deaths, injuries, and property damage, and, if so, by how much. It might not be so easy to generate numbers, even though cost-benefit analysis requires them. Will the regulation save twenty lives annually, or one hundred, or five hundred? The next question is how to turn any such savings into monetary equivalents. For property damage, that might not be so difficult, but how about for savings in terms of lives and serious injuries? I will have something to say about that question.

In some ways, the case of automobile safety is pretty easy. Suppose that a regulation is designed to allow people who use wheelchairs to have access to certain buildings. How should we value their interest in being able to use bathrooms without assistance? That is a dignitary interest, and it is not easy to turn it into some specified sum of money. Or suppose that government wants to inform consumers—say, by telling them about the caloric content of food. What is the benefit of information? Don't we have to know what consumers will do with it?

To make things even harder, suppose that a regulation is designed to reduce the risk of a financial crisis. To identify its benefits, we would need to know the cost of a crisis and the contribution of the regulation to reducing the risk of its occurrence. Any efforts to come up with numbers might involve a visit to fantasy land. Reductions in greenhouse gases present related challenges. To say the least, specialists disagree about the damage from climate change at any specified level of global emissions. Even if we could make a judgment on that subject, we would have to turn it into an economic equivalent. And even if we could do that, we could quantify the monetary benefits of reducing greenhouse gas emissions only if we could say that a ton of emissions produce a specific amount of damage. Is that possible? In due course, I will have something to say about that question.

2 A Foreign Language

Is cost-benefit analysis a foreign language? In many ways, it is. That is its virtue. Because of its foreignness, it distances us from our intuitions and from our immediate, automatic reactions. That distance is important, because our intuitions can lead us astray.

Let's begin with a little experiment that I conducted in late 2016 with 204 Americans. I began by noting that "people debate how the government should go about reducing risks that come from air pollution, unsafe food, and potentially unsafe working conditions." I then asked respondents to state their agreement or disagreement, on a five-point scale (from "strongly agree" to "strongly disagree"), with the following proposition: "The government should assign a dollar value to each human life—perhaps $9 million—and weigh the costs of regulation against the benefits of regulation."

The US government routinely does exactly that. Within both Republican and Democratic administrations, the proposition is not even controversial (though there are occasional debates over the right monetary value; in recent years, estimates have converged at $9 million). Yet most respondents were deeply skeptical.

The most common answer was "strongly disagree," with sixty-eight votes. The second most common was "somewhat disagree," with fifty-two votes. Only four strongly agreed! Just thirty-seven somewhat agreed; forty-two were neutral. The overwhelming majority of American respondents refused to embrace a proposition that most executive branch officials in the United States find self-evidently correct.

I was surprised, but I shouldn't have been. The lack of public enthusiasm for cost-benefit analysis (with this admittedly simplified description) is not exactly shocking. People don't like to assign a monetary figure to human lives. The idea that risk regulation should be based on monetary valuations fits poorly with ordinary intuitions. In deciding whether to protect your child or your spouse against a mortality risk, you do not think: "I will monetize the risk and weigh the costs against the benefits." To be sure, you might do some implicit weighing (you will!), but the language of monetary trade-offs seems quite foreign, even ugly.

When I testified before Congress on regulatory reform in the 1990s, and earnestly argued that the national legislature might want to enact guidelines for the monetary valuation of statistical lives, I was greeted with incredulous stares. Both Republicans and Democrats both seemed to think: "Are you kidding, or are you nuts?" They thought that the idea was absurd, though I am not sure whether their objection was political ("How can I defend any number to my constituents?") or instead substantive ("No monetary figure can possibly make sense"). And when I worked in the Executive Office of the President, a member of the Cabinet with extensive political experience exclaimed to me in the White House in 2011: "Cass, how can you ever put on a value on a human life?" He was exasperated. He wanted to issue a regulation that would save some lives. It would cost a lot of money. He asked: "Do you actually want to stop a regulation that would prevent real people from dying?"

Populists and Technocrats

Consider in this light two stylized approaches to regulatory policy: the populist and the technocratic. Populists emphasize the importance of democratic self-government. They think that, at least as a general rule, public officials should follow the will of the citizenry. They trust people's intuitions, seeing them as a repository of sense, wisdom, and even morality. If people are especially afraid of genetically modified food or abandoned hazardous waste dumps, regulators should pay close attention to that fear, even if experts believe that it is baseless. If people do not like assigning a monetary value to statistical lives, officials should hesitate before assigning a monetary value to statistical lives.

Of course, populist approaches take diverse forms. Within democratic theory, some people believe that crowds are wise and that if most people converge on a belief, they are likely to be right. Other democratic theorists emphasize the importance of deliberation among ordinary people; consider town halls. Within psychology, the most interesting defense of a particular kind of populist approach, coming from Paul Slovic, is that ordinary people display a *rival rationality*, one that has its own logic and that should be treated with respect.[1] Slovic urges that this rival rationality diverges from that of experts and that it is not self-evidently inferior. It contains its own language, its own concerns, and its own moral commitments. For example, ordinary people care about whether a risk is voluntarily incurred, controllable, familiar, fairly distributed, and potentially catastrophic. They may be especially concerned about genetically modified organisms and pesticides, even if experts are not. They do not look only at numbers.

By contrast, technocrats love numbers. They emphasize the importance of facts and in particular of science, statistics, and economics. With respect to regulatory policy, they think that government should do what is right (by the lights of science and economics), not what citizens, with their various intuitions and biases, happen to think is right. Of course, technocratic approaches take diverse forms. Many technocrats insist that some form of cost-benefit analysis is the proper foundation for regulatory policy and that whatever the public believes, the outcome of that analysis should be decisive. If the public is insufficiently fearful of certain risks, such as the risks associated with obesity or distracted driving, regulators should nonetheless proceed if the benefits of proceeding exceed the costs.

Technocrats are greatly concerned about the problem of public complacency, and they see cost-benefit analysis as a corrective. Even if the public is fearful of certain risks, regulators should not proceed if the costs of proceeding would exceed the benefits. Technocrats are also concerned about the problem of public hysteria, and here again they see cost-benefit analysis as a corrective. They are aware, of course, of the limits to their own knowledge, and they are constantly thinking about ways to expand that knowledge.

Cognition

Influenced by behavioral science, some technocrats make an emphatically *cognitive* case for cost-benefit analysis. They believe that that form of analysis is, in a sense, a foreign language—and the right language with which to assess risk regulation. Invoking behavioral findings, they contend that in thinking about risks, both ordinary people and politicians are susceptible to behavioral biases that lead to systematic and predictable errors. Armed with anecdotes and intuitions, those on the political left might be fearful of environmental and other risks that do not pose objectively serious threats. At the same time, they might neglect or downplay the costs of addressing those risks, which may adversely affect real people.

Armed with their own anecdotes and intuitions, those on the political right might favor the opposite policies. Cultural commitments of various sorts might account for those intuitions, leading to both mistakes and polarization. Technocrats distrust populism for that very reason. They think that it threatens to produce serious blunders, with harmful consequences for people's lives.

Availability

Technocrats are especially troubled by the use of the *availability heuristic* in thinking about risks.[2] It is well-established that people tend to think that events are more probable if they can readily recall an incident of its occurrence. Consider, for example, the fact that people typically think that more words, on any given page, will end with the letters *ing* than have *n* as the second-to-last letter (though a moment's reflection shows that this is not possible).[3] Risk-related judgments are often affected by the availability heuristic: people overestimate the number of deaths from highly publicized events (motor vehicle accidents, tornadoes, floods, botulism), but underestimate the number from less publicized sources (stroke, heart disease, stomach cancer).[4]

In 2014, for example, there was a horrible panic in the United States about the risk of getting ebola. Actually the risk was very low, and the number of infections was exceedingly small. But many people were terrified and demanded aggressive regulatory responses. The reason was that the few cases of ebola in the United States received a lot of publicity. As a result, people saw the risk as much greater than it was. The availability heuristic ran rampant. If government responded to what people wanted, it would have imposed all sorts of unjustified restrictions (including restrictions on international travel to and from certain African nations).

There is a big problem here, and it is a formidable objection to populism. To the extent that people lack information or base their judgments on mental shortcuts that produce errors, a highly responsive government is likely to blunder. Alert to the availability heuristic, technocrats insist on the need for scientific and economic safeguards. Cost-benefit analysis is a natural corrective, above all because it focuses attention on the actual effects of regulation—including, in some cases, the existence of surprisingly small benefits from regulatory controls.

Cascades

The availability heuristic does not, of course, operate in a social vacuum. It interacts with emphatically social processes. A signal by one person will provide relevant data to others. When there is little private information, such a signal may initiate an *informational cascade*, with significant consequences for private and public behavior, and with distorting effects on regulatory policy.[5]

Imagine, for example, that A says that abandoned hazardous waste sites are dangerous, or that A initiates protest activity because such a site is located nearby. B, otherwise skeptical or in equipoise, may go along with A; C, otherwise an agnostic, may be convinced that if A and B share the relevant belief, the belief must be true; and it will take a confident D to resist the shared judgments of A, B, and C. The result of this set of influences can be a social cascade, as hundreds, thousands, or millions of people come to accept a certain belief simply because of what they think other people believe. If a particular event starts the whole process, society may experience an *availability cascade*, leading to a strong demand for regulation, even if it is unwarranted.

There is nothing fanciful to the idea. Cascade effects help account for the existence of widespread public concern about abandoned hazardous waste dumps (in most cases, a relatively small environmental hazard), and in recent decades, they spurred grossly excessive public fears of the pesticide Alar, of risks from plane crashes, and of dangers of shootings in schools in the aftermath of particular tragedies. Such effects helped produce massive dislocations in beef production in Europe in connection with mad cow disease; they also helped give rise to growing European fear of genetic engineering of food.

On the reputational side, cognitive errors may be amplified as well. If many people are alarmed about some risk, you may not voice your doubts about whether the alarm is merited, simply in order not to seem obtuse, cruel, or indifferent. And if many people believe that a certain risk is trivial, you may not disagree through words or deeds, lest you appear cowardly or confused. The results of these forces can be cascade effects, mediated by the availability heuristic. Such effects can produce a public demand for regulation even though the relevant risks are trivial.

At the same time, there may be little or no demand for regulation of risks that are, in fact, quite large in magnitude. Self-interested private groups can exploit these forces, often by using the availability heuristic. Consider the fact that European companies have tried to play up fears of genetically engineered food as a way of fending off American competition.

Cost-benefit analysis has a natural role here. If it is made relevant to decisions, it can counteract cascade effects induced by informational and reputational forces, especially when the availability heuristic is at work. The effect of cost-benefit analysis is to subject a public demand for regulation to a kind of technocratic scrutiny, to ensure that the demand is not rooted in myths, and to ensure as well that the government is regulating risks even when the public demand (because of an insufficiently informed public) is low.

Systems and System Neglect

From the cognitive standpoint, there is an even more general problem. Often people focus on small pieces of complex issues, which have mutually interacting parts. The causal effects of one intervention are hard to trace. In these circumstances, unintended consequences are difficult to avoid. There may be big ripple effects, whether good or bad.

The psychologist Dietrich Dorner has performed some illuminating computer experiments designed to test whether people can engage in successful social engineering.[6] Participants are asked to solve problems faced by the inhabitants of some region of the world. Through the magic of the computer, many policy initiatives are available to solve the relevant problems (improved care of cattle, childhood immunization, drilling more wells). But most of the participants produce eventual calamities, because they do not see the complex, system-wide effects of their interventions. Only the rare participant can see a series of steps down the road and thus anticipate the multiple effects of one-shot interventions on the system. In short, most people are subject to *system neglect*.

Regulation often has systemic effects, and it is tough to see them in advance. A decision to ban ozone-depleting chemicals may force manufacturers to stop selling certain kinds of asthma inhalers, which emit such chemicals but are highly beneficial to human health. A decision to forbid asbestos may cause manufacturers to use less safe substitutes. A decision to regulate nuclear power may increase the demand for coal-fired power plants, with harmful environmental consequences, including an increase in greenhouse gas emissions. A decision to require employers to pay a "living wage" may lead them to hire fewer employees and thus hurt the most vulnerable among us.

These are simply a few examples of situations in which a government agency should make "health-health trade-offs" in light of the systemic effects of one-shot interventions. Such trade-offs are necessary whenever reforms designed to improve health turn out to impair health. For sensible policymaking, the two effects must be compared. The good news is that in some cases, a decision may produce unintended health benefits rather than harms, as when regulation of coal-fired power plants, designed to reduce emissions of toxic air pollutants (such as mercury), turns out to reduce emissions of other air pollutants (such as particulate matter) as well, and even reduces greenhouse gas emissions. "Cobenefits" are often a fortunate consequence of policies. But it is also true that unintended consequences can be harmful, and they too must be considered.

A large virtue of cost-benefit analysis is that it tends to overcome people's tendency to focus on mere parts of problems by requiring them to look broadly at the consequences of apparently isolated actions. It is a terrific safeguard against system neglect. Of course, cost-benefit analysts may not be able to learn what they need to know, but their methods, and the questions they ask, dramatically increase the likelihood that they will find out.

Beyond Hysteria and Complacency

It is true but obvious to say that people lack information and that their lack of information can lead to an inadequate or excessive demand for regulation, or simultaneous hysteria and complacency. What is less obvious is that predictable features of cognition can lead to a demand for regulation that is unlikely to be based on the facts. When people ask for regulation because of fears fueled by the availability heuristic, and when large health benefits from the risk-producing activity are not registering, it would be highly desirable to create cost-benefit filters for their requests. When interest groups exploit cognitive mechanisms to create unwarranted fear or diminish concern for serious problems, it is desirable to have institutional safeguards. When people fail to ask for regulation for related reasons, it would be a good idea to create mechanisms by which governments might nonetheless act if the consequences of action would be desirable. If backed by the right institutions and done properly, cost-benefit analysis provides such a mechanism.

Of course, it is entirely possible that the public demand for regulation will result from something other than cognitive errors, even if the relevant risk seems low as a statistical matter. People may think, for example, that it is especially important to protect poor children from a certain risk in a geographically isolated area, and they may be willing to devote an unusually large amount to ensure that protection. What seems to be a cognitive error may turn out, on reflection, to be a judgment of value—and a judgment that can survive reflection. I will return to this point. For now, the basic points are that cognitive errors are common and that cost-benefit analysis can supply a corrective.

Framing Problems

I want to sharpen these points by considering some of the most intriguing research in contemporary social science. It goes by the name of the *foreign-language effect*.[7] The central finding is this: When people are using a language other than their first, they are less likely to make some of the most important errors found in decades of work in behavioral science. In a foreign language, people are more likely to give the right answers and to avoid some of the cognitive traps into which we fall in ordinary life, in business, and in government. To say the least, that's puzzling.

Consider an example. Behavioral scientists have long known that semantically equivalent descriptions of certain questions can produce puzzlingly different responses.[8] For example, people are more likely to choose to have an operation if they are told, "after five years, 90 percent of people who have the operation are alive," than if they are told, "after five years, 10 percent of people who have the operation are dead." So too, if people are told, "if you adopt energy-conservation strategies, you will save $200 per year," they are less likely to adopt such strategies than if they are told, "if you do not adopt energy conservation strategies, you will lose $200 per year."

The reason is that most people are *loss averse*. They dislike losses more than they like corresponding gains, and a "loss frame" can have a much larger impact than a "gain frame." In a sense, framing involves *translating*. It is usually simple to translate from one frame to another. For decision making, such translations often matter, because they can turn a loss into a gain or vice versa.

It is possible, of course, to wonder whether semantically equivalent descriptions might come with suggestive *signals*, to which listeners are rationally attentive. If a doctor tells you that most people who have an operation are alive after five years, she also seems to be saying, "I think it is a good idea for you to have the operation." By contrast, a doctor's emphasis on the percentage of people who end up dying seems to say, "This might not be the best idea." The signal that accompanies people's descriptions of future outcomes might explain some of the effects of different frames.

One of the valuable features of research on the foreign-language effect is that it bypasses questions about the signal contained in one or another frame. If the same words are used in English and French, there is no different signal in one or another language. It is far too weak to say that the descriptions are semantically equivalent. They are equivalent—period. If precisely the same question is described in English and French, and if native English speakers give better answers in French, then it seems clear that using one's own language can lead to mistakes.

The foundational paper on this topic by Boaz Keysar and his colleagues[9] offers two key findings. First, use of a foreign language reduces loss aversion and makes people more likely to make bets (both hypothetical and real) on the basis of expected value. In that sense, people are more likely to act consistently with standard economic accounts of rationality. Second, use of a foreign language reduces framing effects.

Consider the famous Asian disease problem, elaborated by Amos Tversky and Daniel Kahneman:

Problem 1: Imagine that the U.S. is preparing for the outbreak of an unusual Asian disease, which is expected to kill 600 people. Two alternative programs to combat the disease have been proposed. Assume that the exact scientific estimate of the consequences of the programs are as follows:

If Program A is adopted, 200 people will be saved.

If Program B is adopted, there is 1/3 probability that 600 people will be saved, and 2/3 probability that no people will be saved.

Which of the two programs would you favor?

It turns out that most people prefer Program A. Now, consider Problem 2:

Problem 2:

If Program C is adopted 400 people will die.

If Program D is adopted there is 1/3 probability that nobody will die, and 2/3 probability that 600 people will die.

Which of the two programs would you favor?[10]

Most people choose Program D—but a moment's reflection should be enough to show that the two problems are the same. The only difference is that in Problem 1, the outcomes are described by the number of lives saved, whereas in Problem 2, they are described by the number of lives lost. The change produces a major shift from risk aversion to risk taking. That is a demonstration of the power of framing.

When people are answering in a language that is not their own, they are much less likely to display the usual asymmetry between gain frames and loss frames. To that extent, people are more likely to be rational when they are using a foreign language.

What explains these findings? The best answer is that when people are using their native tongue, their emotional reactions help determine their answers, and a loss triggers strong emotions. When they use a foreign language, those reactions are blunted, and people think less automatically and more deliberatively. Keysar and his coauthors contend that "people rely more on systematic processes that respect normative rules when making decisions in a foreign language than when making decisions in their native tongue."[11] They speculate that the central reason is that emotion and affect are attenuated when people use a foreign language, and that attenuation leads to more systematic processing. In now-familiar terms, native speakers are more likely to think fast, whereas foreign-language speakers are more likely to think slowly; they are more distanced from their own immediate reactions.

In recent years, there has been a burst of further research on the foreign-language effect, attempting to specify its boundaries and to understand the underlying mechanisms. The original findings by Keysar et al. have been repeatedly replicated and extended. For example, Albert Costa and his coauthors similarly find that use of a foreign language reduces loss aversion and framing effects.[12] They also find that when speaking in a foreign language, people are less likely to avoid psychological biases and to run the numbers (and hence to arrive at what is, on standard accounts, the correct solution). These findings raise several puzzles, but let's simply note that across a range of problems, people perform better when they are answering in a foreign language, and the reason is that they are thinking hard and slow and are less likely to be trapped by their intuitions and rapid reactions.

Cost-Benefit Analysis as a Foreign Language

A fanciful question: When public officials in English-speaking nations are trying to resolve a difficult problem, should they try to conduct their meetings in French? That would be crazy, of course. But cost-benefit analysis is essentially a foreign language, and it has the same effect identified in research on the foreign-language effect: it reduces people's reliance on intuitive judgments that sometimes go wrong, especially in highly technical areas.

Imagine, for example, that because of some recent event—a railroad accident, an outbreak of food-borne illness—both ordinary citizens and public officials are quite alarmed, and they strongly favor an aggressive (and immediate) regulatory response. Imagine too that the benefits of any such response would be relatively low, because the incident is highly unlikely to be repeated, and that the costs of the response would be high. The language of cost-benefit analysis imposes a firm brake on an evidently unjustified initiative.

Or suppose that a 1 in 50,000 lifetime risk of, say, getting cancer in the workplace, faced by millions of workers, is not much on the government's viewscreen because it seems to be a mere part of the social background, a fact of life. But suppose the risk could be eliminated at a relatively low cost and that it would save at least five hundred lives annually. Cost-benefit analysis would seem to require that risk to be eliminated, even if the public is not clamoring for it.

Whatever the problem, cost-benefit analysis should also reduce and perhaps even eliminate the power of behavioral biases and heuristics (such as availability)—both of which strengthen or weaken the public demand for regulation. It forces officials to speak in a language that people do not ordinarily use and that they even find uncongenial—but insofar as it helps correct biases, it is all the better for that. True, people can frame costs and benefits in certain ways to try to make one or another outcome seem better, but doing that is not exactly easy. If a regulation would cost $900 million annually and prevent thirty premature deaths, it is not clear how to present those facts to make them sound a lot different—and if someone tries, public officials will probably see right through their efforts.

Cost-benefit analysis is essentially a language, one that may defy ordinary intuitions and that must ultimately be evaluated in terms of its fit with what people, after a process of sustained reflection, really value. One of its virtues is that it weakens the likelihood that policymakers will make decisions on the basis of intuitive reactions that seem hard to resist and that cannot survive that reflection.

Work on the foreign-language effect seems to be about psychology, not politics or law. But it clarifies and fortifies the claim that in legislatures, bureaucracies, and courtrooms, as in ordinary life, we often do best to translate social problems into terms that lay bare the underlying variables and make them clear for all to see. In that sense, there is also a democratic argument for cost-benefit balancing.

N'est-ce pas?

3 Willingness to Pay and the Value of Life

When government conducts cost-benefit analysis, some of its numbers come from a single figure, called the *value of a statistical life* (VSL). The whole idea might seem creepy, but the figure is central to monetizing the benefits of life-saving regulations. Whether the issue involves clear air and water or safety in food, at work, and on the road, the major monetized benefits are usually generated by using VSL. That value is now, by the way, in the vicinity of $9 million.

An understanding of VSL, and its importance and limits, gets us to the heart of the arguments for using cost-benefit analysis and leads us directly to important philosophical issues. Much of my engagement in this chapter will be with the utilitarian tradition, represented by John Stuart Mill and Jeremy Bentham, and also the deontological tradition, represented by Immanuel Kant and John Rawls. This is not a work of philosophy; I will not attempt to choose between the two traditions or to explore alternatives (except in passing). My hope is to show that cost-benefit analysis, understood in a certain way, can attract support from diverse foundations. At least across a variety of problems, it is not only compatible with them; it is required by them.

To get a bit ahead of the story: Whether or not regulators say that they are using a VSL, they will inevitably be using one. Any chosen level of stringency depends, at least implicitly, on some judgment about how much money should be spent to save lives. So there is no avoiding some kind of monetary valuation. The real issues are what the value should be, what method we use to come up with it, and whether we should be transparent about it.

Of the three letters in VSL, a bright spotlight should be placed on the *S*. We are not speaking here of identifiable lives—of the lives of your son, your mother, your lover, or your best friend. We are speaking instead of statistical lives, meaning that in a large population subjected to a risk, a certain number of people will die. If we want to be precise, government is assessing the *value of reducing statistical risks of death*.

That claim raises many questions, and I will return to them in due course. But let us notice that in trying to figure out that value, the government's cost-benefit analysts ask this question: How much are people willing to pay to eliminate a risk? In other words, they focus on people's willingness to pay (WTP). But that focus raises immediate questions: Why should government care about WTP at all? Why should it give such authoritative weight to people's willingness to pay to eliminate risks?

Easy Cases, Hard Cases

It is useful to answer these questions by focusing on the *Easy Cases*, in which each individual who benefits from regulatory protection must pay all of the cost. Suppose that you face a 1 in 100,000 risk of dying from contaminants in drinking water. How much would you pay to eliminate that risk? In the Easy Cases, government is giving people protection for which they are going to end up paying. How much should government force people to pay?

I call these the *Easy Cases* for one reason: As a general rule, government should not require people to pay more than they want to pay. People have limited budgets. Instead of paying ninety dollars to eliminate a mortality risk of 1 in 100,000, people might want to use that money for food, medical care, or clothing. In such cases, WTP is usually the right foundation for VSL, because people are hardly helped by being forced to pay for regulatory benefits that they do not believe to be worth buying.

At this point, you might be thinking that the government should protect people against the risk, and it should pay for that protection. Maybe so. But in the Easy Cases, we're not talking about that possibility. The government isn't paying. And if you think that government *should* pay to eliminate a mortality risk, the question remains: How much should it pay?

There are some important qualifications to my claim in favor of use of people's WTP. People might lack information: they might not know what a risk of 1 in 100,000 really is, or they might not have the background that would enable them to understand the concept. Or they might suffer from a behavioral bias—perhaps in the form of *present bias* (focusing on today but not tomorrow, next week, or next year) or *optimistic bias* (thinking, unrealistically, that they are immune from risks). If those qualifications are put to one side, the argument for using VSL is quite powerful in the Easy Cases on grounds of both welfare and (less obviously) autonomy. I shall devote considerable space to defending that claim.

The analysis is much less straightforward in harder cases, in which beneficiaries pay only a fraction of the cost of what they receive. Suppose, for example, that workers are paying $30 million for safety protection, but consumers are paying $90 million, and suppose that the monetized benefits of such protection, enjoyed only by the workers, are $70 million. In such cases, the costs are higher than the benefits, but the workers are net winners from regulation. They are receiving benefits, and they are paying less than the full cost of those benefits.

Of course, there will be many losers as well (consumers), and the costs are higher than the benefits, so the regulation might be unjustified on balance—but unlike in the Easy Cases, arguments from welfare and autonomy may not lead in any obvious direction. As we shall see, it is possible that regulation is justified on welfare grounds *even if the cost-benefit analysis (based on VSL) suggests that it is not.* The reason is that purely in terms of welfare, the winners may win more than the losers lose.

Suppose that in the case just given, the workers are poor, and they gain a great deal in terms of safety, while (wealthy) consumers have to pay more for the goods that the workers produce. Even if the monetized costs exceed the monetized benefits, the welfare gains to workers might be higher than the welfare losses to consumers. Because welfare is the master concept, and because cost-benefit analysis is an imperfect means of assessing welfare effects, this point cannot be ignored, at least as a matter of principle.

In such cases, it is also possible that regulation is justified on redistributive grounds, if it helps those who need help while hurting those who are quite well-off. It is important to see that in general, the best response to unjustified inequality is a redistributive income tax, not regulation—which is a crude and potentially counterproductive redistributive tool.[1] If workers are protected from statistical risks, they might find that their salaries are lower; some of them might lose their jobs. But suppose that we are dealing with the harder cases and that a nation lacks an optimal income tax and seeks greater redistribution. If so, it is possible that regulation is justified even if the monetized costs are higher than the monetized benefits.

The conclusion is that in the Easy Cases, the argument for using VSL, based on WTP, is fairly secure. But in the Hard Cases, the use of VSL may produce a cost-benefit analysis that fails to point in the right directions. At the same time, it is exceedingly difficult to measure welfare directly, and regulation is at best an imperfect redistributive tool. In the Hard Cases, regulators should depart from the outcome of cost-benefit analysis, based on VSL, only when there is compelling reason to believe that the regulation is nonetheless justified on the ground that it will either promote welfare or achieve important distributive goals.

Practice

To produce monetary amounts for statistical risks, agencies in the United States rely on two kinds of evidence.[2] The first and most important involves real-world markets, producing evidence of compensation levels for actual risks.[3] If employers impose a workplace risk on their employees, how much are employees paid to assume that risk? In the workplace and in the market for consumer goods, additional safety has a price; market evidence is investigated to identify that price. The advantage of such real-world markets is that under certain assumptions, they will reveal people's actual preferences, especially when large populations are aggregated. In part for this reason, real-world markets provide the foundation for actual government practice.

A potentially serious disadvantage of these studies is that the underlying decisions are "noisy." A decision to take a construction job is based on a whole host of considerations. Workers are most unlikely to think: "I'll face an annual mortality risk of 1 in 100,000 rather than 1 in 200,000, but it's worth it!" Whenever people take a job, live in a city, or purchase products, it's not exactly easy for them to identify mortality risks. In fact, that seems like a ridiculously impossible task. For this reason, we might object that real-world data about choices, involving options with a large set of characteristics, cannot possibly tell us how much people are willing to pay, or to accept, for mortality risks of particular sizes. There are related questions, taken up below, about whether people are sufficiently informed and whether their decisions are fully rational. For now, consider the standard response from those who rely on real-world evidence: across large populations, we really do find sufficiently steady numbers, justifying the view that on average, people are paid a specified amount to face mortality risks.

The second kind of evidence comes from contingent valuation studies, which ask people, through surveys, how much they are willing to pay to reduce statistical risks.[4] For example: How much would you be willing to pay to avoid a 1 in 100,000 risk of getting cancer from arsenic in drinking water? I have put that question to many law students, and the average answer is usually in the vicinity of seventy-five dollars—suggesting a VSL of around $7.5 million.

The advantage of contingent valuation studies is that they can isolate people's willingness to pay to avoid mortality risks. In this respect, they are far less noisy than real-world data. If we find that the average person is willing to pay one hundred dollars to eliminate a mortality risk of 1 in 100,000, perhaps we can conclude that the VSL is $10 million—not in the sense that a human life is really "worth" that amount, or even in the sense that a 1 in 1000 mortality risk is worth $10,000 or that a 1 in 100 mortality risk is worth $100,000, but in the sense that when government is eliminating a 1 in 100,000 risk faced by a large population, one hundred dollars is the right number to assign.

The disadvantage of contingent valuation studies is that the questions are hypothetical and unfamiliar, and there are many reasons to wonder whether they provide an accurate measurement rather than a stab in the dark.[5] A question about how much you are willing to pay to eliminate a mortality risk of 1 in 100,000 might seem so odd, and so confusing for many people, that the resulting figure tells us very little. And we do tend to get puzzlingly diverse answers. In my own studies, the average conceals a lot of individual differences. Many people say that they are willing to pay $0 to eliminate a risk of 1 in 100,000 and many say that they are willing to pay $200 or more, suggesting a VSL that ranges from $0 to $20 million or higher. Perhaps the diverse answers reflect different risk preferences and different levels of wealth. But perhaps they reflect confusion.

There are other puzzles. How much would you pay to buy safety equipment to eliminate an annual risk of 1 in 100,000 from driving your new car? I have sometimes obtained a high amount in response to that question—an average in the vicinity of $250. How much would you pay to eliminate an annual risk of 1 in 100,000 from contaminants in drinking water? I have sometimes obtained a low amount from that question—an average in the vicinity of fifty dollars. The disparities may reflect a belief that context matters and that all 1 in 100,000 risks are not the same. Or they may reflect confusion, as when a new car purchase (requiring an expenditure of $20,000 or more) biases people in the direction of providing high numbers for risk reduction. A high purchase price might provide an "anchor," inflating the amount that people are willing to pay to eliminate risks.

For government regulators, the relevant risks usually are in the general range of 1 in 10,000 to 1 in 100,000. The calculation of VSL is a product of simple arithmetic. Suppose (as current studies suggest) that workers must be paid $900, on average, to assume a risk of 1 in 10,000. If so, the VSL would be $9 million. Note in this regard that the Department of Transportation, building on that literature, recently adopted a revised VSL estimate of $9.1 million, with suitable adjustments for future years.[6] That estimate fits with existing understandings in the technical literature, which has become increasingly refined over time.

For all their problems, a large advantage of labor market studies is that they avoid the lively disputes over the use of WTP or instead willingness to accept (WTA) in regulatory policy.[7] In both experiments and the real world, people tend to demand far more to give up a good than they are willing to pay to obtain it in the first instance. How much would you be willing to pay for a new lottery ticket? How much would you have to be paid to give up a lottery ticket that you hold? The latter number is usually a lot higher than the former. The disparity between WTP and WTA seems to complicate efforts to assign monetary values to regulatory benefits, including mortality and morbidity. If people are willing to pay twenty-five dollars to eliminate an existing risk of 1 in 100,000 but demand one hundred dollars to incur a new risk of 1 in 100,000, then it is difficult to know how to proceed for purposes of monetary valuation of risks. Should agencies use twenty-five dollars, one hundred dollars, or some intermediate figure? Is the VSL $2.5 million or $10 million?

Fortunately, this problem seems to dissipate in the context of labor market studies. If workers who face a risk of 1 in 10,000 are paid $600 more for doing so, and if workers who decline to face such a risk are paid $600 less, then it is irrelevant whether agencies speak in terms of WTP or WTA. And indeed, there appears to be no difference between the two in this context.[8]

Despite the widespread use of VSL, based on the relevant research, there remains considerable controversy about whether the resulting figures actually capture people's informed choices and whether other methods might be preferable.[9] I will not try to resolve the controversy here (though some of the discussion will bear on it). My basic goal is to see whether VSL, based on WTP, is the right basis for policy, *assuming that we have properly identified WTP*. As we shall see, the answer to that question helps specify the rationale for cost-benefit analysis itself, as well as some of the limits of that rationale.

Forced Exchanges

For the sake of simplicity, assume a society in which people face multiple risks of 1 in 100,000 and in which every person is both adequately informed and willing to pay no more and no less than ninety dollars to eliminate each of those risks. Assume too that the cost of eliminating these 1 in 100,000 risks is widely variable, ranging from close to zero to many billions of dollars. Assume finally that the cost of eliminating any risk is *borne entirely by each individual who benefits from eliminating that risk*.

For example, people's water bills will entirely reflect the costs of a policy that eliminates a 1 in 100,000 risk of getting cancer from arsenic in drinking water. If the per-person cost is one hundred dollars, then each water bill will be increased by exactly that amount. We are assuming, then, that each individual is willing to pay no more and no less than ninety dollars to eliminate each risk of 1 in 100,000, and we are assuming as well that the cost of eliminating each risk will be fully borne by each individual.

With these assumptions, the argument for using WTP to calculate VSL is straightforward. Regulation amounts to a forced exchange. It tells people that they must purchase certain benefits for a certain amount. Why should government force people to pay for things that they do not want?

Welfare

Begin with welfare.[10] By hypothesis, a forced exchange on terms that people dislike will make them worse off. It will require them to buy something that they do not want, undoubtedly because they want other things more. They might want to use their money not to eliminate a mortality risk of 1 in 100,000, but to buy food or education or medical care, or to eliminate a mortality risk of 1 in 20,000 or 1 in 10,000.

At first glance, use of WTP on the assumptions that I am making seems hard to contest. In free societies that are concerned with people's welfare, we should begin by asking people what they want, and if people do not want certain goods, we should start by presuming that they know their own priorities. A forced exchange will decrease their welfare. Indeed, a forced exchange would violate John Stuart Mill's Harm Principle without apparent justification.[11] In Mill's view, the government should not be allowed to control people's behavior unless there is "harm to others." If people are only harming themselves, there is no basis for coercion.

In defense of this position, Mill placed a bright spotlight on welfare and emphasized an essential problem with outsiders, including government officials. He insisted that the individual "is the person most interested in his own well-being" and that the "ordinary man or woman has means of knowledge immeasurably surpassing those that can be possessed by any one else." When society seeks to overrule the individual's judgment, it does so on the basis of "general presumptions"; these "may be altogether wrong, and even if right, are as likely as not to be misapplied to individual cases." Mill's goal was to ensure that people's lives go well, and he contended that the best solution is for public officials to allow people to find their own path.

For purposes of evaluating regulation, it does not matter if the existing distribution of income is unjust or if poor people are, in some intelligible sense, coerced to run certain risks (as they might be if they live in bad or desperate conditions and have few opportunities). The remedy for unjust distributions and for that form of coercion is hardly to require people to buy regulatory benefits on terms that they find unacceptable. In fact, that would be a terrible idea. Suppose that people are willing to pay only sixty dollars to eliminate a 1 in 100,000 risk because they are not rich; suppose also that if they had double their current wealth, they would be willing to pay $120. Government does people no favors by forcing them to pay the amount that they would pay if they had more money. On the contrary, it hurts them.

It follows that in the Easy Cases, it is true but irrelevant that willingness to pay is dependent on ability to pay. Suppose that certain people are willing to pay a very small amount to eliminate a 1 in 100,000 risk, not because they would not obtain much welfare from eliminating that risk, but because they have little money to spend. It might be thought that the welfare gain is not captured by the very small amount that they are willing to pay. That thought is right, but we should not collapse two different questions: (1) Should government force people to spend more than the very small amount that they are willing to pay, because the welfare gain would not be trivial? (2) Should government itself, though a compelled expenditure from consumers or taxpayers, be willing to spend more than poor people are willing to pay to reduce a risk, because the welfare gain would not be trivial?

The answer to (2) might be yes—and if government is concerned with welfare, it might well give that answer. But (1) is a quite different question. Unless there is a problem of lack of information or a behavioral bias, the answer to (1) is clearly no. The welfare gain would not justify the welfare loss. That is the beauty of the WTP approach, which offers an automatic test of the welfare consequences of regulation.

Autonomy

Perhaps regulatory policy should not be based on welfare; perhaps it is unclear what *welfare* really means. Even if so, WTP might be defended instead on the ground of personal autonomy.[12] On this view, people should be allowed to be sovereign over their own lives. It follows that government should respect people's choices about how to use their limited resources (again, so long as those choices are informed and so long as no behavioral bias is at work). We can associate the idea of autonomy with that of dignity. Government should allow people to make choices about how to allocate their resources, not necessarily because people know best, but because they should be treated as adults rather than as infants.

When people decline to devote more than ninety dollars to the elimination of a 1 in 100,000 risk, it is because they would like to spend the money in a way that seems to them more desirable. If regulators do not use people's actual judgments, then they are insulting their autonomy. If people in a free society are entitled to have a kind of mastery over the conduct of their own lives, then they should be permitted to make such allocations as they choose. It is usual to justify use of WTP on welfare grounds, but the same approach is at least equally defensible as a means of respecting the autonomy of persons.

Disaggregating VSL

For VSL, government agencies and departments now use a population-wide number. In general, they do not distinguish among either risks or persons. But the arguments thus far suggest that in the Easy Cases, agencies should disaggregate VSL across both risks and persons, and should not do so on the basis of a population-wide average or median. In principle, every individual in society has a separate VSL, and each of these varies across risks. Recall my own data, finding that in certain populations, people will pay far more to reduce risks from automobiles than to reduce statistically identical risks from drinking water.

Suppose, for example, that people are willing to pay $250 to avoid a 1 in 100,000 risk of dying in a car crash, but pay only one hundred dollars to avoid a 1 in 100,000 risk of dying of cancer.[13] If the government uses a WTP for both risks of $150, it will force people to pay less than they want to avoid the risks associated with car crashes, and more than they want to avoid risks of cancer. Why should government do that? If the argument is convincing in this example, it should apply in numerous cases in which WTP and hence VSL vary across mortality risks. The central question would not be conceptual but instead empirical: How does VSL vary, depending on the nature of the particular risk at issue? We might well expect mortality risks from terrorism to be valued especially highly; perhaps the same is true of mortality risks from food or from air travel in general.

With respect to persons, the central idea is that different people should be expected to have a different WTP to avoid mortality risks. To the extent feasible, regulators should not use a "mass" VSL but should instead attempt to individuate. This argument is more controversial, among other things because it might well treat children differently from adults[14] and the elderly differently from the young,[15] and because it would certainly treat poor people as less valuable (literally) than rich people. The reason is that because they have less money, poor people would have a lower VSL than wealthy people. (Similarly, poor areas, and poor nations, would have a lower VSL than wealthier ones.)[16] But so long as we are dealing with Easy Cases, differences appear to be appropriate here as well.

The reason is not that poor people are less valuable than rich people. It is that *no one, rich or poor, should be forced to pay more than she is willing to pay for the reduction of risks*. In fact, this idea embodies a norm of equality (and the right one). If poor people are unwilling to pay much for the reduction of serious risks, and if government wants to help, the appropriate response is not a compelled purchase but a subsidy, perhaps in the form of cash payments. We might even say that according to the right conception of risk equity, people should not be compelled to pay more than they are willing to pay to reduce risks (unless there is a lack of information or a behavioral bias).

It is tempting to respond that it is a uniform VSL, one that does not distinguish between rich and poor, that embodies the right conception of risk equity, treating every person as equal to every other person and redistributing resources in the direction of poor people. But this is an error. A uniform VSL, taken from a population-wide median, does not produce redistribution toward the poor, any more than any other kind of forced exchange. Government does not require people to buy Volvos, even if Volvos would reduce statistical risks. If government required everyone to buy Volvos, it would not be producing desirable redistribution. A uniform VSL has some of the same characteristics as a policy that requires people to buy Volvos; it forces people to pay for levels of safety for which they do not want to pay. In principle, the government should force exchanges only on terms that people find acceptable, at least if it is genuinely concerned with their welfare. That principle is the correct conception of risk equity.

Note, once again, that the argument for using WTP does not imply satisfaction with the existing distribution of wealth, and it does not mean that the government should not subsidize reductions in risk. The problem with forced exchanges is that they do nothing to alter existing distributions. In fact, they make poor people worse off, requiring them to use their limited resources for something that they do not want to buy.

To be sure, there are strong pragmatic reasons to question use of a more disaggregated WTP. Regulators may well lack reliable information about how to disaggregate, whether the question involves risks or persons. The findings of existing studies may not be sufficiently clear for official use. Market studies, testing actual behavior, may not tell us what we need to know. If so, increased differentiation—for risk characteristics and for individuals outside of the labor market (particularly the very young and the very old)—may require greater reliance on contingent valuation research, which allows researchers to tailor a scenario to particular types of risks and affected populations. For example, we could ask people over sixty-five how much they are willing to pay to reduce certain risks, and we could put the same question to people between the ages of twenty-five and thirty-five. But we have seen that there is good reason to question the reliability of contingent valuation research.

Moreover, many regulatory programs necessarily affect large groups of people at the same time, and it is not possible to tailor the level of stringency to different subgroups, let alone individuals. But if the analysis of the Easy Cases is correct, these concerns involve limitations of knowledge and feasibility; they do not suggest that disaggregation would be a mistake in principle.

Are There Actually Easy Cases?

Are there any Easy Cases?

There certainly are. With the enactment of workers' compensation programs, nonunionized workers faced a dollar-for-dollar wage reduction, corresponding almost perfectly to the expected value of the benefits that they received.[17] For drinking water regulation, something similar is involved. The entire cost of regulation is passed onto consumers in the form of higher water bills.[18] These, then, look like Easy Cases.

To be sure, many real-world cases do not fall in that category. Air pollution regulations are especially important, because they count for a large percentage of both the benefits and the costs of all federal rules, and there is good evidence that the costs of such rules are not fully borne by their beneficiaries. Under the Clean Air Act, relatively poor people appear to obtain disproportionate benefits because they live in especially dirty areas, and they do not have to pay the full costs of what they get.[19] With respect to air pollution, we are not speaking of Easy Cases.

Nonetheless, the Easy Cases do find real-world analogues. And even when beneficiaries do not pay the full cost of what they obtain, they might pay a substantial portion of it. For such cases, the analysis of the Easy Cases is the right place to start.

Objections

There are several objections to the use of WTP to calculate VSL, even in the Easy Cases. They point to some important qualifications of the arguments thus far. They also suggest some puzzles that deserve continuing empirical and conceptual attention. At the same time, many of the objections sound more convincing than they actually are. They point to theoretical possibilities, but they do not, in the general run of cases, impugn the use of WTP in cost-benefit analysis.

Miswanting

The first objection is that people may suffer from a problem of *miswanting*.[20] That is, they want some things that do not promote their welfare, and they do not want some things that would promote their welfare. In many settings, people's decisions appear not to make them happier, and different decisions would do so.[21] *Predicted welfare*, or utility at the time of decision, may be very different from *experienced welfare*, or welfare as life is actually lived.[22] If this is so, then WTP loses much of its underlying justification. People's choices do not actually promote their welfare. (So much for John Stuart Mill.) If government can be confident that people are not willing to pay for goods from which they would greatly benefit, perhaps government should abandon WTP.

A different concern is that people's preferences may have adapted to existing opportunities, including deprivation.[23] Tocqueville writes: "Shall I call it a blessing of God, or a last malediction of his anger, this disposition of the soul that makes men insensible to extreme misery and often gives them a sort of depraved taste for the cause of their afflictions?"[24] Perhaps people show a low WTP for environmental goods, including health improvements, simply because they have adjusted to environmental bads, including health risks. People's beliefs reflect their motivations, and we may be motivated to think that life is safer than it is. Perhaps people's low WTP reflects an effort to reduce cognitive dissonance through the conclusion that risks are lower than they actually are. It's not a lot of fun to think that you face serious dangers, and some people undoubtedly develop an unduly optimistic account of their actual situation (a problem to which I will return).

In some contexts, the idea of miswanting raises serious problems for neoclassical economics and for unambivalent enthusiasm for freedom of choice. As Daniel Kahneman and Carol Varey have explained, "If people do not know their future experience utilities, or if their preferences of the moment do not accurately reflect what they do know, a case can be made for using experience utility rather than preference as the unit of account in utilitarian calculations."[25] If the basis for use of WTP is welfare, then there is a real difficulty, because use of WTP may be imperfectly connected with promoting people's welfare. (See chapter 4 for more details.)

In making these claims, I do not mean to take a contentious position on the nature of welfare. People want their lives to go well, but their understandings of what it means for their lives to go well are diverse and include a diverse array of goods. Hedonic states are important, but they are hardly all that matters. People choose certain activities not because they are fun or joyful, but because they are right to choose, perhaps because they are meaningful. People want their lives to have purpose; they do not want their lives simply to be happy.[26] People sensibly, even virtuously, choose things that they will not in any simple sense "like."[27]

For example, they may want to help others even when it is not a lot of fun to do so. They may want to do what they are morally obliged to do, even if they do not enjoy it. An important survey suggests that people's projected choices are *generally* based on what they believe would promote their subjective well-being—but that sometimes people are willing to make choices that would sacrifice their happiness in favor of promoting an assortment of other goals, including (1) promoting the happiness of their family, (2) increasing their control over their lives, (3) increasing their social status, or (4) improving their sense of purpose in life.[28] The point here is not that people seek to promote a narrow conception of welfare, but that, whatever their preferred conception, they make mistakes, and these mistakes can be reflected in their WTP.

This point bears on autonomy as well. The idea of autonomy requires respect not merely for whatever preferences people happen to have, but also for preferences that are informed and developed in a way that does not reflect coercion, unjustified limits in available opportunities, or background injustice. With respect to some risks, the relevant preferences may be nonautonomous. Consider the fact that in human history, many women have faced a risk of male harassment or domination (or even violence) under circumstances in which they believe that little can be done—and hence adapt.[29]

In the context of ordinary regulatory policy, however, this objection has more theoretical than practical interest. Typically, regulation involves the reduction of low-level mortality risks (say, 1 in 100,000). In the abstract, there is no reason to believe that the use of people's WTP (say, ninety dollars) is a product of adaptive preferences or a problem of miswanting. It is true that when WTP does result from adaptive preferences, judgment about the Easy Cases must be revised—but in the real world of regulatory practice, there is no reason to think that problem arises often or that it is sufficient to "impeach" the evidence on which regulators rely in using VSL.

Information and Behavioral Market Failures

A closely related objection would point to an absence of information and to bounded rationality, meant as an umbrella concept for a wide range of findings from behavioral economics. We can use the term *behavioral market failures* to refer to a set of behavioral problems that may make markets work imperfectly, including present bias, unrealistic optimism, myopia, and self-control problems.

Here is a way to make the point: Imagine a population of people. Let us call them Simpsons (after the character Homer Simpson in the television show *The Simpsons*). Simpsons make choices, but the choices reflect systematic errors in the sense that they are unrealistically optimistic, neglectful of the long term, and reckless. The Simpsons will have an identifiable WTP to avoid mortality risks (and other risks). By hypothesis, the WTP and the corresponding VSL will be low. But the fact that it is low does not mean that the government should use a low VSL in regulatory policy for the Simpsons. What matters is the welfare of the Simpsons' population, and the Simpsons' welfare is not adequately captured by the Simpsons' WTP. Regulators should use preferences that are informed and rational and that extend over people's life histories. The Simpsons' preferences do not satisfy those criteria.

No nation consists of the Simpsons, but as behavioral economists have shown, people often suffer from present bias and unrealistic optimism, and they have difficulty dealing with low-probability events. If people are unaware of the risks that they actually face, or if they have a poor understanding of such risks, their WTP, as measured by market evidence, might be too low (or too high). Suppose that workers receive a ninety-dollar wage premium for risks of 1 in 100,000. What does this mean, concretely? Are workers actually trading off risks and money? Do they even know about the relevant probabilities? If these questions do not have clear answers, the market evidence might not be reliable if we care about welfare. (Note that this is not an objection to basing VSL on informed WTP; it is merely a concern that existing evidence does not allow us to be certain that we are eliciting informed WTP.)

Or perhaps the availability heuristic will lead people to underestimate mortality risks. If people cannot recall a case in which some activity produced illness or death, they might conclude that a risk is trivial even if it is not. Perhaps market evidence will reflect such mistakes. Or perhaps the same heuristic, and neglect of the question of probability, will lead people to exaggerate risks, producing a WTP that is wildly inflated in light of reality. And if people are unable to understand the meaning of ideas like 1 in 100,000 or to respond rationally to such ideas, then there are serious problems with relying on contingent valuation studies to produce WTP.

If present bias is at work, people's WTP may reflect excessive discounting of future health benefits. If workers are disregarding the future or applying an implausibly high discount rate, then there is a good argument for not relying on their WTP. In the context of climate change, for example, the temporally distant nature of the harm might well lead to insufficient concern for a potentially catastrophic risk. The same is true for less dramatic risks that people face in their daily lives. Young smokers undoubtedly give too little attention to the long-term health risks associated with smoking. Those who choose a poor diet and little exercise often fail to consider the long-term effects of their behavior. Self-control problems are an important part of bounded rationality. If a low WTP shows a failure to give adequate attention to the future, then there is reason not to use WTP.

To be sure, a dollar today is worth less than a dollar tomorrow, in part because a dollar today can be invested and made to grow. For money, some kind of discount rate makes a great deal of sense—and for rational reasons, people might prefer welfare today to welfare tomorrow. For all of us, there is at least some chance of death tonight, which argues for welfare today. The question how rational people distribute welfare (as opposed to money) over time does not admit of an easy answer. But if people care very little about their future selves, and are willing to impose a great deal of future suffering in return for a small benefit in the present, then something has likely gone wrong. An appealing welfarist approach emphasizes preferences that are fully informed and fully rational and that extend over life histories. If people's choices do not satisfy these constraints, they are "impeached" from the standpoint of welfare.

When a behavioral market failure is involved, appropriate adjustments should be made to WTP, and the VSL that emerges from WTP should be corrected accordingly. It is possible, of course, that across large aggregations of workers, behavioral market failures are not a serious problem, and hence existing numbers are trustworthy. As noted, no nation consists of Simpsons. But further conceptual and empirical work needs to be done on these issues.

Rights

A quite different objection would point to people's rights. Perhaps people have a right not to be subjected to risks of a certain magnitude, and the use of WTP will violate that right. It is tempting to think that whatever their WTP, human beings should have a right not to be subject to risks above a particular level. Imagine that poor people live in a place where they face a 1/20 annual risk of dying from water pollution. That risk is intolerably high. It makes sense to say that the government, or the international community, should take steps to reduce that risk even if the relevant population is poor, even if people are willing to pay only one dollar to eliminate it, and even if the per-person cost is ten dollars.

As an abstract claim about people's rights, the objection seems correct. Something has gone badly wrong if people are exposed to serious risks and their WTP prevents them from doing anything in response. It would be foolish to suggest that WTP is determinative of the appropriate use of government resources. (Would it make sense to say that government would give poor people a check for one hundred dollars only if they were willing to pay one hundred dollars for the check?) And in many cases, people are subject to risks whose magnitude is indeed a violation of their rights. But for several reasons, this point has little force against my conclusions for the Easy Cases.

The initial problem with this objection is that in the cases under discussion, rights of this kind are usually not involved; we are speaking here of statistically small risks. Suppose that this initial response is unconvincing and that rights are indeed involved. If so, there is a still more fundamental response. When rights are involved, the proper response is not to force people to buy protection that they do not want, but to provide a subsidy that will give them the benefit for free or enable them to receive the benefit at what is, for them, an acceptable price. Nothing here is meant to deny the possibility that government should provide certain goods via subsidy, or indeed that subjection to risks above a certain level is a violation of rights. The question instead is one of regulation under the stated assumptions. So long as that is the question, use of WTP does not violate anyone's rights.

Democracy and Markets

An independent objection would stress that people are citizens, not merely consumers. It would urge that regulatory choices should be made after citizens have deliberated with one another about their preferences and values. The argument against forced exchanges treats people as consumers; it sees their decisions about safety as the same as their decisions about all other commodities. For some decisions, this approach is badly misconceived. Well-functioning constitutional systems promote deliberative democracy, and many social judgments should be made by citizens engaged in deliberative discussion with one another, rather than by aggregating the individual choices of consumers. Consider some examples:

• The permissible level of race and sex discrimination is not set by using market evidence, or contingent valuation studies, to see how much people would be willing to pay to discriminate (or to be free from discrimination). Such discrimination should banned, even if discriminators would be willing to pay a lot to avoid associating with members of unpopular groups. Through democratic processes, citizens have decided that certain forms of discrimination are illicit, whatever people's WTP.

• The prohibition against sexual harassment does not emerge from consulting people's WTP. Many harassers would be willing to pay something, perhaps a great deal, for the privilege of harassing. In imaginable circumstances, the harassers' WTP might exceed their victims' WTP to prevent harassment. Nonetheless, harassment is forbidden. One reason is that a goal of the civil rights laws is to alter existing preferences and beliefs, not entrench them.

• Laws that forbid cruelty to animals, and that impose affirmative duties of protecting animals on human beings, stem not from WTP, but from a belief that morality justifies such laws. When laws require protection of animals against cruelty or suffering, it is hardly decisive that those who are regulated might be willing to pay a significant amount to avoid the regulation. Of course, the cost of the regulatory burden might play a role in deciding whether to impose it. But the underlying moral judgment is rooted in a belief in the prevention of suffering that does not essentially turn on WTP.

Stressing the limits of any approach that takes "preferences" to be the foundation of regulatory policy, Amartya Sen emphasizes that "discussions and exchange, and even political arguments, contribute to the formation and revision of values."[30] He urges that in the particular context of environmental protection, solutions require regulators "to go beyond looking only for the best reflection of given individual preferences, or the most acceptable procedures for choices based on those preferences."[31]

Sen's claims are both fundamental and correct. They point to some serious limitations on the use of WTP. But it is important not to read such objections for more than they are worth. When trading off safety, health, and money in their private lives, people do not have static values and preferences. Much of the time, human choices are a product of reflection, even if choosers are simply acting as consumers. Reflection and deliberation, including discussion with other people, are hardly absent from the market domain.

To be sure, moral questions should not be resolved by aggregating private WTP (even if willingness to pay to protect moral commitments should count in the analysis; see chapter 6). Sometimes people's preferences, even though backed by WTP, are morally off-limits (consider sexual harassment), and policy should not take account of them. In addition, people may be unwilling to pay a great deal for goods that have strong moral justifications; animal welfare is a potential example. In these circumstances, the market model is inapplicable and WTP reveals very little.

What about the Easy Cases? Do these arguments suggest that government should override individual choices about how much to spend to eliminate low-level risks, even when those choices are adequately informed? For environmental protection generally, it is indeed important to go beyond "the best reflection of given individual preferences." But this point does not mean that people should be required to pay one hundred dollars to eliminate mortality risks of 1/100,000 when they are willing to pay only seventy-five dollars. If people's WTP reflects an absence of information, behavioral biases, or insufficient deliberation, then it is important for other people, in government and elsewhere, to draw attention to that fact. And in some cases, a low WTP might be overridden on the ground that it is rooted in errors, factual or otherwise. But these points should not be taken as a general objection to my conclusion about the Easy Cases, or to suggest that government should force people to reduce statistical risks at an expense that they deem excessive.

Third-Party Effects

A final objection would point to effects on third parties. If outsiders would be harmed if a risk comes to fruition, and if their welfare is not being considered, then the WTP calculus is seriously incomplete. This point demonstrates a general and badly neglected problem for WTP as it is currently used: agencies consider people's WTP to eliminate statistical risks, without accounting for the fact that others—especially family members and close friends—would also be willing to pay something to eliminate those risks.

John might be willing to pay twenty-five dollars to eliminate his own risk of 1/100,000, but his wife, Jane, also might be willing to pay twenty-five dollars to eliminate John's risk. When John is hurt or killed, John is not the only person who pays the price. If regulators add the WTP of John's friends and relatives, the the total WTP will soon exceed one-hundred dollars. This is a real problem for existing uses of WTP. In principle, regulators should consider the full range of people who are adversely affected, not only the person directly at risk.[32] A great deal of work remains to be done on this topic.

This is a legitimate point, but thus far the discussion has been assuming that there are no third-party effects. In the Easy Cases, the argument for using WTP, on the stated assumptions, is that government should not force people to buy goods that are not worthwhile for them.

Harder Cases

There is an obvious artificiality in the assumptions thus far. Most important, people do not always bear the full social costs of the regulatory benefits that they receive. Sometimes they pay only a fraction of those costs—or possibly close to nothing. When this is so, the analysis is more complicated.

We have seen that in the context of air pollution regulation, there is a complex set of distributional effects; on balance, poor people and members of minority communities may well turn out to be net gainers. Suppose that the result of an air pollution regulation is to improve public health in poor communities and that those who benefit pay only a small part of the cost. Suppose too that strictly in terms of welfare, they benefit a great deal, perhaps because they are less likely to get sick, perhaps because they live longer lives. Suppose that most of the cost is paid by people who can easily bear it (and hence do not much suffer from paying).

In such cases, a cost-benefit analysis, based on WTP, might not produce an adequate account of the welfare effects of air pollution regulation. The reason is that in terms of welfare, the people who gain may end up gaining more than the people who lose end up losing. Use of WTP, and hence of VSL, may produce a cost-benefit analysis suggesting that the regulation is a net loser—but on welfare grounds, the analysis might be misleading. It might point in the wrong direction.

The case of rich and poor may be the most vivid, but it is merely illustrative. We could imagine many cases in which cost-benefit analysis, based on WTP, produces outcomes that do not promote welfare. A safety regulation, designed to protect workers, might increase welfare even if the cost-benefit analysis suggests otherwise. This is true not only if and because WTP does not capture informed, rational preferences over a lifetime, but also if and because the welfare effects are not sufficiently captured by the monetary figures. Of course, it may also be true that a regulation that has positive net monetary benefits is also bad from the standpoint of promoting welfare. Indeed, we could distinguish among four kinds of cases: (1) net monetary benefits and net welfare benefits, (2) net monetary benefits but net welfare costs, (3) net monetary costs and net welfare costs, and (4) net monetary costs but net welfare benefits. For present purposes, cases (2) and (4) are the interesting ones.

In any case, the welfare effects might not resolve the question about what to do, because the distributional gains are important to consider. Executive Order 13563, issued by President Barack Obama, explicitly makes "distributional impacts" relevant. If poor people are gaining a great deal, and wealthy people are losing slightly more, the regulation might be justified on distributional grounds. Consider the idea of *prioritarianism*, which suggests (to summarize a long and interesting story) that the social goal should be to increase overall welfare, but with priority given to the most disadvantaged.[33]

Here, in short, is what distinguishes the Easy Cases from the harder ones. We have seen that in the Easy Cases, it does not make much sense to require people to pay more than they are willing to pay. But in the harder cases, people are not paying all the cost of the benefits that they receive. If so, it is possible that they will gain on balance from the relevant regulation, even if their WTP is significantly lower than the cost of the regulation. The more relevant possibility is that on net, society will gain in terms of welfare as well. This point suggests a potentially serious objection to the use of WTP in regulatory policy when those who benefit from regulations do not pay for them. In such cases, even a unitary VSL may produce misleading results if welfare is our guide. A more disaggregated VSL, suggesting a lower figure for poor people, may be especially misleading if poor people stand to gain a great deal in terms of welfare.

Indeed, the use of a unitary rather than disaggregated VSL, in which poor people are given more than they are willing to pay for, might be justified in such circumstances. Thus, W. Kip Viscusi suggests that by "using a uniform VSL across different populations, agencies engage in an implicit form of income redistribution, as benefits to the poor receive a greater weight than is justified by their VSL and benefits to the rich are undervalued."[34] The argument does not work in the Easy Cases, in which a uniform VSL forces poor people to spend more than they want to spend; that is hardly a form of income redistribution from the rich to the poor. But in some of the harder cases, Viscusi's argument is right, because use of a uniform VSL helps ensure that poor people will benefit from redistribution in the form of protection against mortality risks.

Some of the most intuitively plausible defenses of cost-benefit analysis speak in terms of the Kaldor-Hicks criterion (sometimes called potential Pareto superiority), which asks whether the winners win more than the losers lose. The central idea is that if the winners could compensate the losers, and there would be a surplus, then satisfaction of the Kaldor-Hicks criterion shows a net welfare gain. The criterion raises many doubts and puzzles, but let us simply stipulate that regulation is ordinarily justified if it produces such a welfare gain. The problem is that under certain circumstances, a net loss in terms of cost-benefit analysis may coexist with a net gain in terms of welfare. Because welfare is the master concept, and because monetized numbers are mere proxies, it would seem clear that the proxies would have to yield in favor of the master concept. (I will have more to say about this issue in chapter 4.)

It is sometimes argued that if agencies use cost-benefit analysis, then everyone, or almost everyone, will benefit in the long run. John Hicks made an argument of this kind about the Kaldor-Hicks criterion, suggesting that "although we could not say that all the inhabitants of that community would be necessarily better off than they would have been if the community had been organized on some different principle, nevertheless there would be a strong probability that almost all of them would be better off after the lapse of a sufficient amount of time."[35] Note that this argument is about welfare and not about cost-benefit analysis—and it would take a great deal of work to show that if agencies use such analysis as a criterion of decision, based on VSL, almost everyone "would be better off after the lapse of a sufficient length of time." There is also good reason to question Hicks's argument.[36] But my basic point is that if government could measure welfare directly and make individual decisions to promote it, it would unquestionably do better on welfare grounds.

With respect to harder cases, related points can be made with respect to autonomy. If poor people do not bear all the costs of programs that benefit them, the autonomy argument for use of WTP is greatly weakened. Poor people are enjoying a benefit (in whole or in part) for free. Whether right or wrong on other grounds, it does not insult people's autonomy to give them a good on terms that they find acceptable.

I have noted that if redistribution is the goal, it should be produced not through regulation but through the tax system, which is a much more efficient way of transferring resources to people who need help.[37] But suppose that redistribution is not possible through the tax system. If so, then regulation in the harder cases cannot be ruled off-limits (despite its inefficiency). To be sure, the fact that a regulation is helpful to the most disadvantaged is not decisive in its favor. We need some method for comparing benefits to the most disadvantaged against costs to others. If a regulation is trivially helpful to the most disadvantaged, and if it inflicts huge costs on everyone else, little can be said for it. Everything depends on the magnitude of the relevant effects. A program that produces large gains for the least well-off might well be justified even if it imposes, in terms of WTP, slightly higher costs than benefits on balance.

Concrete Problems

I have been exploring the relationship between cost-benefit analysis and welfarism, arguing that the latter has priority over the former and that in some cases, cost-benefit analysis will fail to capture welfare effects. I have also suggested that distribution matters, and that an initiative may fail cost-benefit analysis but have a distributional justification, which may make it worthwhile, all things considered.

Some of the most penetrating theoretical work on these issues has been done by Matthew Adler, who reaches broadly similar conclusions with somewhat different terminology.[38] Adler argues that cost-benefit analysis is inferior to prioritarianism (which, it will be recalled, gives special weight, or priority, to changes that affect the least well-off). Adler also urges that if the goal is to promote well-being, cost-benefit analysis is inferior to utilitarianism. Whether we give special weight to the least well-off or focus on the sum total of well-being (as utilitarians do), we will reject cost-benefit analysis as a guiding principle. In the abstract, Adler's arguments are quite powerful, but in practice, it is not easy to know what to do with them. Consider some cases.

First: A clean air rule has an assortment of benefits and an assortment of costs. No group is disproportionately affected. At all ends of the income distribution, consumers pay for goods that are now more expensive; the goods include gasoline and electricity. At the same time, the air is cleaner for all.

On plausible assumptions, cost-benefit analysis works pretty well in such cases. It is very difficult to investigate welfare directly, and the analysis of costs and benefits should capture what most matters. (I will qualify this claim in chapter 4). Because no particular group faces disproportionate effects, we need not worry about distributional effects or about prioritarianism. As it happens, there are numerous rules of this kind.

Second: An occupational safety rule benefits poor workers, and wealthy consumers pay for it. The rule has costs in excess of benefits. Nonetheless, it might be justified on utilitarian grounds, and also on prioritarian grounds. In my own experience, this kind of rule is highly unusual—but there are some.

Third: A food safety rule has benefits that exceed costs. But the costs are mostly imposed on poor people, whose salaries are cut (they make the food), and the benefits are enjoyed mostly by people who are wealthy. Although the rule passes a cost-benefit test, it might be unjustified on utilitarian or prioritarian grounds.

In my experience, this kind of rule is also highly unusual. Note, however, that an instructive study of safe drinking water rules identifies a similar problem.[39] Although people at all parts of the income distribution benefit from such rules, and pay the same amount for them, the payment imposes particular hardship on poor people, who have less money to spend on goods that (to them) may well have higher priority, such as housing and health care. The problem is not as stark as the hypothetical food safety rule, but the conclusion is the same: A rule that passes a cost-benefit test might be unjustified on utilitarian or prioritarian grounds.

As we have seen, some rules are essentially a transfer from one group of people to another group of people. In the simplest case, a regulation takes $100 million from one group and gives it to another. Such regulations may be justified on utilitarian grounds; the beneficiaries may obtain more utility, or welfare, than the losers lose. For obvious reasons, they might also be justified on prioritarian grounds. Regulations of this kind are quite common.

Optimal Taxation and Administrability

Notwithstanding these considerations, regulators do not make direct inquiries into welfare, and although Executive Order 13563 allows them to take account of distributional effects, they do not often do so. Why?

I have noted that in my own experience in government, I received a surprising answer. It turns out that there are very few cases in which (1) a regulation imposes costs that exceed the benefits but (2) the same regulation disproportionately helps poor people, or others who have a strong claim to public health, so that (3) there is a redistributive argument for a regulation that fails cost-benefit analysis. A main reason is practical: Because VSL is so high, a life-saving regulation that protects many poor people will have high benefits, likely exceeding costs. In theory, though, we can imagine regulations that would fail cost-benefit analysis but help the poor at the expense of the rich. Should regulators proceed in such cases?

Probably so, but one issue involves administrability. In the real-world cases, regulators might well think that a direct inquiry into welfare, bypassing WTP, would be extremely difficult or perhaps even impossible to operationalize. Regulators might rely on WTP not because it is perfect as a proxy for welfare, or even close to it, but because any more direct welfare inquiry is not tractable. Regulators lack welfare meters, and for that reason alone, they might use standard cost-benefit analysis instead, at least outside of extreme cases. (I will return to this question in chapter 4.)

If regulators decide that distributional considerations are relevant, they might fear that interest-group warfare would be the consequence, rather than distribution to those who particularly need and deserve help. Recall that it is not easy to identify regulations for which poor people are the clear beneficiaries while rich people foot the bill. It is far more usual for the costs and benefits of regulations to be widely distributed, so that a variety of demographic groups both enjoy the benefits and pay the costs. To the extent that regulation increases the price of goods and services, it may even be regressive, and there is good reason to think that is the general pattern. A great deal of additional work needs to be done on this topic, in order to specify the distributional effects of regulation with far more precision than has been done to date.

Under current circumstances, a reasonable approach would be for regulators to use WTP as the foundation for decisions, and generally follow the results of cost-benefit balancing, but to inquire into welfare or distribution in cases in which there is compelling reason to do so.

Consider cases in which the monetized benefits are only mildly higher than the monetized costs, but in which the costs are borne by those who are well-off and the benefits are enjoyed mostly by those who are struggling. Regulators might decide to proceed in such circumstances. In fact, this is generally the correct approach, because it is right in principle and because it does not impose undue information-gathering burdens on regulators.

What Is to Be Done?

In many contexts, the use of the WTP criterion is controversial, and for legitimate reasons. But for valuation of statistical mortality risks, that criterion makes a great deal of sense, at least as a place to start. In the Easy Cases, people should not be asked to spend more than they are willing to pay for the elimination of risks, even mortality risks. To be sure, it is possible to doubt whether we have accurately measured people's informed choices.

In the Hard Cases, the analysis is more complicated. Use of VSL may lead to cost-benefit analyses that do not capture the welfare effects of regulations. In some cases, those effects may be positive even if a regulation has net monetary costs. In addition, distributional effects deserve consideration, and they may support regulation even in the face of net costs (consider prioritarianism). At the same time, regulators do not have good tools for measuring welfare effects directly, and consideration of distributional effects may also create serious challenges. In these circumstances, the best approach is to proceed as suggested by cost-benefit analysis, but to allow departures when there are compelling reasons to believe that rules nonetheless increase welfare or are strongly supported by distributional considerations.

4   Welfare: The Master Value

Suppose that the Environmental Protection Agency (EPA) is considering a new regulation, designed to reduce levels of particulate matter in the ambient air. Suppose that the total cost of the regulation would be $900 million. Suppose that the mortality benefits would be precisely equal to that, because the regulation would prevent one hundred deaths, each valued at $9 million. Suppose as well that if the EPA includes morbidity benefits (in the form of nonfatal illnesses averted), the regulation would have an additional $150 million in benefits, ensuring that the monetized benefits significantly exceed the monetized costs.

Now assume two further facts. First, the mortality and morbidity benefits of the regulation would accrue mostly to older people—those over the age of eighty. Second, the rule would have significant disemployment effects, imposing a statistical risk of job loss on many people and ultimately causing three thousand people to lose their jobs. The EPA believes that the overwhelming majority of those three thousand people would find other jobs, and probably do so relatively soon. But it does not have a great deal of data on that question, and it cannot rule out the possibility of long-term job loss for many people. In accordance with standard practice, the EPA does not include either of those further facts in its cost-benefit analysis.

If the goal is to promote social welfare, we might well think that it is far too simple for EPA to conclude that because the monetized benefits exceed the monetized costs, it should proceed with the regulation. On welfare grounds, the regulation might be a bad idea, and in any case, the monetary figures do not tell us everything we need to know. One question is whether and how, in *welfare* terms, to take account of the relatively few additional life years that the regulation will save. In welfare terms, is a rule that "saves" people over eighty to be deemed equivalent to one that "saves" an equivalent number of people who are much younger? (Many people think that the best answer is a firm "No.")

Another question is the welfare consequences of the $900 million expenditure. Suppose that concretely, that admittedly high cost will be spread across at least two hundred million people, who will be spending, on average, a little over four dollars annually for the regulation. What are the welfare consequences of that modest expenditure? Might they be relatively small? (The answer is emphatically yes. Most people will lose essentially no welfare from an annual four-dollar loss.)

A further question is the disemployment effect. We know that in terms of subjective welfare, it is extremely bad to lose one's job.[1] People who lose their jobs suffer a lot; it is humiliating to be jobless, and one's days are often far worse without a job. We know too that in terms of money, the loss of a job often creates a nontrivial long-term loss in income.[2] If you are out of work for a year, the economic toll might be very high over a lifetime. We know that a long-term loss of employment has more severe adverse consequences than a short-term loss— but that both are bad. Shouldn't those welfare effects be included?

Now suppose that the Department of Transportation is considering a regulation that would require all new automobiles to come equipped with cameras, so as to improve rear visibility and thus to reduce the risk of backover crashes.[3] Suppose that the total estimated annual cost of the regulation is $1.2 billion (reflecting an average cost of fifty dollars per vehicle for a large number of vehicles, to be sold over a relevant time period). Suppose that the regulation is expected to prevent sixty deaths annually, for monetized annual savings of $540 million, and to prevent several nonfatal injuries and cases of property damage, for additional annual savings of $200 million. On the basis of these numbers, the department is inclined to believe that the benefits of the rules are significantly lower than the costs.

At the same time, suppose that the department is aware of four facts that it deems relevant, but is not at all clear how to handle. First, a majority of the deaths would involve young children—between the ages of one and five. Second, most of those deaths would occur as a result of the driving errors of their own parents, who would therefore suffer unspeakable anguish. Third, the cost of the rule would be diffused across a large population of new car purchasers, who would not much notice the per-vehicle cost. Fourth, the cameras would improve people's driving experience by making it much easier for them to navigate roads, even when they do not prevent crashes. (The department speculates that many consumers do not sufficiently appreciate this improvement when deciding which cars to buy.) Is it so clear, in light of these four facts, that the agency should not proceed?

I have said that in principle, cost-benefit analysis is best defended as the most administrable way of capturing the welfare effects of policies (including regulations). But if we actually *knew* those effects, in terms of people's welfare, and thus could specify the actual consequences of policies for welfare, we would not have to trouble ourselves with cost-benefit analysis. As we have seen, an initial problem is that cost-benefit analysis depends on willingness to pay, and people might be willing to pay for goods that do not have substantial positive effects on their welfare (and might be unwilling to pay for goods that would have substantial positive effects). Willingness to pay is based on a prediction, and at least some of the time, people make mistakes in forecasting how various outcomes will make them feel. You might think that if you don't get a particular job or your favorite sport team loses a crucial game or even someone you really like refuses to date you, you'll be miserable for a good long time. Chances are that you're wrong—and that you'll recover far more quickly than you think.

We have also seen that a separate problem involves the *incidence* of costs and benefits, which can complicate the analysis of welfare effects, even if we put "pure" distributional considerations to one side. Suppose that a regulation would impose $400 million in costs on relatively wealthy people and confer $300 million in benefits on relatively poor people. Even if the losers lose more than the gainers gain in *monetary* terms, we cannot exclude the possibility that the losers will lose less than the gainers gain in *welfare* terms.

The most general problem is that once agencies specify costs and benefits, the resulting figures will inevitably have an ambiguous relationship to what they should care about, which is welfare. To be sure, it is possible that some of the problems in the two cases I have given could be significantly reduced with improved cost-benefit analysis. If children should be valued differently from adults, and elderly people differently from younger, cost-benefit analysis might be able to explain why and how. Perhaps parental anguish could be monetized as well. The same might well be true of the increased ease of driving. But even the best proxies remain proxies, and what matters most is the thing itself.

Proxies

In recent years, social scientists have become greatly interested in measuring welfare. One of their techniques is to study "self-reported well-being," meaning people's answers to survey questions about how satisfied they are with their lives. The promise of this technique is that it might be able to offer a more direct, and more accurate, measure of welfare[4] than could possibly come from an account of costs and benefits (especially if that account depends on willingness to pay). Suppose that we agree, with the economist Paul Dolan,[5] that welfare consists in significant part of two things: (1) people's feelings of pleasure (broadly conceived) and (2) people's feelings of purpose (also broadly conceived). People might enjoy watching sports on television, but they might not get much of a sense of purpose from that activity. Working for a good cause might not be a lot of fun, but it might produce a strong sense of purpose.

If pleasure and purpose matter, and if we want to measure them, we might be able to ask people about those two variables. How much pleasure do people get from certain activities? How much of a sense of purpose? Dolan has in fact asked such questions, with a range of illuminating results.[6] We are learning a great deal about what kinds of activities are pleasurable or not, as well as about what kinds of activities seem to give people a sense of purpose or meaning. In the abstract, what we learn seems to tell us a lot about people's welfare, and it might offer a more direct and accurate account than what emerges from an analysis of costs and benefits. The reason is that measures of pleasure and purpose offer information about the actual experience that people have during their lives, and that seems to be what most matters.

With respect to ascertaining subjective well-being, the most popular existing measures take two forms. First, researchers try to assess people's "evaluative" welfare by asking questions about overall life satisfaction (or related concepts, such as happiness).[7] With such measures, it is possible to test the effects of a range of variables, such as marriage, divorce, disability, and unemployment.[8] Second, researchers try to assess people's "experienced" welfare, through measures of people's assessments of particular activities (working, commuting, being with friends, watching television).[9]

In fact, researchers have uncovered some systematic differences between people's overall evaluations and their assessments of their particular experiences.[10] Marital status is more closely correlated with experienced well-being than with evaluative well-being, though there is conflicting evidence on this point.[11] French people report significantly lower levels of satisfaction in their lives than Americans, but the French appear to show equal or even higher levels of experienced well-being.[12] (Daniel Kahneman suggests a partial explanation: in France, if you say you are happy, you are superficial; in the United States, if you say you are unhappy, you are pathetic.) Health states are more closely correlated with experienced well-being, though they also affect evaluative well-being.

There is a lively debate about the choice between the two measures.[13] The current consensus appears to be that useful but different information is provided by each.[14] On one view, questions about experienced welfare focus people on their existing emotional states and thus provide valuable information about those states. By contrast, questions about evaluative welfare encourage people to think about their overall goals or aspirations. On this view, evaluative welfare "is more likely to reflect people's longer-term outlook about their lives as a whole."[15] If this is so, then the two measures do capture different kinds of values, and both are important. In my view, an important issue remains: we do not yet know whether people's answers to questions about evaluative well-being in fact reflect their broader aspirations, or whether they are instead an effort to summarize experienced well-being, in which case the latter is the better (because more accurate) measure.

There is also an active debate about the reliability of both measures of welfare: some people are skeptical about how much we can learn from them.[16] Just as with willingness to pay, it is important to consider issues related to the quality, reliability, and applicability of different studies.[17] Making a frontal assault on the whole program, the economist Deirdre McCloskey disparages what she calls the *1-2-3 hedonists*, who celebrate *happyism*,[18] by which McCloskey means to caricature people who put excessive emphasis on whether people say that they are "happy." McCloskey doesn't trust the surveys, and she appears to think that it's pretty superficial to think that the goal in life is to be happy. In my view, such disparagement is a big mistake. The measures tell us a great deal; happiness matters even if it isn't everything, and those who are trying to improve people's welfare are not narrow happyists.[19]

True, the idea of *welfare* allows for a great deal of ambiguity, and if it is invoked for policy purposes or by governments, any particular account is highly likely to end up in contested terrain. As Dolan makes clear, a purely hedonic measure, focused only on pleasure and pain, would be inadequate; people's lives should be meaningful as well as pleasant. But even if we adopt a measure that goes beyond pleasure to measure a sense of purpose as well, we might be capturing too little. We might be ignoring *qualitative differences among goods* and the general problem of *incommensurability*.

We value some things purely or principally for use; consider hammers, forks, or money. We value other things at least in part for their own sake; consider knowledge or friendship. But that distinction captures only a part of the picture. Intrinsically valued things produce a range of diverse responses. Some bring about wonder and awe; consider a mountain or certain artistic works. Toward some people, we feel respect; toward others, affection; toward others, love. People worship their deity. Some events produce gratitude; others produce joy; others are thrilling; others make us feel content; others bring about delight. Some things are valued if they meet certain standards, like a musical or athletic performance or perhaps a pun.

In this regard, Mill's objections to Bentham are worth quoting at length:

Nor is it only the moral part of man's nature, in the strict sense of the term—the desire of perfection, or the feeling of an approving or of an accusing conscience—that he overlooks; he but faintly recognizes, as a fact in human nature, the pursuit of any other ideal end for its own sake. The sense of honour, and personal dignity—that feeling of personal exaltation and degradation which acts independently of other people's opinion, or even in defiance of it; the love of beauty, the passion of the artist; the love of order, of congruity, of consistency in all things, and conformity to their end; the love of power, not in the limited form of power over other human beings, but abstract power, the power of making our volitions effectual; the love of action, the thirst for movement and activity, a principle scarcely of less influence in human life than its opposite, the love of ease. ... Man, that most complex being, is a very simple one in his eyes.[20]

These points suggest the importance of having a capacious conception of welfare, one that is alert to the diverse array of goods that matter to people. Consistent with Mill's plea, a large survey by the economist Daniel Benjamin and his coauthors tests people's concern for a list of factors that includes not only measures that are widely used by economists, such as happiness and life satisfaction, but also "other items, such as goals and achievements, freedoms, engagement, morality, self-expression, relationships, and the well-being of others."[21]

The central and important (though not especially surprising) result is that people do indeed care about those other items.[22] The perhaps ironic conclusion is that if measures of reported well-being neglect those items, *they will end up losing important information that cost-benefit measures ought to be able to capture.* I have said that a significant advantage of the willingness to pay measure is that it should, in principle, take account of everything that people care about, including those things that matter for Mill's reasons. If people value cell phones because they want to connect with their children, or if they want to save (rather than spend) money so that they can give it to poor children in Africa, or if they want to spend money on a vacation because of their love of nature, then their concerns, however diverse in qualitative terms, should be adequately captured by the willingness to pay criterion, however unitary.

That is a point for cost-benefit analysis. Notwithstanding its apparent crudeness, and notwithstanding the simplicity of the monetary measure, it honors qualitatively diverse goods that people care about for diverse reasons. In that way, it is not simple at all. For that reason, cost-benefit analysis has advantages over some measures of happiness or subjective welfare. Nonetheless, that form of analysis cannot have priority over excellent or full measures of welfare. What is required are measures that are sufficiently reflective of the diverse set of goods that matter to people but that avoid the various problems associated with cost-benefit analysis.

The Big Problem

With respect to regulatory policy, the largest problem with invoking self-reported well-being is this: even if such surveys provide a great deal of information, we cannot easily "map" any particular set of regulatory consequences onto changes in welfare.

Although we are learning a great deal about what increases and what decreases welfare, what we are learning is relatively coarse; it frequently involves the consequences of large life events, such as marriage, divorce, and unemployment. We do not know nearly enough about how to answer hard questions about the welfare effects of health and safety regulations. How much happier are people when the level of ozone in the ambient air is decreased from seventy parts per billion to sixty parts per billion? For the median person, what is the welfare effect of having to spend $50 or $100 or $300 on a regulatory initiative, noting that the money could have been used for other purposes? In terms of welfare units, how should we think about a loss of a job or a life year? Should we use those units, or some other kind (monetary?), in conducting analyses on the basis of studies of self-reported well-being? If we use those units, then what exactly is the relevant scale?

Return to the problems with which I began. We have seen that in terms of welfare, cost-benefit analysis, at least in its current form, may not adequately handle (1) unusually large or unusually small numbers of life years saved; (2) adverse unemployment effects; (3) questions about the welfare effects of small economic losses faced by large populations; (4) intense emotions associated with certain outcomes, such as parental anguish; and (5) hedonic benefits associated with increased ease and convenience. As I have suggested, improved forms of cost-benefit analysis might be able to reduce these problems. But ideally, we would want to know about welfare itself. The problem is that measures of self-reported well-being are far too crude to enable us to do that.

No one should doubt that cost-benefit analysis itself presents serious challenges, sometimes described under the rubric of the *knowledge problem* (see chapter 5); agencies must compile a great deal of information to make sensible extrapolations. But to map regulatory outcomes onto self-reported well-being, the challenges are far more severe.

To be sure, creative efforts have been made to extrapolate relevant values from measures of self-reported well-being.[23] Examining an EPA pulp and paper regulation from the late 1990s, law professor John Bronsteen and his colleagues argue that cost-benefit analysis and reported welfare analysis point in quite different directions and that, as a proxy for welfare, the latter is far superior to the former. They conclude that while the regulation would be expensive in monetary terms (with EPA's options ranging from $262 million to $1 billion in cost), that expense would have trivial harmful effects on welfare. In other words, the monetary cost figure is misleading, because it suggests adverse welfare effects that would not actually occur.

Here is their explanation: The EPA's regulation would require affected individuals to bear several hundred dollars in annual costs. What is the welfare consequence of asking the average person to pay out $200 next year? To answer that question, they enlist a study, finding that people with a threefold increase in income experience a gain in well-being units of 0.11, and those with a two-thirds decrease in income experience a 0.11 decrease in such units.[24] (Pause for a moment over those figures. What exactly do they mean?) On the basis of this study, and doing a little arithmetic, Bronsteen and his colleagues find *near 0* in aggregate welfare losses for a modest annual expenditure of several hundred dollars. As they put it, "The monetary costs of the regulation, which dominated the CBA, are nearly irrelevant here."[25] To this extent, the monetary costs that loomed so large in EPA's analysis end up playing essentially no role in a welfare analysis.

By contrast, the unemployment effects matter a great deal in that analysis. On the basis of another study, Bronsteen and his coauthors conclude that those who are unemployed lose 0.83 well-being units per year while unemployed; even after finding new employment, those who were unemployed lost an average of 0.34 well-being units per year during the next seven years after they began working again. Because the EPA regulation would result in several thousand lost jobs, it would produce a massive welfare loss. Stunningly, the estimated welfare loss from lost jobs is *well over 400,000 times* the estimated welfare loss from the total monetary cost. But is that enough to doom the regulation?

Not at all. We must also look at the welfare gain. Bronsteen et al. also note that the average American has a life satisfaction of 7.4 on a scale of 0 to 10. To capture the welfare gain from avoiding fatal cancers, they multiply 7.4 by the significant number of life years that would be saved by the regulation. Without getting into the details, the result of the exercise is that the total welfare gains are very high—high enough to justify the welfare costs that come from job loss.

The problem with this impressively creative exercise is that it involves far too much guesswork to be invoked credibly by government regulators. We do not really know how to translate the various consequences into quantifiable effects on human welfare. Some of the central numbers are both speculative and unclear, provoking a range of questions and doubts. (1) Can we really extrapolate, from one or two (or more) studies of the effects on reported well-being of massive increases or decreases in annual income, the welfare effects across a large population of losing several hundred dollars a year? (2) Is it credible to suppose that regulations that impose such costs on such large populations should be treated as having essentially no adverse effects on welfare? Would a tax of $200, on, say, two hundred million Americans, have no such adverse effects? (3) Should the same be said of five, or ten, or fifty regulations of this kind? (4) What does it even mean to say that the average worker loses 0.83 well-being units while unemployed? If an employed person's experience of his life is 7.4, is an unemployed person's 6.57? In terms of what, exactly?

For now, these questions lack good answers. The most sensible conclusion is that studies of reported well-being cannot be used as anything like a substitute for cost-benefit analysis, and most of the time, they should not play a significant role in regulatory analysis.

Does this conclusion mean that today and in the near future, regulators should rest content with cost-benefit analysis and put entirely to one side, as speculative and unreliable, whatever we might learn from directly considering welfare? That would be too strong a conclusion. Most important, disemployment effects deserve serious consideration, not least because of the significant adverse welfare effects of losing one's job. It is also relevant to know whether a regulation would protect children and hence provide a large number of life years, or instead protect older people and hence provide a relatively smaller number of life years. The Department of Transportation was correct to emphasize this point in considering the regulation designed to reduce backover crashes.

It is also possible that a large cost, spread over a very large population, might turn out to have relatively modest adverse effects on welfare. Agencies should consider this possibility, especially in cases in which costs and benefits are otherwise fairly close. If agencies would help people who suffer from mental illness of one or another kind, then the welfare gain might be substantial, even if the benefits cannot be adequately captured in willingness to pay figures.

Emphasizing the promise of research on subjective well-being, the economist Raj Chetty contends: "Further work is needed to determine whether and how subjective well-being metrics can be used to reliably measure experienced utility, but they appear to offer at least some qualitative information on ex post preferences than can help mitigate concerns about paternalism in behavioral welfare economics."[26] Chetty's conclusion is sound, but it could be much stronger. Work on subjective well-being can serve not only to mitigate concerns about paternalism, but also, at least on occasion, to inform analysis of the welfare effects of regulations (and policies in general). For now, cost-benefit analysis remains the best proxy for what matters, but it is not too optimistic to think that in the fullness of time, it will be supplemented or even superseded by a more direct focus on welfare.

5 The Knowledge Problem

With respect to the past and future of regulation, there are two truly indispensable ideas. Unfortunately, they are in serious tension with one another.

The first indispensable idea is that it is immensely important to measure, both in advance and on a continuing basis, the effects of regulation of social welfare. The second idea, attributable above all to Friedrich Hayek, is that knowledge is widely dispersed in society.[1] As Hayek and his followers emphasize, government planners cannot possibly know what individuals know, simply because they lack that dispersed knowledge. The multiple failures of plans and the omnipresence of unintended consequences can be attributed, in large part, to the absence of relevant information.

Are cost-benefit analysts planners? In a way, they certainly are. How can they possibly obtain the knowledge that would allow them to compare costs and benefits? Often they cannot.

Hayek was particularly concerned about socialist-style planning. He contended that even if socialist planners are well-motivated and if the public interest is their true concern, they will fail, because they will not know enough to succeed. Hayek celebrated the price system as a "marvel"—not for any mystical reason, but because it can aggregate dispersed information, the information held by countless individuals, and do so in a way that permits rapid adjustment to changing circumstances, values, and tastes.

Hayek's arguments offer a serious cautionary note for planners of all kinds, including contemporary regulators who are committed, at least as a general rule, to free markets and freedom of contract. Even if they despise socialism and are simply correcting market failures (as, for example, in the domains of pollution, health care, or occupational safety), they might well lack indispensable information.

Suppose that they are seeking to reduce levels of particulate matter in the ambient air. What, precisely, are the health benefits of a reduction of existing levels to twelve parts per billion (ppb), or 11 ppb, or 8 ppb? And what would be the costs, economic and otherwise, of mandating such reductions? When should reductions be required? How should they be obtained? Should small businesses receive exemptions? Of what kind? What are the alternative approaches, and of these, which is best? How can regulators possibly know?

The problem should not be overstated. With respect to costs, regulators often have a reasonable sense of potential outcomes, in part because of information from the regulated sector. To be sure, that information might well be self-serving, but regulators often have sufficient experience to discount alarmist or excessive claims. With respect to benefits, quantification and monetization present separate issues. In many domains, existing knowledge is sufficient to permit the identification of sufficiently narrow ranges with respect to, say, mortalities averted or accidents prevented. Well-established and continuously improving tools are also in place to convert various values into monetary equivalents. In the day-to-day life of cost-benefit analysis, regulators are hardly making a stab in the dark. Usually they have, or are able to accumulate, a great deal of relevant information.

Nonetheless, modern followers of Hayek are correct to emphasize what they call the knowledge problem, which can be a problem for contemporary regulators of all kinds, working, for example, to implement the Clean Air Act, the Occupational Safety and Health Act, the Affordable Care Act, and the Dodd-Frank Wall Street Reform and Consumer Protection Act. If cost-benefit analysis is essential to sensible judgments, incomplete knowledge, when it exists, would appear to be a serious and potentially devastating problem. In some cases, agencies do face serious challenges in cataloguing costs and benefits. Retrospective analysis attests to those challenges, because it has identified a number of mistakes.

In short, the source of the tension is that regulators have to focus on costs and benefits (the first indispensable idea), but they will sometimes lack the information that would enable them to make accurate assessments (the second indispensable idea). In light of the knowledge problem, is cost-benefit analysis akin to socialist planning? Can regulators produce reliable cost-benefit analyses, or any other kind of projection of the human consequences of what they seek to do and of potential alternatives? We have seen that cost-benefit analysts are technocrats, charged with measuring and assessing consequences, but their technocratic enterprise runs into a serious objection. The force of the objection will depend on the context, but in some situations, the effort to assess the likely effects of a regulatory intervention (involving pollution, health care, energy, transportation safety, communications, disability rights, or homeland security) might go badly wrong.

Four Reforms

Four reforms can help. I am not suggesting that Hayek himself would be satisfied. Consider this remarkable passage:

This is, perhaps, also the point where I should briefly mention the fact that the sort of knowledge with which I have been concerned is knowledge of the kind which by its nature cannot enter into statistics and therefore cannot be conveyed to any central authority in statistical form. The statistics which such a central authority would have to use would have to be arrived at precisely by abstracting from minor differences between the things, by lumping together, as resources of one kind, items which differ as regards location, quality, and other particulars, in a way which may be very significant for the specific decision. It follows from this that central planning based on statistical information by its nature cannot take direct account of these circumstances of time and place and that the central planner will have to find some way or other in which the decisions depending on them can be left to the "man on the spot."[2]

This is a complex passage, but I fear that Hayek's claim here is a mystification, at least as applied to the regulatory context, and at least in the modern era, when collection of massive data is possible, and when algorithms, making fine-grained distinctions, are often astonishingly accurate. Statistical information "by its nature" can indeed "take direct account of these circumstances of time and place." How many refrigerator companies are affected by an energy-efficiency requirement? Which ones would pay how much? How much would they have to pay in total? Increasingly, regulators are in a position to obtain answers to questions of this kind, and many more, thus suggesting that "statistical information by its nature" can indeed "take direct account of these circumstances of time and place." On this view, Hayek meant to state a logical truth, but he was really speaking about the epistemic limits of the available tools in his time.

Of course it is true that companies differ from one another, and the cost-benefit analyst may not know that for some of them, the cost will be far higher or far lower than anticipated. Whether that knowledge is available depends on the state of the art. And of course it is possible that for some purposes and activities, statistical knowledge remains inadequate in light of existing tools. Perhaps most important, social interactions can make predictions difficult; if people are affected by what other people do, then before-the-fact projections can be difficult. It is for this reason that successful predictions about the success or failure of songs, movies, and books can be challenging or perhaps impossible; even the best analysts, and the best algorithms, may not be able to foresee who will influence whom at a certain time, or when a cascade will start to develop, eventually creating a flood. But if the goal is to understand the damage done by air pollution or the cost of reducing it, statistical knowledge can bring us much of the way home. On, then, to the four reforms.

The first involves the process of notice-and-comment rulemaking, updated for the current era and with a clear sense of the underlying substantive goal, which is to obtain dispersed information about the likely consequences of regulations (including costs and benefits).

The second involves retrospective analysis of rules, which can both produce changes in those rules and lead to significant improvements in prospective analysis. Sometimes retrospective analysis can be performed a few years after a regulation has been issued, to see if it is having the anticipated effects. Much more ambitiously, new technologies should enable regulators to learn essentially immediately and to see, in weeks or months, whether regulations are achieving their intended goals or having adverse side-effects. There is a pressing need to enlist those technologies to provide that learning. (We're going to get there.) To realize its potential, retrospective analysis should be undertaken with public comment.

The third reform involves careful experiments—above all, randomized controlled trials, which can provide far better information than expert judgments.[3] Use of randomized controlled trials is exceedingly promising, but it does present challenges in terms of feasibility. Here as well, there is reason for optimism. Increasingly, those challenges can be, and are being, surmounted.

The fourth involves *measure and react*. The basic idea is that it is increasingly possible to measure, in real time, the effects of policies and thus to learn, by December, how they worked in November. With measure-and-react approaches, officials need not rely on ex ante predictions about costs and benefits. They can see both. Such approaches are not always feasible—often, they are not—but they are the most promising of all, and we will eventually see far more use of them.

An Old Debate

During and after Franklin Delano Roosevelt's New Deal, the United States saw an intense debate about government regulation.[4] The competing sides were the New Deal enthusiasts, receptive to the larger regulatory state,[5] and the New Deal critics, insisting that the new administrative institutions were a betrayal of constitutional ideals. One of the enduring products of that debate was the Administrative Procedure Act (APA), enacted in 1946. The APA contained a genuine innovation, now called *notice-and-comment rulemaking*. The basic idea is that regulators do not merely consult with one another and then issue final regulations. Instead, they must provide the public with advance notice of what they are planning to do and why, and then they solicit comments. It was expected that when agencies finalized rules, they would incorporate what they learned from the public.

Why did Congress call for notice-and-comment rulemaking? The historical record does not give an unambiguous answer, but we can isolate two quite different factors. The first involves the idea of self-government itself. During and after the New Deal, some people have been greatly concerned that regulators are not directly accountable to the people and have contended that they may suffer from some kind of "democracy deficit." In an extreme view, the result is a crisis of legitimacy. For such critics, notice-and-comment rulemaking may not be sufficient, but it is an important way to help legitimate the administrative process, by increasing accountability and responsiveness. A form of democratic participation is built into the very idea of notice-and-comment rulemaking. That admittedly technical idea is designed to help ensure ultimate rule, or at least involvement, by We the People. If administrators are not directly accountable through elections, they must listen and respond to the public insofar as its members are willing to raise objections and concerns.

The second idea is less abstract and high-flown, and it is, I think, even more important. It involves information, not legitimation, and it has roots in Hayek's concerns. It is also closely connected with the ideals of the cost-benefit revolution. We have seen that if government is attempting to make air cleaner or food safer, to reduce deaths in the workplace or on the highways, or to increase homeland security, it might well have incomplete information about the effects of its plans.

Some nonhypothetical examples: If regulators take steps to make the food supply safer, they might impose high costs on farmers, including small farmers, and potentially create serious economic dislocations. If government imposes high costs on electricity producers, it might produce spikes in the cost of electricity, which would be particularly harmful for the poor. If regulators require motor vehicles to be more fuel-efficient, they might make motor vehicles more dangerous, and thus cause losses of life.

To make sensible decisions, regulators need to obtain a great deal of information about questions of this kind. As hard as they might try, they will not know everything, and they may have significant gaps in their knowledge. Within government, those with technical expertise will try to fill those gaps, but their efforts might be insufficient. Here is the potential of the notice-and-comment process. If regulators have made mistakes or been too optimistic, there is a real chance that members of the public will tell them about it. Regulators' assessment of the costs of a proposed rule might depend on unrealistic assumptions. If so, someone might well object on that ground. Regulators might not have seen how a well-intended rule would affect small business. With respect to benefits, their scientific projections might not be consistent with recent scientific findings. They might have neglected local circumstances, failing to understand that what makes sense in Los Angeles and New York is unnecessary or even harmful in Carson City and Boise.

They might have missed the potential effects of a low-cost technology. They might not have appreciated the possibility that radically different approach would have far higher net benefits.

On this view, the most important goal of notice-and-comment rule-making is to increase the likelihood that agencies will obtain relevant information. Some of that information might come from technical specialists outside of government, who can correct agency errors (e.g., about the carcinogenic properties of silica, the social cost of carbon, or the likely costs of emissions controls). Some of it might come from private associations with distinctive knowledge of particular sectors. Some of it might come from people with highly localized knowledge, which might escape the regulators' attention. Some of it might show, consistent with Hayek's cautionary notes, that efforts to lump people together might go badly wrong. If the knowledge problem cannot always be eliminated—and it would be foolish to think that it can be— at least it can be reduced, in part through institutions that increase the likelihood that public officials will learn from what members of the public know.

To be sure, reliance on free markets might be a lot better than regulation. To know whether to regulate at all, we need to know whether there is some kind of market failure, and even if such a failure exists, regulation might make things worse rather than better. But in some contexts, the argument on behalf of regulation is convincing. When it is, enlisting dispersed information can greatly reduce the likelihood of error.

It is important to emphasize that the notice-and-comment process is hardly the only way for agencies to obtain dispersed knowledge. Regulators often engage in extensive consultations before rules are even proposed—sometimes through informal routes, sometimes through formal *requests for information* (published in the Federal Register), sometimes through advance notices of proposed rulemaking. All of these strategies are indispensable. Executive Order 13563, issued in the Obama administration, goes so far as to state, "Before issuing a notice of proposed rulemaking, each agency, where feasible and appropriate, shall seek the views of those who are likely to be affected, including those who are likely to benefit from and those who are potentially subject to such rulemaking."[6] The various forms of information-gathering—preliminary to proposed rulemaking—can be essential to accurate cost-benefit analysis.

Unrealized Potential

In the initial decades after enactment of the APA, some people greatly admired the notice-and-comment idea, celebrating its immense potential for providing valuable information—but it did not realize that potential. There were two reasons.

The first is that for decades, many regulatory agencies relied on adjudication, rather than rulemaking, to make public policy. Instead of proposing a new regulation, for example, the Federal Trade Commission would initiate a proceeding against someone who engaged in apparently deceptive advertising, and it would produce the functional equivalent of a new rule as a result of that proceeding. Needless to say, this kind of approach—policymaking by adjudication—was far from ideal, in part because regulators would be unlikely to hear from enough people.

Moreover, cost-benefit analysis does not precede or accompany the orders that emerge from adjudication. For multiple reasons, the decisions that follow adjudication, involving a small number of parties, might turn out to be inadequately informed. But since the 1980s, and in part for this very reason, agencies have chosen to rely far more on notice-and-comment rulemaking (with the continuing and disappointing exception of the National Labor Relations Board, which mostly relies on adjudication to this day).

The second reason is that from the standpoint of most members of the public, the notice-and-comment process has been quite arcane—technical, obscure, perhaps even unfathomable. For many people, it has not been simple to send comments to regulators or for regulators to read and assess everything that they receive. At least part of the problem can be captured in a single word: paper. So long as everything was received and read in hard copy, there were significant limits to the notice-and-comment process. Among other things, those who sought to file comments could not necessarily or easily see the comments sent by other people. For the process to work as well as it might, that kind of visibility, along with a substantive back-and-forth, could be exceedingly important. There is an enduring ideal of *government by discussion*; that ideal cannot be realized if substantive ideas are not broadly visible.

The Age of Online Rulemaking

We have now entered the age of online rulemaking, thanks in part to Executive Order 13563, issued by President Obama in 2011 and continuing to serve, during the Trump administration, as a kind of mini-Constitution for the regulatory state. (Regulations.gov is the key website.) As we shall see, that Executive Order promises to reduce the tension between the two indispensable ideas with which I began by increasing the likelihood that regulators will have access to dispersed information.

Among other things, Executive Order 13563 requires regulations to be adopted "through a process that involves public participation." It directs agencies to "afford the public a meaningful opportunity to comment through the Internet on any proposed regulation, with a comment period that should generally be at least 60 days." Importantly, it requires agencies to "provide, for both proposed and final rules, timely online access to the rulemaking docket on Regulations.gov, including relevant scientific and technical findings, in an open format that can be easily searched and downloaded."

Do not be fooled by the technical jargon ("rulemaking docket") in that last sentence. It means in essence that members of the public are allowed to see the technical support for regulations, including the analysis of costs and benefits, and also to see public comments themselves. That form of transparency is exceedingly important, because it triggers public scrutiny of what regulators think they know (including with respect to costs and benefits) and generates a great deal of additional information.

Regulations.gov may not be everyone's favorite website, and for most people, it isn't a lot of fun, but it has transformed notice-and-comment rulemaking. When the agency proposes a rule, all the world can find it and see it, usually with great ease. Both the rule and the technical analyses are standardly available. If the proposal contains a mistake, or veers in a bad direction, there is a genuine opportunity to comment and to get the problem fixed.

Indeed, there is an app that contains all relevant information. RegInfo Mobile allows you to find the key information on your cell phone.

When I served as administrator of the White House Office of Information and Regulatory Affairs, I was surprised by one thing above all: many regulators pay exceedingly close attention to public comments, and they spend a lot of time on regulations.gov. These comments are carefully read, typically by officials who have the actual authority to move regulations in better directions. (These include officials in the rulemaking agency, in OIRA, and in various White House offices, such as the Domestic Policy Council and the National Economic Council.) Very often, they do so as a direct result of what they learn. For this reason, the notice-and-comment process is hardly a charade. With respect to regulation, it is a central part of official decision making.

In the modern era, regulators are in a far better position to collect the dispersed information of the public. In its best form, the goal of notice-and-comment rulemaking is emphatically *not* to take an opinion poll, to take some kind of political temperature, to see how much applause a proposal is able to attract, to defuse public opposition, to engage in some communications strategy, or to collect the digital equivalent of postcards (though a number of those are sometimes received). Instead, the goal is overwhelmingly substantive: to fill gaps in knowledge and to see what might have been overlooked. In particular, the agency's assessment of the likely consequences is subject to close scrutiny. If the agency has inaccurately assessed costs and benefits, public participation can and often will supply a corrective. Democratization of the regulatory process through the comment process has an *epistemic* value. It helps collect dispersed knowledge and to bring it to bear on official choices.

Complexity

It is true that many rules continue to be lengthy and complex. For the public comment process to work, regulations should be comprehensible rather than opaque, and technical language and sheer length can reduce comprehensibility. Executive summaries, now required for long or complex rules, can help, but they are not sufficient. Experiments with the idea of a "regulation room," a website offering informal, plain-language versions of regulatory proposals, are designed to promote broader understanding, but those experiments have not been a big success; in my view, they have been a failure. Some of the public comments in those experiments look like simple expressions of enthusiasm or skepticism, and because they do not provide new information, they do not inform regulatory judgments.

To come to terms with the challenge of complex rules, it is important to distinguish between two conceptions of the purpose of the public comment process. According to one conception, connected with the old idea of legitimation, the goal is to allow We the People—anyone, really—to participate in the process. If this is the goal, then intelligibility and clarity are indispensable, and complexity is a fatal problem. Another conception, focused on the knowledge problem, sees the goal as information acquisition. If that is the goal, then intelligibility and clarity are important, but because the process often has a large technical component, the absence of genuine plain language need not be a fatal flaw, so long as those who have information to contribute are in a position to do so.

Of Hubris and Risks

It is important to acknowledge that even in its most ambitious forms, the public comment process might fail to solve the knowledge problem. Centralized planning of the old socialist sort could hardly be redeemed by the notice-and-comment process. Sure, Soviet-style five-year plans would be likely improved by efforts to receive public comments, but we should not, for that reason, embrace five-year plans.

Dedicated followers of Hayek would urge that the process of aggregating information will inevitably be imperfect and (in their view) probably worse than that. Can the comment process ensure accurate judgments about the optimal level of particulate matter in the ambient air? Markets encode the local knowledge and values of everyone who produces or purchases relevant products. By contrast, most citizens—including many with substantive contributions to make—are unlikely to know about notice-and-comment rulemaking or to have the commitment and background that would enable them to participate. Hayek's followers would rightly demand a convincing demonstration of some kind of market failure before embarking on regulation. Even if a market failure is shown, market-friendly responses (such as disclosure of information, corrective taxes, or some kind of nudge, such as a default rule, a reminder, or a warning) deserve pride of place, in part because they reduce informational demands on regulators and can enlist rather than displace private knowledge.

There is an independent point. It would be reasonable to fear that well-organized groups of one or another kind (perhaps wealthy companies, perhaps purported public interest groups) will inevitably play the most important part in notice-and-comment rulemaking, and even dominate it. They will disclose what it is in their interest to disclose, and so press public officials in their preferred directions. If so, there will be a kind of epistemic "skew" on the part of regulators. The supposed solution to the knowledge problem may make things even worse. The most frequent comments, and the most competent ones, will come from those whose self-interest is at stake, thus creating a distinctive form of capture, one that is epistemic in nature.

This risk cannot be dismissed in the abstract. It may well be realized in practice. But public officials are often able to discount self-serving arguments and give critical scrutiny to external arguments and claims. During my period in government, I witnessed this process every day. Within the executive branch, people work exceedingly hard to produce solutions that are sensible, regardless of whether powerful interest groups like those solutions. Insofar as diverse regulators are working together to produce sensible regulations, justified by costs and benefits, members of the public, the media, and academic observers overstate the role of interest groups and even of political pressures. For regulators, the principal problem is not such pressures; it is a lack of information. On that front, notice-and-comment rulemaking turns out to be crucial, even if there is a risk of epistemic skew.

We should not be too optimistic. In some times and places, public officials pay most attention to the interest groups they trust. Their time and attention are limited; they are drinking from a fire hose. If the Chamber of Commerce or the Sierra Club says that a certain course of action is best, they will follow its guidance. That approach can lead to terrible mistakes. An idealized notice-and-comment process is not always the real world's notice-and-comment process. Administrations differ from one another, and they differ from month to month. The only point is that the ability to obtain public comments, and to learn from people outside of government, can and often does produce essential information, and can and does correct misconceptions within the government.

In the coming decades, the ability to elicit and compile information will inevitably expand at an extraordinarily rapid rate. A pressing question is how to use that information to reduce the risks of regulatory error, not least with respect to cost-benefit analysis itself. We could easily imagine large-scale improvements as massive data sets become increasingly simple to compile and analyze. Algorithms and machine learning will be a great help. In the fullness of time, notice-and-comment rulemaking will become, far more than it is today, a major contributor to forms of data acquisition that are indispensable to accurate cost-benefit analysis.

Retrospective Analysis

Agency rulemaking occurs before the fact, when information gathering is highly likely to be imperfect. An agency issues a rule involving food safety, occupational health, or energy efficiency—and then it moves on. Even with a lot of public participation, the original rule may be based on speculative projections. The costs are expected to be $400 million and the benefits are expected to be $700 million, but no one really knows for sure. Often both costs and benefits are anticipated to fall within wide ranges—say, from $400 million to $900 million—and the agency cannot produce a point estimate. The agency might also be aware of potential unintended bad consequences, but it might think that they are unlikely in the extreme. It might be wrong. Or it might not anticipate some terrible consequence, which occurs two months, two years, or five years after it has acted. Life is full of surprises, and even the most well-meaning planners, engaged in cost-benefit analysis, are unable to foresee them.

A sensible regulatory system gives continuing scrutiny to regulatory requirements to test whether they are working as anticipated. A central question is whether the ex ante estimates square with what is known ex post. If they do not, regulations can be changed. There is another advantage to retrospective analysis: it can help inform and improve prospective analysis, as agencies learn about their own mistakes and can become less likely to make them in the future. In this respect, retrospective analysis can lead to major changes in prospective analysis.

On these fronts, existing knowledge remains incomplete; we remain in early stages. But some valuable research can be found, and it continues to grow. Consider, for example, Winston Harrington's careful study.[7] Building on previous work, Harrington explored sixty-one rules for which benefit-cost ratios could be compared before and after the fact. He found significant errors—but no systematic bias. In his account, agencies overestimated both benefits and costs with about equal frequency. In sixteen of the sixty-one cases, the cost-benefit ratios were found to be essentially accurate. In twenty-four cases, the ratio was better, not worse, than the agency had anticipated. In twenty-one cases, the ratio was worse than anticipated. Harrington's general conclusion is that though both costs and benefits tend to be lower than estimated, no bias can be found in estimates of benefit-cost ratios.

Harrington's study is highly illuminating, but it leaves many questions unanswered. The sample size is exceedingly small. Harrington focuses on benefit-cost ratios, which is certainly a relevant question but not the central one. If we care about social welfare, what most matters is not ratios, but *net benefits* and whether agencies have accurately calculated them. (A rule might have a cost-benefit ratio of 1 to 2, which is good, but the net benefits, from such a ratio, might be $1, $1,000, or $1 billion.) Nor does Harrington specify the degree to which benefits and costs were underestimated or overestimated. Other studies do explore the question of underestimation or overestimation. One such study analyzed twenty-one environmental and occupational safety regulations for which retrospective estimates could be found.[8] The basic conclusion is that agencies display a modest tendency to overestimate costs. For thirteen rules, agencies overestimated costs; they estimated costs accurately for four; they underestimated for three; and the costs were indeterminate for one.

In 2005, the Office of Management and Budget, and in particular the Office of Information and Regulatory Affairs, provided an overview of retrospective analyses based on an examination of forty-seven case studies.[9] Its particular concern was the risk that ex ante estimates might be inadequately informed and therefore erroneous. The overview offers three key conclusions. First, agencies were far more likely to overestimate benefits than to underestimate them. Agencies overestimated benefits 40 percent of the time; they underestimated benefits only 2 percent of the time. Second, agencies tended to overestimate the benefit-cost ratio, and in that sense be a bit too optimistic about the consequences of their rules. Agency estimates were accurate 23 percent of the time, whereas the ratio was overestimated 47 percent of the time and underestimated 30 percent of the time. Third, agencies were slightly more likely to overestimate than to underestimate costs. Agencies were accurate 26 percent of the time, overestimated costs 34 percent of the time, and underestimated costs 26 percent of the time.

From existing work, the most sensible general conclusion is that agencies do make many mistakes, attesting to the reality of the knowledge problem), but there does not appear to be a large systematic bias in any one direction. That is useful and important to know. At the same time, it is even more important to acknowledge that we need to know a great deal more than we do now. The existing studies cover only a trivially small fraction of rules on the books. Much more can and should be done to compare prospective estimates to what actually happens in the world. One of the most important goals should be to see when particular rules are working as anticipated and when they are not—and to fix them when they have gone wrong.

Retrospective Analysis, with Public Comment

I have noted that in 2011, President Obama issued Executive Order 13563, which requires retrospective analysis of existing rules. A key purpose was to reduce the knowledge problem—not by assembling information in advance, but by bringing to bear information about how rules are actually operating, and with explicit reference to the dispersed information of the public.

After the order was issued, the initial step was the production of preliminary plans for retrospective review, which were required within 120 days. This was an aggressive timeline, especially considering the fact that public officials have numerous responsibilities. Many agencies began by asking for suggestions from the public, requesting ideas about which regulations needed to be revisited. For example, the Environmental Protection Agency and the Departments of Commerce, Transportation, the Interior, Homeland Security, State, and the Treasury posted notices in the Federal Register, asking for comments about how the process should work and which rules should be streamlined or repealed. Several agencies held public meetings nationwide.

In a short period, a small subset of the initiatives that emerged from this feedback on streamlining or repealing of rules produced savings of more than $10 billion. Many of the resulting initiatives also provide benefits that are hard to monetize but likely to be significant. For example, it is not easy to quantify the economic benefits, including the jobs created, of reducing restrictions on exports and simplifying the requirements imposed on those who do business across national borders. Nonetheless, those benefits are probably high.

In 2012, President Obama issued a supplemental executive order, still in effect, with three key components.[10] First, agencies are required to reach out to the public, on a continuing basis, to solicit ideas about reforms. Second, agencies must give priority to reforms that would have a significant impact—for example, those with substantial economic savings. New initiatives are supposed to make a real difference; they should not be symbolic measures or mere updating. Third, and perhaps most important, agencies have to report on their progress to OIRA and to the public on a continuing basis. This final step is designed to promote accountability—to ensure that if agencies are not doing much, the public will be able to see that and provide a corrective. In all of these ways, the process of retrospective analysis is expected to be informed by the dispersed information of the public. Ultimately, the Obama initiatives produced over $30 billion in five-year savings.

In 2017, President Trump left these requirements in place, but he took some major additional steps, and these should be enthusiastically applauded. One of the most important took the form of an executive order that calls for the official designation of *regulatory reform officers* and *regulatory reform task forces* within each department and agency of the federal government. The reform task forces have a specific job. They are required to provide a report to agency heads, identifying specific regulations that are ripe for repeal, replacement, or modification. They are charged with calling out those rules that eliminate jobs or inhibit job creation; that are outdated, unnecessary, or ineffective; or that impose costs in excess of benefits. The task forces are specifically directed to seek input from those affected by regulations, including small businesses; consumers; nongovernmental organizations; trade associations; and state, local, and tribal governments. All this is highly constructive.

For all their differences, Obama and Trump, by endorsing retrospective review, have demonstrated alertness to the knowledge problem and have sought to create institutional safeguards to provide correctives when it proves severe. But their measures are inadequate. It would be good, and less clumsy, for regulations to be issued so as to promote continuing scrutiny and review—perhaps even in real time. I will return to this point shortly.

Experiments and Rapid Learning

To get the facts right, it is important to engage in far more evaluation and experimentation than we now do. The central goal is not to rely on expert judgments about likely effects, but instead to compile evidence from the real world—not retrospectively, but in advance. In the past decade, there has been growing interest in the use of randomized controlled trials as a means of learning the effects of policy initiatives. In medicine, of course, it is standard to rely on such trials to see if a drug is safe and effective. For drugs, it would not be enough simply to guess, to rely on informed hunches, or even to make before-and-after assessments. Suppose we learn that people who use a certain asthma medicine do better after taking the medicine than before. If so, we know something important—but we do not know nearly enough. The risk of before-and-after assessments is that they may not control for confounding variables. Perhaps people are doing better because of some change in the environment that is not adequately understood by those who are making the assessment. In the medical domain, the great value of randomized controlled experiments is that they have the potential to provide a clear sense of the actual effects of the intervention.

Esther Duflo, an economist at Massachusetts Institute of Technology (MIT), has helped pioneer the use of randomized controlled trials for purposes of policy evaluation.[11] In principle, such trials are the best way to solve the knowledge problem; they provide the closest thing to the gold standard, and in at least in some contexts, they should adequately respond to the Hayekian concern about regulators' lack of information. Duflo has demonstrated that in many cases, small measures can have significant effects. In the regulatory area, the use of such trials remains in a lamentably preliminary state. Analysis of costs and benefits is rarely informed by them, but it is easy to imagine serious evaluations. Consider a few examples:

• Would state regulators save lives by banning the use of cell phones while driving? This is a disputed question. Laboratory experiments, showing that people's reaction times slow down when they are distracted, strongly suggest that the answer is affirmative—and indeed that driving while talking on a phone is not unlike driving while inebriated, producing a fourfold increase in relative crash risk.[12] But those experiments may be an unreliable guide to the real world. We could test whether a ban on cell phone use would have major effects on safety by comparing similarly situated localities, one with such a ban and one without. Or we could test whether accidents increase during periods in which cell phone use goes up—for example, when rates decrease after 9 p.m. (In fact, precisely that question has been studied, with a surprising finding of no such increase.[13]

• What are the effects of different methods of increasing rear visibility in cars? If monitors are placed in the dashboard, do accidents drop? How much, and compared to what? Do improved mirrors have a significant effect? What about sonar devices, making beeping noises? Do they work as well as cameras? Randomized trials might help (assuming that sufficiently large sample sizes could be obtained).

• It is important to evaluate different disclosure requirements. We might test whether different fuel-economy labels have different effects on similarly situated consumers. Does one label produce different choices? How different? If labels draw attention to annual fuel costs, are people affected? Do people care about environmental factors? How much? The same kinds of questions might be asked about disclosure requirements for credit cards, mortgages, cell phones, and school loans.

In important areas, experimentation might take the form of advance testing of regulatory alternatives through randomized controlled trials. Steps in this direction would have major advantages over current approaches, such as focus groups, which are often highly artificial and which sometimes test what people like rather than what they would actually do. A presentation of information might be pleasing without having much of an effect on what people understand and do.

In the United Kingdom, there has been a great deal of interest in using randomized controlled trials, above all through the work of the Behavioral Insights Team (sometimes called the Nudge Unit).[14] What are the effects of different kinds of communications in reducing tax delinquency? In producing higher rates of organ donation? In reducing overprescription of antibiotics? All of these questions can be and are being tested. Related efforts have been made in the United States and elsewhere. If randomized trials are not feasible, we might be able to design experiments in order to improve understanding of actual behavior by asking people concrete questions about what they would do if provided with certain information or if given a range of options.

Of course, there are constraints—involving not merely law but also resources and feasibility (and perhaps equity as well)—on using randomized controlled trials in the regulatory context. Among other things, sufficient sample sizes might be difficult to obtain. But in some cases, they would be both appropriate and useful. We should expect far more progress in the future.

Measure and React

In 2016 and 2017, I served on the Defense Innovation Board, created by the Department of Defense to promote more innovative practices. Many members of the board came from Silicon Valley—and they knew a lot about innovation. In an early meeting, I suggested that the department should be using cost-benefit analysis far more than it now does. To my great surprise, one of the members of the board, from Silicon Valley, was skeptical. He said, roughly, "We don't do that." I asked him to explain. He answered that for many things that Silicon Valley does, there just isn't enough information, available in advance, to allow quantification of costs and benefits. Instead, companies experiment. They do so not only through randomized controlled trials, and perhaps not even mostly through such trials, but by trying something and measuring what happens.

He was speaking of what Duncan Watts calls the *measure-and-react strategy*.[15] By way of explanation, Watts points to the Spanish clothing retailer Zara, which acknowledges its limited foresight and its inability to predict what consumers are going to buy. Instead of trying to make predictions, it hires people to go to shopping malls to see, in real time, what people are buying and wearing. On the basis of that information, it produces a big portfolio of the styles, fabrics, and colors that seem popular and sends that portfolio to stores, so as to test consumer behavior. Zara has a fast and flexible system for manufacturing and distribution, which makes it possible to design and produce new clothing and ship it all over the world with tremendous speed. Apparently, Silicon Valley does something like that as well. I don't know for sure, but I am willing to speculate that in the future, that will be a winning business model for numerous companies.

The measure-and-react strategy is not a randomized controlled trial, but it serves the same functions. It is increasingly used by private-sector actors, who know what they do not know and try to adjust to what people are doing on the fly. Can governments do the same thing? In many contexts, they certainly can. With respect to security lines at airports, for example, they can make rapid adjustments as the number of travelers varies over time. With respect to traffic fatalities, they can test interventions and monitor diverse situations to test what works and what does not. The sky is the limit here. We should see far more use of measure-and-react strategies in the future.

Less Tension

Let's underline the more general point. There can be a serious tension between the commitment to cost-benefit analysis and a realistic appreciation of the limits of official knowledge. In their own way, cost-benefit analysts are planners. Without significant efforts to learn, their numbers might be inadequately informed. They might move governments in the wrong directions. In some cases, regulators might appropriately decide to abstain entirely, concluding that the market failure is not clear and that any cure might be worse than the disease. Whenever regulators face significant informational deficits, it is important to explore tools that take advantage of what the private sector knows;

market-friendly tools, such as nudges and economic incentives, have important advantages in that arena.

In other cases, however, Congress has required agencies to act, or the argument for action is too compelling to be ignored. As a result of modern technologies, the old tool of notice-and-comment rulemaking has new promise for acquiring dispersed information. This point holds not only for new rules, which lack a track record, but also for retrospective analysis of old rules, for which the private sector often has important information about both costs and benefits. It would be extravagant to contend that notice-and-comment rulemaking can eliminate the knowledge problem, even in the modern era, but it can produce a great deal of help. By enlisting retrospective analysis of regulations—itself spurred and informed by public comment and undertaken on a continuing basis—and experimental evidence alongside measure-and-react strategies, officials should be able to reduce the enduring tension between two ideas that belong at the heart of contemporary thinking about the regulatory state.

II Frontiers

6 Moral Commitments

What is the role of moral commitments in cost-benefit analysis? Do such commitments have a place in this particular revolution? Consider the following cases:

1. Congress has directed the Securities and Exchange Commission (SEC) to issue a regulation to ensure disclosure of *conflict minerals*—minerals used to finance mass atrocities.[1] The SEC is required to catalog the costs and benefits of its regulation (to the extent feasible). It is aware that many consumers are interested in the relevant information. How, if at all, should the SEC monetize that interest?

2. The Dolphin Protection Consumer Information Act[2] imposes labeling requirements to inform consumers if tuna used in tuna products was caught using drift nets and other methods that harm dolphins. It includes standards by which companies may label their products *dolphin safe*.[3] Many consumers care a great deal about the protection of dolphins and want to see those labels. How, if at all, should the Department of Agriculture incorporate that concern in issuing standards? Should it attempt to monetize it?

3. Many consumers are concerned about genetically modified (GM) food.[4] Some of them are concerned about health and the environment, but others believe that genetic modification of food is "just wrong." Congress has required the Department of Agriculture to label GM food as such.[5] How, if at all, should the department take account of consumer sentiment in cataloging the rule's benefits?

In important contexts, governments regulate products because some or many people believe that their production is immoral, or at least morally problematic. The regulation might involve protection of children, of people in other nations, of victims of some kind of wrong-doing, of animals, or even of nature. In most cases, their production involves concrete harms, such as lives lost, which are what trigger the moral concern. The goal of regulation—in the form of a mandate, a ban, or a labeling requirement—is to reduce those harms.

In some cases, it is difficult or perhaps impossible to identify concrete harms, but people nonetheless favor regulation as a way of expressing and realizing their moral commitments (as in the context of GM food). The principal question in this chapter is how regulators should take account of moral commitments in undertaking cost-benefit analysis.

My simple answer, put too briefly, is that they should ask: How much are people willing to pay to honor those commitments? This answer is jarring, because the question of what morality requires is usually not answered by asking how much people are willing to pay to protect their moral convictions. Nonetheless, that is an important question. Suppose that a consumer, Eden, cares about an assortment of things, including her longevity, her health, her comfort, and dolphins. Suppose that a substantial component of her welfare is the welfare of dolphins. If they suffer, she suffers—but how much does she suffer? Here as elsewhere, and whatever its limitations, her willingness to pay is the best available measure.

An alternative view is that even though they matter, moral commitments should not be taken to be part of a cost-benefit analysis; they raise entirely independent issues and must be engaged seriously but separately. On that view, analysis of costs and benefits is important but not exhaustive; it turns on a narrower set of factors, such as effects on income and health.

It is true that moral commitments often signal values that are not adequately captured by private willingness to pay. If the goal is to prevent mass atrocities in a foreign country, Americans' willingness to pay to prevent mass atrocities hardly exhausts the welfare effects of preventing mass atrocities. Fair enough. But people's welfare may well be affected—even profoundly—by violations of their moral commitments, as demonstrated by willingness to pay. If people lose welfare because of the suffering or death of others—people in other countries, those they love, their own children, rape victims, dolphins, members of future generations—then their loss ought to be counted.

To be sure, the welfare loss might be hard to measure,[6] and in many cases it might turn out to be relatively or even trivially small, not least because people's budget constraints might mean that they are unwilling to spend a great deal to vindicate any particular moral commitment. In principle, however, there is no justification for refusing to include people's willingness to pay to protect such commitments in a cost-benefit analysis. If an agency ignores the resulting number and thus treats people's moral concerns as valueless, there is a strong argument that it is acting arbitrarily and therefore in violation of the Administrative Procedure Act.[7] The resulting regulation will be too weak.

The issue is hardly fanciful. In recent years, the Environmental Protection Agency has issued regulations designed largely to protect fish from discharges from power plants. On standard assumptions, the direct benefits of such protection in terms of human welfare—perhaps in the form of ecological benefits and improved recreation—are relatively small, and far less than the costs.[8] But it has been vigorously urged that apart from those standard benefits, people would be willing to pay something more to provide such protection, because they care about protecting fish—and that once that figure is aggregated across the population and included in the benefits figure, aggressive regulation is amply justified.[9]

Indeed, a court of appeals struck down a damage measure from the Department of Interior that refused to consider people's willingness to pay to protect the continued existence of pristine areas and the animals that live there.[10] In the court's view, it was unlawful for the agency to focus entirely on use value and to ignore private willingness to pay— which would depend, in that case, on moral considerations. That conclusion has potentially broad implications, suggesting that in certain contexts, a refusal to use contingent valuation methods to account for *existence value*[11]—reflecting people's concern for the value of the continued existence of a wilderness beyond its utility for recreation and food—would be arbitrary and therefore unlawful.

Nothing here is meant to take a stand on the continuing controversy over contingent valuation methods,[12] and my claim is emphatically not meant to suggest that willingness to pay captures all the welfare benefits of regulations that are designed to protect third parties. The ultimate goal of the Dolphin Protection Consumer Information Act is to protect dolphins. But insofar as people's welfare is increased by the protection of dolphins, their willingness to pay is part of the cost-benefit analysis.

In prominent cases, government regulators have essentially accepted this argument. For a regulation designed to reduce the incidence of prison rape, regulators enlisted a contingent valuation study suggesting that (unimprisoned) Americans would pay over $300,000 to eliminate a case of prison rape; they added that in light of that number, the regulation likely had benefits in excess of costs.[13] Recall too that in a case involving protection of children from backover crashes, the Department of Transportation pointed to, without monetizing, parents' desire to provide that protection.

The question of how to address people's moral commitments in cost-benefit analysis is of great importance, and not only because many regulations advance moral goals. The problem for agencies is that when Congress commands them to advance such goals, it rarely provides guidance about the level of costs that should be imposed on the private sector in the course of achieving those goals. The SEC calculated that its conflict minerals regulation would cost industry about $5 billion, and in light of the statutory mandate, it deemed that amount a reasonable price to pay in order to enhance disclosure of conflict minerals use.[14]

But what if a slightly more effective regulation would have cost $50 billion or $500 billion? Should the SEC have imposed huge costs on the private sector in order to improve disclosure by only a small amount? Critics of cost-benefit analysis, who claim that moral gains are not monetizable and therefore that agencies should not use cost-benefit analysis at all, have not given a satisfactory answer to this question. If agencies monetize the moral benefits of regulations, they will be in a better position to decide on the stringency of regulations in a nonarbitrary way. In many cases, monetization of moral benefits will justify stronger regulations.

The central argument, concrete though it is, touches directly on some of the most abstract and fundamental issues in legal and political theory—and it is important to identify limiting principles. Some moral commitments, such as belief in racial segregation or suppression of sexually explicit speech, are inconsistent with the Constitution or with statutes authorizing regulatory action; it is legitimate for regulators to conclude that those commitments cannot be counted in the analysis. Some people might also insist on ideas, associated with the liberal political tradition, that forbid interference with purely self-regarding behavior by reference to the moral concerns of outsiders. For example, people might be willing to pay something to stop same-sex marriages, use of contraceptives, sales of alcohol, and indoor tanning. Welfarists may or may not be willing to take account of third-party preferences of this kind, but it is possible to embrace the thrust of the argument here while also insisting on such a limitation on its domain.

Some moral commitments operate at an exceedingly high level of generality, as when people suffer or rejoice as a result of the very fact of regulation. On strict welfarist principles, such commitments should be counted, but it seems safe to say that regulators ought to ignore them on the ground that the analysis becomes too unruly and too untethered if they are taken into account. In due course, I shall explore all of these arguments.

Willingness to Pay for Moral Reasons

Many regulations are animated by moral concerns that go far beyond their effects on those who choose the relevant products. For example, a regulation might be designed to protect workers who are affected by certain purchasing decisions, or people who do not live in the nation in which the products are bought. Indeed, the principal purpose of some regulations is to protect something other than human beings. Return to the Dolphin Protection Consumer Information Act. The statute was enacted in response to a belief that tuna harvesting caused excessive harm to dolphins, not to human well-being.

To understand the problem, compare Jane and Sam. Jane suffers from seafood intolerances, as a result of which she greatly benefits when food products include labels that disclose whether trace amounts of seafood are present in the product. Before the Food Allergen Labeling and Consumer Protection Act was enacted, she bought organic foods from specialty stores that cost about $1,000 per year more than comparable food products sold in supermarkets. As a result of the law, Jane can shop at supermarkets; she is at least $1,000 better off per year and can use this money to buy goods that she could not afford in the past.

So long as she uses this money for saving and consumption, the $1,000 amount is a reasonable approximation of the impact of the law on her well-being; it might well be a lower bound.

Sam does not suffer from food intolerances, but he cares deeply about the well-being of dolphins. He donates $1,000 per year to a charity that lobbies for laws that protect dolphin populations from harm by drift nets used to catch tuna. When Congress enacts the Dolphin Protection Consumer Information Act, Sam is very happy, but he is not sure whether the law should affect his charitable giving. He still cares about dolphins and thinks that the $1,000 he donates might be used to lobby for a stricter law that bans drift nets or for some other law that will help dolphins. But he also needs to pay his mortgage.

The Allergen Labeling Act improves Jane's well-being in a straightforward way. Does the Dolphin Act improve Sam's well-being? It is tempting to think that though the law helps advance one of Sam's moral commitments, the answer is "no." After all, it does not improve his health or safety, give him goods or services to consume, or (directly) enhance his wealth. Another way to make this point is to imagine a world in which people like Sam largely disappear, so that almost no one cares about dolphins anymore. A respectable view in moral philosophy is that even so, it remains wrong to kill dolphins with drift nets. Most utilitarians believe that the well-being of animals has independent moral importance. That was Bentham's view, in fact, and I share it. On this view, the moral worth of dolphins does not depend on whether Sam exists or on whether many or few people agree with Sam.

This view seems to have a surprising implication. If cost-benefit analysis is a welfarist decision-procedure, then there is an argument that insofar as regulators are engaging in that form of analysis, they will account for Jane's self-regarding preferences and disregard Sam's moral beliefs. To understand this argument (which I shall shortly reject), consider the Benthamite view. If one hundred thousand dolphins exist, then their continued existence has moral value reflecting the well-being of those dolphins. If we take Sam's $1,000 charitable donation as an approximation of his willingness to pay to keep the dolphins alive, this would imply that the moral value of the existence of the dolphins is $1,000. If one thousand people agree with Sam, their moral value equals $1 million. And if the Sams disappeared, the moral value of dolphins in a cost-benefit analysis would fall to $0. But the moral value of the dolphins is not a function of the number of people who care about dolphins. This means that the cost-benefit analysis should not treat Sam's willingness to pay as a reflection of their moral value.

On this view, a regulatory agency charged with implementing the Dolphin Act should conduct cost-benefit analyses, but insofar as it is doing so, it should ignore moral valuations (including those that are expressed in charitable donations). To be sure, moral arguments, captured in the commitment to the well-being of dolphins, matter and deserve independent consideration; under the relevant law, they might complement or override cost-benefit analysis. With respect to that form of analysis, however, Sam's moral views are irrelevant.

But this conclusion is wrong. The first and more minor point is that when Sam donates $1,000 to the dolphin charity, he has $1,000 less to spend on his own well-being. If we want to be precise, we need to analyze Sam's motivations with some care. If the regulation causes Sam to spend the entire amount on himself, then the regulation does make him better off by $1,000. If a regulation that helps dolphins causes Sam to reconsider his moral priorities and donate the money elsewhere, then it is harder to know whether and to what extent it improves Sam's well-being.

But there is a far more fundamental point, which bears directly on that question. Suppose that Sam's subjective welfare is affected by what happens to dolphins. When he hears about them being caught in drift nets, he experiences a loss of welfare, probably captured in a pang of unhappiness. This sense of empathy is a psychological reaction, in some ways akin to disgust, anger, and fear, and it is highly relevant to Sam's welfare. In principle, cost-benefit analysis should take account of the positive psychological effect that people experience as a result of protecting those about whom they care. People are willing to pay to improve their welfare, and affective states are an important component of welfare.

It follows that if the entire dolphin population were eliminated, or if significant numbers of dolphins were killed, then there would be two separate effects: a *moral effect* and a *welfare effect*. (To be sure, the moral effect is a kind of welfare effect, but it does not involve consumers or even human beings.) Both effects should count. If you are a moral realist, a moral wrong has taken place, and it is independent of the welfare effects on human beings. The elimination of dolphins also harms human welfare by causing unhappiness or other welfare losses among people who care about dolphins. This harm can be measured, at least in principle, and is of course a function of the size of the human population that cares about dolphins.

Here, in short, is my central claim: When regulators conduct cost-benefit analysis, they should include valuations that reflect how much people are willing to pay to see their moral beliefs vindicated or to reduce the level of psychological harm they feel if those beliefs are not vindicated. At least this is so to the extent that people's welfare is reduced if their moral commitments are violated. Monetary valuations will hardly capture everything that matters, but they are an important point of a full accounting.

Limiting Principles

This claim is a concrete and relatively straightforward suggestion for how to conduct cost-benefit analysis. But it turns out to bear on some of the most fundamental questions in legal and political theory. Taken for all that it is worth, it might seem unacceptably broad.

To see the concern, suppose that some people think that pornography is morally unacceptable and are willing to pay something to ban it; that some people have strong moral objections to the use of contraceptives, and they would pay to see them banned; that the very idea of alcohol consumption is, to many people, morally problematic, and they would gladly pay to reduce it; that certain religious practices seem morally offensive to people who would be willing to pay to stamp them out; that many people object to opening stores on Sunday and would happily pay something for Sunday-closing laws; that some people greatly dislike the very idea of transgender people and would pay something to require that they use the bathroom available to people of their biological sex. Under a standard view of liberal political theory, the government is not permitted to take account of these kinds of moral commitments when it regulates. One reason—some people say—is that if government does take account of such commitments, freedom itself will be at risk, simply because people want to put freedom at risk.

The examples could easily be proliferated. In these circumstances, it seems important to identify limiting principles. Indeed, some people might be tempted to suggest that if identifying such principles proves difficult, there should be a general prohibition on including moral commitments in cost-benefit analysis at all. That conclusion might be defended on the ground that though such a prohibition leads to a problem of underinclusiveness (in welfarist terms), it reduces unacceptable complexity for public officials and avoids a problem of overinclusiveness (in welfarist or other terms). To make the argument less compressed: If we exclude moral commitments, we make cost-benefit analysis a lot easier. It is true that we will end up excluding values that ought to count (because they matter to welfare). But if we include moral commitments, we might end up including some values that should not count (for welfarist or other reasons; consider the examples listed above). In the end, the best approach might be a simple rule: do not include moral commitments in cost-benefit analysis.

As a practical matter, that argument is not crazy. It is possible to agree that in theory, violations of moral commitments produce welfare losses that should be counted in cost-benefit analysis, but also to agree that in practice, it is too hard to come up with the relevant numbers, that they are not likely to be large, and that limiting principles are too hard to specify.

That conclusion is not obviously wrong, but it is greatly weakened if we make progress toward identifying limiting principles. If we can do so, we will be able to consider moral commitments when they should be considered, and to exclude them when they should be excluded. The most obvious limiting principles come from the Constitution. If people like the idea of racial segregation or think that sex discrimination is wonderful, their willingness to pay for regulations that promote racial segregation or sex discrimination cannot be counted, because the Constitution rules those moral commitments out of bounds. If people want to ban sexually explicit speech, their willingness to pay for such bans cannot count, because the Constitution protects sexually explicit speech. It is true that a strict welfarist, armed with a perfect method for calculating welfare effects, might want to consider all such effects. But it is safe to suggest that regulatory welfarism, implemented through cost-benefit analysis, may not take account of moral commitments that offend the Constitution.

So too, some moral commitments are inconsistent with statutory requirements. Some people might believe that civil rights laws violate what morality requires, because they intrude on freedom of association, or insist that minimum-wage and maximum-hour laws have the same defect. Committed libertarians would object to many regulations on this general ground. Here again, a strict welfarist would be open to the possibility that preferences of this kind must be counted in a cost-benefit analysis, at least if they are backed by willingness to pay. But for purposes of actual practice, regulators can certainly refuse to take account of moral commitments that are inconsistent with existing sources of law.

I have noted that a significant strand in liberal political theory, associated with John Stuart Mill, insists that the government may not interfere with people's freedom of action unless there is *harm to others*. Taken for all that it is worth, the argument here is inconsistent with that view. It suggests that even if there is no harm to others, people's actions might be regulable if it offends other people's moral sensibilities—at least if those who are offended are willing to pay for the interference. To be sure, most of the cases I have given are in no tension with the liberal position, because harm to others is involved, but the argument could easily be taken to cut more broadly. Suppose, for example, that people would be willing to pay to stop their fellow citizens from reading certain materials, from dancing in certain ways, or from singing certain songs. For those who believe in a certain understanding of freedom, their willingness to pay is neither here nor there. So long as there is no harm to others, people should be allowed to do as they wish—or so a significant strand in the liberal position holds.

For reasons that have produced an extensive debate in economics and political philosophy, a welfarist would indeed have some trouble with that strand of the liberal position. But for those who broadly embrace that strand, it would be possible to accept the argument here while limiting its domain to cases in which harm to others is involved. Indeed, most of the cases explored here do involve that harm and hence fit comfortably within liberal constraints.

There is an additional point. It is not fanciful to suppose that some people rejoice, and others feel dismay, at the very issuance of regulations—perhaps because of their attitudes toward regulation as such, perhaps because of the general areas in which some regulations fall. Should regulators survey the American people, or the people of their nation, to see whether rejoicing or dismay would accompany the issuance of their regulations and try to elicit the corresponding willingness to pay? Here again, a strict welfarist might be tempted to answer yes. But that answer seems daft. To say the least, it is hard to generate numbers that are reliable in this context.

In any case, it would be most surprising if the welfare effects, from abstract reactions of this kind, turned out to have the same magnitude as the effects from the more concrete commitments identified here. It is also possible that at this level of abstraction, valuations in different directions will cancel each other out. People who are philosophically opposed to economic regulation in general might be willing to pay a small amount to block any type of regulation, but then there are people who welcome government oversight, and they are likely to be willing to pay a small amount for further government involvement in economic life.

More broadly, some utilitarians have said that some preferences, such as sadistic or malicious preferences, should not be included in the utilitarian (or welfarist) calculus.[15] To be sure, it is reasonable to wonder whether any such conclusion is ultimately justified on utilitarian (or welfarist) grounds or whether it requires some kind of nonutilitarian (or nonwelfarist) explanation. It is not necessary to answer that question to insist that private willingness to pay for certain outcomes (favoring, say, assault, acute human suffering, sexual harassment, or rape) ought not to be counted, even if those outcomes would please people.

Implementation: Two Questions

Subject to the foregoing limitations, what are the practical implications of the argument that moral commitments should count in cost-benefit analysis?

What Congress Wants

The first question is simple: If Congress asks agencies to protect dolphins because it believes that dolphins have independent moral value, shouldn't agencies obey Congress' instructions? Of course they should. And if Congress wants agencies to disregard cost-benefit analysis in protecting dolphins, then they should do that as well. As we shall see, sometimes Congress requires agencies to act, and the outcome of a cost-benefit analysis (whether it is unfavorable to action or leaves unanswered questions) cannot justify inaction.

At the same time, we have also seen that prevailing executive orders require an accounting of both costs and benefits, and ignoring a class of benefits will ensure that the accounting is inaccurate. It is also clear that in many important cases, Congress does not want agencies to disregard cost-benefit analysis, and agencies should not do so. The reason is rooted in the nature of regulation. As I have noted, the issue is often not whether to regulate, but how strictly to regulate. An analysis of costs and benefits is usually relevant to that issue. If, for example, numerous dolphins would be protected by an expensive regulation, the argument for that regulation is stronger than if it would protect few dolphins. And if people's willingness to pay to protect dolphins is very high, then the argument for that regulation receives additional fortification. To that extent, moral commitments must be counted.

A Daunting Task

The second question concerns *how* agencies should use moral commitments in cost-benefit analysis. Should an agency really try to figure out private willingness to pay? In principle, the answer is yes—but the task can be daunting. It is impossible to rule out the possibility that in some cases, reliable quantification is not possible, and the most that the agency can do is point to the existence of a positive amount without specifying it. One reason involves the potential unreliability of the only available tools.

Suppose, for example, that the question is how much Americans would pay to reduce some harm done to fish in the Atlantic Ocean. It is easy to imagine a contingent valuation study that would produce some number for the average American—say, five dollars annually, which would yield an annual benefit figure in excess of $1 billion. The problem is that for countless regulations that produce moral benefits, it would likely be easy to produce the same number, which might suggest that the average American would be willing to have a "moral budget" of perhaps $5,000 or more, and that might seem to defy belief. People might be willing to pay a nontrivial amount to help solve one problem, but if they were given a full universe of problems, the amount that they would be willing to pay to help solve any particular one might get very small.

The problem, in short, is that contingent-valuation studies often ask for willingness to pay to solve certain problems in isolation, rather than requiring respondents to consider how payments to solve one problem would reduce funds available to solve numerous others. As a result, the method may produce unreliable answers. Perhaps appropriate studies can overcome this problem—but perhaps not.

My major goal is to notice rather than to resolve the measurement problem and to insist on a basic principle: people experience welfare losses from social outcomes that offend their moral commitments, even if those outcomes do not involve their own wealth or health. Private willingness to pay is the best way to measure those losses. Eliciting the relevant values can be extremely challenging, but agencies have techniques for doing that, at least as general approximations. On welfarist grounds, and subject to the identified limitations, there is no justification for ignoring the losses that people experience from morally abhorrent outcomes.

7 On Mandatory Labeling

When should government mandate labels? When would mandatory labels have desirable consequences for social welfare? How can those consequences be measured? When would labels do more good than harm? There is a clear link to the topic just discussed, because labels are often mandated on moral grounds.

My principal goal here is to offer a guide suitable for use in many contexts—including calorie labels, energy-efficiency labels, fuel-economy labels, graphic warnings, and much more. Sometimes agencies quantify both benefits and costs, or at least significant subsets of them, either by using endpoints (economic savings or health benefits) or by measuring private willingness to pay for labels. Sometimes they engage in breakeven analysis. Sometimes they point to human dignity, equity, or distributional concerns. As we will see, private willingness to pay is the best approach in theory, but its measurement raises serious empirical and conceptual challenges.

Product Labeling in General: Market Failure?

It is easy to imagine labels that are unnecessary, that are costly to impose, that are widely ignored by consumers, or that promote the interests of powerful private groups. It is also easy to imagine labels that help consumers save money, to avoid serious risks, to protect third parties, or to register their deepest moral commitments. Under the standard economic approach, the initial question is whether there is a market failure. In many cases, we can expect the market to produce the necessary information on its own.[1] In other words, sellers are expected to disclose relevant information voluntarily. Mandatory disclosure is needed only when voluntary disclosure fails.

Consumer Demand and Incomplete Information

A standard market failure, often invoked by agencies themselves, involves *incomplete information*. Sometimes consumers lack information that would enable them to make (sufficiently informed) choices, and government provides that information to make the market work efficiently.

It is true, of course, that consumers sometimes insist on product-related information, and hence the market will provide it; there is no need for a mandate. But consumers might not have the information that would put them in the position to demand disclosure of (further) information—and it might not be rational for them to attempt to acquire that information. Consider the health risks posed by trans fats, which raise highly technical questions. Rational ignorance on the part of consumers might lead them not to acquire information from which they would ultimately benefit. Without that information, they might lack the knowledge that would lead them to ask for labels. For that reason, a government response might be appropriate.

A further problem stems from the fact that information has the characteristics of a public good, which means that the market will not generate enough of it. Acting on his or her own, each consumer might not seek information from which all or most consumers would benefit. Mandatory labels overcome a collective action problem.

Yet another problem arises when the point of disclosure is to protect third parties. Often consumers want to know whether products are harming people; even if they do not, disclosure might be required to reduce that harm. Suppose, for example, that disclosure of information is designed to reduce the risks of secondhand smoke, to prevent harms to animals (such as elephants or dolphins), to protect vulnerable groups (as with labels for products from companies that have frequently violated occupational-safety laws), or to protect American jobs (as with *country of origin* or *made in America* labels).

If third parties are at risk, we have a standard argument for government intervention. It is true, of course, that the preferred response to such risks is some kind of corrective tax, not disclosure. But if a tax is unavailable, for political or other reasons, then disclosure might seem to be a reasonable second best.

There are behavioral issues as well. If risks are not sufficiently salient, then consumers might not demand relevant information about them, even if those risks are not exactly trivial. In principle, disclosure could increase consumer welfare. Or suppose that health risks are long-term; if so, then present bias might lead consumers not to demand information about them. It is true that in the face of present bias, disclosure might not do much good; present-biased consumers might not care about what they learn. But perhaps information could be provided in a way that would reduce present bias. For example, labels might be graphic or specifically focus people on what might happen in the long term.

Producer Behavior

Notwithstanding these points, a standard unraveling argument predicts voluntary disclosure even if consumers do not demand it. For purposes of illustration, assume that for whatever reason (rational or not), consumers would choose non-GM foods if they were given the information that would enable them to do so. Specifically, assume that consumers are willing to pay ten dollars for GM salmon and twenty dollars for salmon if it is not genetically modified. Further assume that GM salmon costs five dollars to produce, whereas non-GM salmon costs seven dollars to produce. Finally, assume that, initially, half the salmon on the market is genetically modified and half is not. Without any labeling, the consumer would not know what kind of salmon she is buying and would therefore be willing to pay fifteen dollars (= 0.5*$10 + 0.5*$20). This state of (consumer) ignorance benefits the producers of GM salmon and harms the producers of non-GM salmon.

But this state of ignorance is not an equilibrium. The non-GM sellers will voluntarily add a "No GMOs" label so that they can charge twenty dollars rather than fifteen dollars per salmon (so long as the cost of adding such a label is less than five dollars per salmon). The GM salmon will not be labeled, but GM labeling would not be necessary; rational consumers would infer that nonlabeled salmon is genetically modified.[2]

As a real-world example, analogous to the question of GM food, consider the example of gluten-free foods. Some people (including those with celiac disease) are allergic to food that contains gluten. At least to date, we do not observe statutory disclosure requirements ("Warning: this product contains gluten"). Instead we see voluntary labels, saying, for example, that products are "gluten-free." The FDA has issued guidance for such labels.[3] On optimistic assumptions, voluntary labels provide sufficient information.

Markets That Do Not Unravel

This happy unraveling story, however, does not always play out. Failure of voluntary disclosure occurs for several reasons—some neoclassical and some behavioral. Starting with the standard, neoclassical reasons, note that the unraveling result assumes that voluntary disclosure is truthful. But imperfect enforcement might lead to false disclosures, which government must correct—and once government is in the business of correction, it might be getting close to mandating a label.

Voluntary disclosure might also fail when there is no standardized format or metric for disclosing information. Without standardization, consumers might not be able to make the required distinctions, in which case voluntary disclosure will be insufficient. And if the point of disclosure is to protect third parties, the unraveling story might not work, because consumers might not care enough about third-party effects to respond to the various informational signals. True, consumer indifference would also mean that mandatory labels would be ineffective. But it is plausible to think that consumers care some—enough to make mandatory labels work but not enough to promote unraveling.

Behavioral economics suggests an additional and perhaps stronger reason for skepticism about voluntary disclosure. The unraveling result assumes that consumers attend to and draw rational inferences from the absence of a label. But attention is limited,[4] and such inferences can be quite difficult to draw, especially when consumers are receiving numerous signals at the same time (as is true for food) and when there are multiple quality levels or continuous quality dimensions. Suppose that some products come with labels saying "low fat" or "low sugar." Would consumers necessarily infer that products lacking such labels are high in fat or sugar? Or would many of them not think much or at all about the question of fat or sugar?

A standard neoclassical argument is that competition might occur over easily observed characteristics, such as price, and less or not at all over less observable characteristics, such as ingredients. The behavioral suggestion (or exclamation point) is that in view of the scarcity of attention, this limited kind of competition is highly likely. Even if consumers pay attention to the relevant ingredient (salt, sugar, fat), they might be unable to draw the rational inference from the absence of disclosure.

For example, those who are purchasing cereal or milk might attend to a variety of product attributes; unless high fat or high sugar content is brought to their attention, many of them might not consider those ingredients at all. If many consumers would not pay attention or draw a negative inference (or a sufficiently negative inference) from the absence of a label, voluntary disclosure might fail. Such failure justifies the consideration of mandatory disclosure, at least in principle. The Affordable Care Act, for example, mandates calorie labels, and there is a plausible argument on their behalf, based on the considerations just sketched.

"Does Not Contain" Labels vs. "Contains" Labels

There are important differences between a system in which a product without some characteristic has a label stating it "does not contain x" and one in which a product with some characteristic has a label stating that it "contains x." As we have seen, "contains x" offers far more salient information to consumers with bounded attention. In addition, "contains x" might have a distinctive signal, suggesting that private and public institutions think that something is wrong with x. "Does not contain x" might also promote a desirable form of sorting. Suppose that 10 percent of the population is troubled by x, whereas 90 percent is not; suppose also that both groups are informed and rational. If so, there is no need for "contains x." Those who want to avoid x can easily do so, and those who have no interest in avoiding x need not be troubled by the issue.

On a certain view of the facts, "does not contain x" is the right approach both to gluten-free and to GM food. People who are allergic to gluten should know what to look for. The principal problem is that if they are inattentive, they might become sick simply by virtue of the fact that the issue has not been brought to their attention. (Compare labels saying "contains peanuts" or "contains shellfish," which may be especially important if consumers are inattentive or if it is not self-evident that the relevant food contains either.) With "does not contain" labels, consumers can easily avoid GM food if that is what they want to do. But this approach is not a solution if GM food has harmful systemic effects or threatens to cause environmental harm (or if relevant interest groups want to stigmatize GM food).

Four Approaches

Agencies have not always responded well to the difficulty of quantifying the costs and benefits of disclosure requirements. With respect to benefits, they have adopted four distinctive approaches, imposing increasingly severe information-gathering demands on agencies. It is not always easy to explain why they choose one or another in particular cases.

The first approach—and it may be the most candid—is to confess a lack of knowledge by acknowledging that, in light of existing information, some costs and (especially) benefits simply cannot be quantified. The problem with this approach is that it suggests that the decision to proceed is essentially a stab in the dark.

The second approach is *breakeven analysis*. When benefits cannot be quantified, breakeven analysis is a significant part of federal agency practice. It is also a part of ordinary life. Suppose that you are deciding whether to take a vacation in Denmark, to drive to an adjacent state to purchase a desirable product, or to join a sports club. In all these cases, you might have a clear sense of the costs but only a vague sense of the benefits, which may not be quantifiable. You might think: What would the benefits have to be to justify the costs? Breakeven analysis, thus understood, plays a significant role in ordinary life.

It plays a role in business as well. Suppose that a real estate investment company does not know for how much certain apartments will rent, but it does know that other, less desirable apartments in the area rent for $900 per month. Suppose too that the company knows that the investment will be worthwhile if it can rent its apartments for more than $800 per month. If so, it makes sense to proceed. Or consider the decision whether to purchase insurance in circumstances in which potential purchasers cannot quantify the probability of a bad outcome. In deciding whether to proceed, potential purchasers might well engage in a kind of informal breakeven analysis.

Agencies should, and often do, respond to nonquantifiable benefits by engaging in a kind of *conditional cost-benefit analysis*, stating that the benefits would justify the costs if certain assumptions hold and certain conditions are met. Suppose that an agency is imposing a new disclosure requirement on the automobile industry, designed to ensure greater clarity about the economic and environmental benefits of increased fuel economy. The cost of the requirement is $15 million. The agency knows (on the basis of evidence) that with the new requirement, the public will have a significantly better understanding of those benefits and thus be able to make more informed decisions and save money. The agency believes that the social gains will be substantial, especially because it anticipates sales of over sixteen million cars annually.

At the same time, it is not able to specify those social gains. The agency does not know how to monetize more informed decision making as such, and it does not know how much consumers will save as a result of the new requirement. But the agency is inclined to conclude that under breakeven analysis, the requirement is justified, because millions of people are likely to incorporate the information and save money, and as a lower bound, the value of those savings exceeds $15 million. If the average consumer obtains just $1 in benefit from the label, it is worthwhile. We could easily imagine cases in which breakeven analysis demonstrates that an initiative would not be worthwhile, because at the upper bound, its benefits could not justify its costs.

In principle, this approach is better than a simple confession of ignorance, and it is often the best path forward. Sometimes it is sufficient. But it may well involve a high degree of guesswork. Without some discipline, it may not be altogether different from a confession of ignorance.

The third approach is to attempt to specify outcomes in terms of, say, economic savings or health endpoints. The advantage of this approach is that it points to concrete benefits, and it attempts to measure and to monetize them. Nevertheless, it too runs into difficulties. The first is that agencies may lack anything like the information that would enable them to venture such a specification. The second and more interesting is that, for reasons I will explore, even an accurate specification will not give a complete picture of the actual benefits; in crucial respects, it will almost certainly overstate them. In brief, the problem is that people might experience significant losses as well as gains from labels (e.g., if they switch to a product that is inferior along certain dimensions), and an account of endpoints will ignore those losses.

The fourth approach is to identify consumers' willingness to pay. As a matter of abstract principle, that approach is (mostly) the right one, because it should capture the full universe of losses and gains from labels. At the same time, it runs into serious and perhaps insuperable normative, conceptual, and empirical challenges. As we shall see, the most obvious problem is that it is difficult to elicit people's *informed and unbiased* willingness to pay for labels.

Costs

On the cost side, some of the questions are relatively straightforward. For example, regulators may well be able to learn the total cost of producing fuel-economy labels and placing them on new vehicles. The principal difficulty arises when *the information itself imposes costs on consumers*. It is a mistake to ignore those costs, even if they prove difficult to quantify, and even if consumers benefit on net. Those costs come in several different forms. Some of them will usually be low—but not always.

A Small Cognitive Tax

First, a cost is involved in reading and processing the information. For each consumer, that cost is likely to be quite low, but across a large number of purchasers, it might turn out to be significant. Information disclosure is, in a sense, akin to a paperwork burden. To be sure, consumers are not compelled to read and process what is disclosed. But it may be hard to ignore it. Even for those who seek to do so, the very presence of information may operate as a kind of cognitive tax. (True, it may be a benefit rather than a cost for some people.)

A Hedonic Tax on Those Who Do Not Change Their Behavior

Second, and more importantly, the cost may be hedonic, not cognitive. Suppose that smokers are given information about the adverse health effects of smoking or that visitors to chain restaurants are given information about the caloric contents of food. Many members of both groups will suffer a hedonic loss. Consider smokers who cannot quit and customers who decide to choose high-calorie foods notwithstanding the labels. In hedonic terms, such people will lose, rather than gain, if they are miserable—or at least a bit sadder—at the time of purchase.

To be sure, there is a serious normative question whether regulators should count, as a cost, the adverse hedonic effect of truthful information. Is it a cost or a benefit if people learn, truthfully, that they have diabetes or cancer? I think that there is a cost, even if the net effect is positive. The hedonic loss must be treated as such. It might turn out to be low, but regulators should not ignore it (as they typically do).

A Hedonic Tax on Those Who Do Change Their Behavior

Even if people are able to quit smoking or choose lower-calorie items, and will hence benefit greatly on net, they will incur a cost by learning something that inflicts pain. In principle, that cost should also count, even if it is greatly outweighed by benefits. The point, then, is not that the hedonic cost is a trump card; if people make different choices once they are informed, the presumption should be that they are better off. But by how much?

To answer that question, the hedonic cost must be taken into account. For many people, a calorie label imposes a serious cost, because it informs them that the delicious cheeseburger they are about to eat is also going to make their belly bulge. As a friend remarked to me after hearing that the calorie-labeling requirement in the Affordable Care Act would be applied to movie theaters: "They just ruined popcorn."

A Consumer Welfare Loss

There is a fourth loss, in the form of foregone consumer surplus. Suppose that people decide that on balance, they should have a salad rather than a cheeseburger, on the ground that the latter has many more calories. If they choose the salad because of the label, they are probably better off on balance; in a sense, they are sadder but wiser (and healthier). They are sadder to the extent that they enjoy their meal less. Assessment of the magnitude of the loss poses serious challenges, but there is no question that it exists and that it might turn out to be a significant fraction of the benefits. In principle, a decision to forego the hamburger might make people only modestly better off if the hedonic loss is almost as high as the health gain.

Suppose that consumers are choosing between two essentially equivalent cars; that the more fuel-efficient one would cost $2000 less annually to operate because of its fuel efficiency; that the less fuel-efficient one would cost $500 more upfront; and that because of the fuel economy label, consumers select the fuel-efficient car. For each such consumer, we might be tempted to say that the label has produced $1500 in gains. But in practice, the effects of a fuel-economy label will be more complicated to assess. Some consumers will purchase cars that are more fuel-efficient but inferior along some other dimension, so they will gain $1500 minus X, where X refers to the desirable features of the unchosen car that they otherwise prefer. It is hard for public officials to know whether X is, on average, $100, or $1,000, or $1,450.

Benefits

On the benefits side, the assessment is even more challenging.[5] If the government mandates a fuel-economy label, agencies should project the economic and environmental benefits from the mandate. To do that, they have to *know the effect of the label on behavior.* In principle, a randomized controlled trial would be valuable and perhaps necessary for that purpose. If one group sees a particular label and a similar group sees a different label (or no label), regulators should be able to specify the effect of the label on purchasing decisions. Armed with that information, they could estimate economic and environmental consequences, at least if they could generalize from the trial.

Unfortunately, it is sometimes difficult or impossible to run randomized controlled trials. In these circumstances, making any kind of projection of how consumers will react to a label can be difficult. An additional problem is that for the reasons given thus far, the projection would not give an adequate estimate of the (net) benefits. We have seen that if people are buying cars that are more fuel-efficient but along some other dimension undesirable, there will be a welfare loss. For that reason, regulators might explore the issue from another direction.[6] Rather than asking about the economic savings from the fuel-efficient car, they might ask an entirely different question: How much would consumers be willing to pay for a fuel-economy label?

Under ideal conditions, that is the right question for regulators to ask; they should not focus on the economic benefits that consumers might receive if, for example, they purchase more fuel-efficient cars. The reason is that on optimistic assumptions, the willingness-to-pay question ought to capture everything that matters to consumers. (Of course, it is true that this question will not fully capture third-party effects.)

As an empirical matter, however, it is not easy to obtain a reliable answer to that question, or anything close to it. We might simply ask people, but for their answers to be relevant it would be important to provide pertinent information—for example, about the potential benefits (purely economic and otherwise) of labels. Providing that information is no simple endeavor, not least because offering some numbers about those potential benefits would be important, and any numbers might bias their answers. Suppose that the risk of bias could be overcome and that informed consumers would be willing to pay ten dollars on average for fuel-economy labels. If so, we might have some sense of the benefits, at least if behavioral biases are not distorting people's answers.

Unfortunately, however, such biases might well produce distortions; consider present bias and optimistic bias, which may lead to unduly low willingness to pay. In any case, survey evidence is imperfectly reliable, in part because of the familiar problems with contingent-valuation studies and in part because of the immense difficulty of informing consumers in a sufficiently neutral way.

For health-related disclosures, the problem is even harder. One goal of calorie labels is to reduce obesity, which causes an assortment of health problems, including premature mortality. We have seen that a statistical life is now valued at about $9 million. How many premature deaths would be prevented by calorie labels? What would be the effect of such labels on adverse health outcomes short of death?

To answer such questions, regulators must undertake several tasks. First, they must make some prediction about the effect of calorie labels on what people choose to eat. Second, they have to specify the health consequences of lower levels of caloric intake. If they accomplish those tasks, they will have some sense of the benefits of the labels, once (and this is a third task) they turn the various consequences into monetary equivalents. After undertaking all three tasks, regulators will have specified endpoints—but for the reasons given, a specification of endpoints will overstate benefits, because it will not include various cognitive and hedonic losses. (Recall that people might be healthier and live longer, but life might be less fun.)

Alternatively, we could (again) ask how much people would be willing to pay for calorie labels.[7] As before, asking that question is, in principle, preferable to an effort to assess health states, because the answer will capture all variables that matter to consumers. Also, as before, there are formidable challenges in using surveys to elicit reliable numbers free from biases of various kinds.

In light of these challenges, regulators have two reasonable options. First, they can work on the two relevant tracks to try to produce answers: exploring endpoints and enlisting surveys. On prominent occasions, they have tried the former.[8] Second, they can acknowledge the difficulties, confess that they cannot surmount them, and use breakeven analysis. Suppose that an energy-efficiency label for refrigerators would cost $10 million annually and that eight million refrigerators are sold in the United States every year. Even if the average consumer saves only $1.50 annually as a result of the label, the benefits will justify the costs.

Third Parties—and Morality

Some actual or imaginable labels are meant to protect third parties, not consumers as such. Recall the discussion in the previous chapter: some consumers are concerned about the use of certain minerals to finance mass atrocities, and they favor labeling or some kind of disclosure requirement. In some such cases, the third-party effects are not obscure; the real challenge is how to quantify them.

As before, it is necessary to begin by making some projections about consumer behavior. To what extent would consumers change their purchasing habits in response? Even if that question could be answered, it would be necessary to tie any such changes to reduced harm or increased benefit for third parties. And even if that problem can be resolved, it would be necessary to quantify and monetize the resulting effects. It is no wonder that in the context of conflict minerals, the Securities and Exchange Commission concluded that quantification was not possible. Perhaps it should have engaged in some form of breakeven analysis, explaining that the requirement was likely to survive cost-benefit analysis even if its effect was modest. But perhaps it lacked the information that would have allowed it to make that analysis plausible.

Some disclosure requirements are justified because considerations of equity, distributional effects, or human dignity are involved. Under the law, it might be sufficient for agencies simply to point to such considerations and not to fold them into a cost-benefit analysis. If the statutory goal is to achieve distributional goals by transferring resources from some people to others, then cost-benefit balancing is not the rule of decision, and it is not all that matters. A rule might have costs in excess of benefits, in the sense that the losers lose more than the winners gain, but perhaps the winners are poor or otherwise deprived, and perhaps they have a special claim to attention under the relevant law or as a matter of principle. Some disclosure requirements might be justifiable on these grounds; recall the case of conflict minerals.

I have suggested that if quantification of the benefits of labels is required, the question might be: How much would (informed) consumers be willing to pay for such labels? Within a certain framework, that question is the right one. But that framework is not always the right one. If the issue involves human dignity, equity, or distributional considerations—or any kind of harm to third parties—why should the proper analysis depend on how much people are willing to pay for it? It seems senseless to say that labels motivated by distributive goals should be imposed to the extent that people are willing to pay for them.

To say this is not to say that welfarist considerations do not matter at all. Insofar as harms to third parties are involved, cost-benefit analysis can be used, acknowledging the empirical problems sketched thus far. Insofar as the issue involves equity or dignity, breakeven analysis might be useful, to see whether it is worthwhile to incur the costs. To the extent that distributive goals are involved, a key question is whether such goals would, in fact, be promoted by labels or disclosure. That question would seem relevant to the conflict minerals problem. Some kind of *means-ends analysis*, explaining how the means are connected to the ends, would seem indispensable to an evaluation of labels that are designed to promote distributive goals (or, for that matter, equity or human dignity). Agencies should be expected to undertake that analysis—or to explain why they cannot.

Genetically Modified Foods

To illustrate the points discussed thus far, I now turn to the question of mandatory labels for GM foods. Under existing law, the US Department of Agriculture (USDA) is required to produce such labels within the next few years. I offer two general conclusions. The first is that it will not be easy for the USDA to show that the benefits of the mandate justify the costs. The second is that, of the USDA's various options, the best (or least bad) is probably to use breakeven analysis, accompanied by an account of consumers' desire to be informed or by reference to the remaining uncertainties about the environmental risks of GM foods.

A Little Science

The World Health Organization defines genetically modified organisms (GMOs) as "organisms … in which the genetic material (DNA) has been altered in a way that does not occur naturally."[9] According to a common understanding, a GMO is "one that has been deliberately created to contain a piece of 'foreign' DNA, usually a full-length 'foreign' gene incorporated in its genome."[10] As a result of the underlying technology, sometimes called *recombinant DNA technology* or *genetic engineering*, certain individual genes are transferred into one organism from another.[11] The magnitude of the benefits of GM foods is disputed, but they can potentially grow faster, taste better, resist diseases, have a lower reliance on pesticides, cost less to produce, and prove more nutritious.[12]

In the United States, GM food has become pervasive. According to the UDSA, adoption of GM "crop varieties by U.S. farmers has reached about 90 percent of the planted acres of corn, soybeans, and cotton."[13] American "consumers eat many products derived from these crops— including cornmeal, oils, and sugars"—even though they are generally unaware of that fact.[14] In American supermarkets, it has been estimated that GM ingredients can be found in about 70 percent of processed foods.[15] Among them are pizza, cookies, ice cream, salad dressing, corn syrup, and chips.

Do GM foods have significant benefits? The answer is sharply disputed, and I hardly mean to settle it here The standard arguments on behalf of GM ingredients are that they can produce superior foods with not only more nutritional value and greater resistance to herbicides (requiring less use of pesticides) but also improved texture and taste.[16] GM food is often engineered for longer shelf life, furthering the reach of shipping fresh food. For example, the Innate potato has been engineered to prevent bruising and browning and to reduce the amount of the possible carcinogen acrylamide released when the potato is fried.[17]

The most famous nutritional supplementation may be Golden Rice, a variety engineered to provide vitamin A.[18] In hopes of combatting protein malnutrition, cereals such as maize, canola, and soybean have been engineered for greater amounts of lysine, an essential amino acid.[19] Some products are alternatives to less healthy foods, such as the sweet protein brazzein, developed in maize as an alternative to sugar as a sweetener.[20] Scientists have also been able to reduce the harmful effects of food products, in one instance isolating proteins that cause allergic reactions in the development of a hypoallergenic peanut.[21] In addition, GM foods have been engineered to act as inexpensive vaccines; for example, Applied Biotechnology Institute has developed a hepatitis B vaccine in maize.[22]

Health

With respect to safety, the consensus of the scientific community seems unambiguous: GM foods do not present health risks.[23] In 2012, the American Association for the Advancement of Science summarized the consensus, writing that "the World Health Organization, the American Medical Association, the U.S. National Academy of Sciences, the British Royal Society, and every other respected organization that has examined the evidence has come to the same conclusion: consuming foods containing ingredients derived from GM crops is no riskier than consuming the same foods containing ingredients from crop plants modified by conventional plant improvement techniques."[24]

In 2016, the National Academies of Sciences, Engineering, and Medicine issued a book-length report,[25] strongly reaffirming what American and European scientists have long found: food from GM crops is no more dangerous to eat than food produced by conventional agriculture. In the words of the report, there is "no substantiated evidence" that genetic modification of crops produces less safe foods.[26] In the United States, Canada, the United Kingdom, and Western Europe, "no differences have been found that implicate a higher risk to human health safety" from genetically engineered foods.[27] In its summary, the report states: "On the basis of its detailed examination of comparisons between currently commercialized GE and non-GE foods in compositional analysis, acute and chronic animal toxicity tests, long-term data on health of livestock fed GE foods, and epidemiological data, the committee concluded that no differences have been found that implicate a higher risk to human health safety from these GE foods than from their non-GE counterparts."[28]

This conclusion tracks that of many others. In 2015, the American Association for the Advancement of Science spoke unequivocally. In its words, "The science is quite clear: crop improvement by the modern molecular techniques of biotechnology is safe."[29] The European Commission has similarly proclaimed: "The main conclusion to be drawn from the efforts of more than 130 research projects, covering a period of more than 25 years of research and involving more than 500 independent research groups, is that biotechnology, and in particular GMOs, are not *per se* more risky than e.g. conventional plant breeding technologies."[30] The World Health Organization, the National Academy of Sciences, and the Royal Society in the United Kingdom are in agreement.

Ecology and the Environment

There would also be an argument for labeling if GMOs created ecological risks, rather than dangers to human health. Here the answer is less unambiguous. The 2016 report of the National Academies of Sciences,

Engineering, and Medicine finds no clear evidence that GM crops cause environmental harm.[31] At the same time, the report is written with considerable caution. It acknowledges the importance of continuing monitoring, but pointedly declines to embrace the widespread view that those crops have been responsible for declines in monarch butterfly populations.[32] Other studies are less equivocal, finding no special risks to the environment from GM agriculture. The American Medical Association has endorsed this general view.[33]

It must be acknowledged that in some circles, the prevailing scientific judgments are intensely disputed.[34] Some people believe that with respect to both health and the environment, the scientific consensus is influenced by powerful private-interest groups, which have an interest in denying both health and environmental concerns. In their view, any such consensus is not trustworthy, especially insofar as it purports to discount low-probability risks. Many observers point to what they see as a series of ecological risks, including toxicity to nontarget organisms (such as butterflies and bees), invasiveness in natural settings, and threats to biodiversity.[35] Some scientists and regulators have also expressed grave concern that if they are widespread, GMOs will lead to resistance and the loss of a "public good"—susceptibility of insect pests to certain proteins.[36]

It should be acknowledged that some people fear long-term effects that are not only ecological in nature, but also cultural and distributional, including the adverse effects of GM products on small farmers. It is hardly impossible that their concerns will be vindicated over time. For present purposes, the central point is that the prevailing scientific judgment appears to be that the health risks are nonexistent and that the standard environmental concerns are highly conjectural and have not been demonstrated to be serious.

Risk-Risk Trade-offs

It should be clear in this light that if GM labels are effective in changing consumer behavior, there could well be a risk-risk trade-off. On one view, such labels might help diminish ecological risks. At the same time, they might increase risks to health and to the environment; longer shelf lives save resources, and GM food reduces use of pesticides, which create hazards of their own.[37] The point is not to reach a final judgment about the magnitude of these effects, but to signal the fact that risks are not only on one side of the equation.

What People Want, and Why

The public-opinion evidence is at least as clear as the science: people do not believe that GM food is safe, and they strongly favor mandatory labels. It is not easy to find a domain in which public opinion is so unambiguously at odds with the scientific consensus. A typical survey finds that only 37 percent of Americans believe that GM food is safe to eat (as compared with 88 percent of members of the American Association for the Advancement of Science).[38] According to my own recent survey, 86 percent of Americans favor labeling of GM food: 89 percent of Democrats, 80 percent of Republicans, and 87 percent of independents.[39]

What explains such high levels of support for mandatory labels? The simplest answer is that people favor labels because they think that GM food is harmful, and they believe that consumers should be allowed to make an informed choice about whether to consume it.[40] To that extent, the judgment in favor of labels for GM food is quite similar to the corresponding judgment with respect to products that contain high levels of salt or that otherwise are taken to create health risks.[41] Without carefully engaging with questions about costs and benefits, people make an intuitive judgment that government should mandate labels to allow consumers to avoid products that might be dangerous.

On the basis of existing research, the simplest answer appears to be correct, but Sydney Scott, Paul Rozin, and Yoel Inbar offer some important and illuminating complications.[42] Scott et al. asked a representative sample of Americans whether they supported or opposed genetically engineering plants and animals. The authors also asked respondents to register agreement or disagreement with the statement, "This should be prohibited no matter how great the benefits and minor the risks from allowing it."

Consistent with previous studies, 64 percent of participants opposed genetic engineering. In fact, 71 percent of the opponents—46 percent of the entire sample—were absolutists: they want to ban genetic engineering *regardless* of the benefits and risks. To that extent, their opposition to GM foods is not based on an assessment of costs and benefits at all. To explain the psychology behind that apparently puzzling finding, Scott and her coauthors presented their participants with a scenario in which a random person eats GM tomatoes (either knowingly or unknowingly). They asked people how angry or disgusted they were when imagining the scenario. Opponents of genetic modification were angrier and more disgusted than its supporters, but the absolutists were especially disgusted. Controlling for demographic and other differences, Scott et al. found that "disgust was the best predictor" of whether people would proclaim absolute opposition to genetic modification.[43] The authors' conclusion is simple: People who most strongly oppose genetic modification are not weighing consequences. Their opposition is a product of the fact that they find the idea disgusting.

That claim requires its own exploration. By itself, the idea of GM food does not seem to be the sort that would trigger disgust; it is not as though we are speaking of bodily fluids or the ordinary sources of something like nausea.[44] In this context, disgust would seem to be a placeholder for some kind of intense emotion, signaling disapproval. We might speculate that many people have an immediate, intuitive sense that what is healthy is what is "natural," and that efforts to tamper with nature will inevitably unleash serious risks—involving so-called Frankenfoods.

This speculation raises two puzzles of its own. First, we might question whether and to what extent people really are absolutists about GM food. It is one thing to say, in the abstract, that GM foods should be regulated or banned regardless of the benefits and risks. It is another thing to favor regulation or prohibition after receiving concrete information about benefits and risks. If people are asked to assume that GM food reduces costs by 20 percent or promises to save thousands of lives annually, and that it poses no risks to health or to the environment, would they really favor regulation or prohibition? Many of those who purport to be absolutists in the abstract or in response to general questions tend to become more welfarist and more amenable to some form of cost-benefit balancing when they are presented with concrete numbers.[45]

Second, it is not obvious how regulators should respond to regulatory intuitions of the kind that existing surveys seem to capture. If people are using a heuristic ("unnatural is unsafe"), and if that heuristic is producing an error ("GM food is unsafe"), then regulators should correct the error so that consumers can make informed decisions. But if consumers are simply disgusted, then they are registering a taste, not an erroneous judgment. Consider a purer case of disgust: Some people are disgusted by Jell-O. (I confess that I am among them. Yuck.) They can decide to avoid Jell-O. Should regulators mandate labels ("This product contains Jell-O") in the face of such a taste? Even if no health issues are involved? In such circumstances, there would not seem to be a compelling argument for mandatory labeling (to say the least). I will return to these issues shortly.

Costs and Benefits

To assess costs, the USDA must begin by projecting the expense of labeling itself. The projection is likely to be disputed, but it does not present serious conceptual difficulties; the only issues are ones of fact. We have seen that there are costs as well to consumers who see the label (and are less happy when they do) and to consumers who, having seen the label, buy goods that are either more costly or inferior (the lost consumer surplus).

The latter costs will be extremely difficult to specify, and the USDA might be forced to produce some upper or lower bound or even to say that those costs are not quantifiable. It might also be reasonable for the USDA to conclude that those costs are unlikely to be large. Merely seeing the label would not impose high costs on consumers. To project the lost consumer surplus, agencies would need to project the likely effect of the label on consumer behavior and the monetized loss. Undertaking that projection might well turn out to be daunting—even impossible—and the agency might be unable to produce specific numbers or even a reasonably bounded range.

If we focus, as agencies frequently do, on health benefits from mandatory labels, then GM labels seem difficult to defend. As we have seen, the health benefits appear to be zero. We have also seen that environmental benefits cannot be ruled out—but on the basis of the existing science, they are probably impossible to quantify. I will return to that issue; for the moment, the simple conclusion is that it would not be so easy to argue that the environmental benefits of labels would justify a significant expenditure.

In this respect, agencies would face a difficult challenge in using their conventional approach to benefit estimates to justify the conclusion that mandatory labeling would survive a cost-benefit test. As compared to the case of calorie labeling, for example, it would be hard to specify health or environmental endpoints, or even ranges, that could make their way into a conventional Regulatory Impact Analysis.

Options

Confronted with this problem, the USDA has several options. First, it might simply announce that the benefits of GM labels are not quantifiable. As we have seen, agencies have taken that route in the past, and it has survived judicial scrutiny, at least under statutes that require agencies to act. The problem with this approach is that when agencies have previously imposed disclosure mandates without quantifying benefits, they could usually say that they expect significant benefits (in terms of money or health). If the expectation of significant benefits is reasonable, a failure to quantify may not be objectionable, at least if quantification is not feasible.

In this context, by contrast, the problem is that there would seem to be no benefits at all (bracketing the question of environmental harm, to which I will return). When benefits are in the general range of zero, it is not enough, or even reasonable, to say that they are speculative. Because the statute requires the USDA to act, the inability to project benefits is unlikely to be objectionable purely as a matter of law, but it does require serious challenges for the agency when it attempts to produce an RIA and to survive the scrutiny of analysts within the executive branch.

Faced with those challenges, the USDA might engage in some form of breakeven analysis, especially if the costs of mandatory GM labels can be described as low. We can easily imagine creative efforts in this vein, asking, for example, about whether it would be worthwhile to charge the average American $X annually (where $X is very little) in return for GM labels. Suppose that the cost of a label is $2.30 per person per year.[46] It might well be suggested that the mandate obviously survives breakeven analysis. Isn't that modest cost worth incurring, given widespread consumer preference for labels and good-faith concerns about ecological risks? Perhaps so. But one problem is that for the assumption about the per-person cost, the aggregate cost is over $700 million—hardly a trivial amount. It would be easy, and misleading, to say that *any* annual $700 million expenditure is justified because the annual per person cost is merely $2.30 for all Americans. The real question is what people are obtaining for that $700 million.

As an independent method of valuation, or as part of some breakeven analysis, it might seem reasonable to put a spotlight on consumers' willingness to pay for GM labels. On the basis of survey evidence suggesting that consumers favor such labels, it would not be implausible to think that the amount would be significant population-wide— and, per person, at least $2.30 per year. Ideally, regulators would have some evidence of people's willingness to pay, which they could compare with some estimate of costs. In the absence of such evidence, they might nonetheless engage in breakeven analysis.

What Consumers Want

We can easily imagine cases in which the law should not mandate labels even if consumers would be willing to pay for them. Suppose, for example, that consumers want to know whether African Americans or Jews were involved in the production of some commodity. To the extent that the consumer demand reflected racism or prejudice, it should not be honored. But the call for GM labels does not run afoul of this principle, because no invidious discrimination is involved.

Consider a more relevant comparison: Suppose that consumers are alarmed about some ingredient in food—call it Omega P—even though there is no reason for alarm. Suppose that there is an online health scare about Omega P and that people want to know whether the food they are eating contains it. In principle, a label is not a good idea. It would cater to public ignorance, and it would have no benefits. For government, the right response is to inform people that Omega P is safe. Note that in this case, the standard argument for use of willingness to pay is decisively undermined. People might be willing to pay *something*—perhaps even a great deal—for Omega P labels, but because such labels would not promote their welfare, there is no good reason to mandate them. The challenge for the USDA will be to show that labels for GM food are relevantly different from labels for Omega P.

But Morality?

For some people, arguments about health and the environment miss the central points. On one view, the objection to GM foods is theological: GMOs tamper with God's creation. On another view, it is moral: there is something wrong with treating nature in this way. On a third view, GM food benefits large corporations and the wealthy at the expense of small farmers, poor nations, and the poor in general. The third view can easily be translated into an argument about adverse effects on third parties. Under all three views, GM labels are a modest step in the right direction insofar as they allow consumers to know what they are buying and to register their preferences, their values, and their commitments.

At the very least, we should be willing to agree that if labels do have some kind of moral motivation, they might be justified, even if quantitative cost-benefit analysis turns out to be challenging, impossible, or beside the point. We have seen analogies, in the form of labels designed to prevent cruelty to animals. Could GM labels be defended on some similar grounds? It should not be sufficient merely to point to the *fact* of moral concern; the question is whether the moral concern has some plausible basis. In the abstract, an affirmative answer can hardly be ruled out; many people hold moral concerns about GM food in good faith.

The difficulty lies in specifying some intelligible moral principle that does in fact call for labels. It is not at all clear that there is a plausible religious objection to GM foods (and if there was, it could not easily be invoked by the Department of Agriculture without raising First Amendment issues). It is hard to make sense of the argument that GM foods are "mistreating nature." Nor is it clear that GM labels can be defended on distributional grounds in light of the considerable difficulty of demonstrating that GM foods are objectionable on such grounds and of showing that even if they are, labels are helpful in meeting that challenge. I do not mean to reach a judgment on the particulars here—only to suggest the form of a possible justification and the serious challenges that the USDA, or anyone else, might face in offering it.

Taking Stock

I have covered numerous issues here, so let's take stock. With respect to costs, the USDA must calculate the expense of producing the labels themselves. The analysis should be reasonably straightforward. There are also costs to consumers who see the label (and are less happy when they do) and also to consumers who, having seen the label, buy goods that are more costly or (in their view) inferior. The latter costs are more important but will be extremely difficult to specify; the USDA might do best simply to say that they are not quantifiable. It might be reasonable for the agency to conclude that the costs are unlikely to be large, though informed conjecture or (better) evidence would of course be necessary to support that conclusion.

The benefits issue is far more challenging. It is not possible to identify health endpoints that would justify mandatory labels, nor is it simple to specify environmental risks or to connect a disclosure mandate to reduction of those risks. In principle, the willingness-to-pay figure is the right one, but it is highly doubtful that the USDA could produce reliable estimates. Even if it did, the numbers might well be a product of consumer errors in the form of a mistaken belief that GM foods produce health risks.

In these circumstances, the USDA will not have an easy time demonstrating that the benefits of mandatory labels justify the costs. As I have noted, the law requires the agency to proceed even if it cannot make that demonstration, but under prevailing executive orders, no agency likes to proceed when costs plainly exceed benefits, and the process of scrutiny within the executive branch will produce a serious demand for a plausible cost-benefit justification. For the USDA, the best option is probably to offer a breakeven analysis, invoking consumers' wishes, the risk of irreversible environmental harm (perhaps with special attention to biodiversity), or both. If the per-person cost of labels indeed is very low, a breakeven analysis might turn out to be plausible. That claim brings us to our final topic.

Precautions

When a product or activity creates a risk, even a small one, many people argue in favor of precautions and, in particular, in favor of the

Precautionary Principle. The idea takes diverse forms, but the central idea is that regulators should take aggressive action to avoid environmental risks, even if they do not know that those risks will come to fruition, and indeed even if the likelihood of harm is very low. Suppose, for example, that there is some probability, even a small one, that genetic modification of food will produce serious environmental harm or some kind of catastrophe. For those who embrace the Precautionary Principle, it is important to take precautions against potentially serious hazards, simply because it is better to be safe than sorry. Especially if the worst-case scenario is very bad, strong precautions are entirely appropriate. Compare the medical situation, in which it is tempting and often sensible to say that even if there is only a small probability that a patient is facing a serious health risk, doctors should take precautions to ensure that those risks do not come to fruition.

In an illuminating account, the Precautionary Principle is understood as holding "that if an action or policy has a suspected risk of causing severe harm to the public domain (affecting general health or the environment globally), the action should not be taken in the absence of scientific near-certainty about its safety. Under these conditions, the burden of proof about absence of harm falls on those proposing an action, not those opposing it."[47] The Wingspread Declaration puts it more cautiously: "When an activity raises threats of harm to human health or the environment, precautionary measures should be taken even if some cause and effect relationships are not fully established scientifically. In this context the proponent of an activity, rather than the public, should bear the burden of proof."[48]

The influential 1992 Rio Declaration states, also with relative caution: "Where there are threats of serious or irreversible damage, lack of full scientific certainty shall not be used as a reason for postponing cost-effective measures to prevent environmental degradation."[49] In Europe, the Precautionary Principle has sometimes been understood in a still stronger way, suggesting that it is important to build "a margin of safety into all decision making."[50] This stronger version takes the form a suggestion that when an activity, product, or situation *might* create risks, it is appropriate to take precautions against those risks, even if the probability of harm is very low.[51]

Some of the central claims on behalf of the Precautionary Principle involve uncertainty, learning over time, irreversibility, and the need for epistemic humility on the part of scientists. With respect to uncertainty: any consensus might turn out to be wrong; today's assurance might be tomorrow's red alert. With respect to learning over time: in a decade, we are likely to have a lot more information than we have today; why should we allow practices to continue when we might learn that they are dangerous? With respect to irreversibility: some practices threaten to cause irreversible harm, and for that reason, we might want to pay something, possibly a great deal, to prevent that harm from occurring. For those who emphasize irreversibility, the general attitude in the face of uncertainty is "act, then learn," as opposed to the tempting and often sensible alternative of "wait and learn." With respect to epistemic humility: knowing that we do not know, we might want to take precautions, rather than to proceed on the assumption that we are omniscient.

The risk of irreversibility is of special importance. An influential essay, by Kenneth Arrow and Anthony Fisher, demonstrates that the ideas of uncertainty and irreversibility have considerable importance in many domains.[52] Arrow and Fisher imagine that the question is whether to preserve a virgin redwood forest for wilderness recreation or instead open it to clear-cut logging. Assume that if the development option is chosen, the destruction of the forest is effectively irreversible. Arrow and Fisher argue that it matters whether the authorities cannot yet assess the costs or benefits of a proposed development. If development produces "some irreversible transformation of the environment, hence a loss in perpetuity of the benefits from preservation," then it is worth paying something to wait to acquire the missing information. Their suggestion is that "the expected benefits of an irreversible decision should be adjusted to reflect the loss of options it entails."[53]

Fisher generalizes this argument to suggest that "where a decision problem is characterized by (1) uncertainty about future costs and benefits of the alternatives, (2) prospects for resolving or reducing the uncertainty with the passage of time, and (3) irreversibility of one or more of the alternatives, an extra value, an option value, properly attaches to the reversible alternative(s)."[54] The intuition here is both straightforward and appealing: more steps should be taken to prevent harms that are effectively final than to prevent those that can be reversed at some cost. If an irreversible harm is on one side and a reversible one on the other, and if decision makers are uncertain[55] about future costs and benefits of precautions, an understanding of option value suggests that it is worthwhile to spend a certain amount to preserve future flexibility by paying a premium to avoid the irreversible harm.

GMOs are often thought to trigger the Precautionary Principle, with special emphasis on the need for continued monitoring, residual uncertainty, and potentially irreversible or catastrophic environmental risks. This is no mere theoretical point. As one commentator explains, European "legislation that governed GMOs used a precautionary approach, and precaution was one basis for the de facto moratorium on authorizations of GM varieties."[56]

In its various forms, the Precautionary Principle has been subject to a great deal of analysis, some of it quite skeptical[57] and some of it highly supportive.[58] A central question involves the appropriate approach to "worst-case" thinking. This is not the place for a full analysis, which would require investigation of some complex issues in decision theory,[59] but three points seem obvious, and keeping them in mind can prove helpful (bracketing hard questions about quantification).

First, if a product or activity has modest or no benefits but significant costs, the argument for taking precautions is far stronger than if the benefits are significant. Second, if a product or activity creates only a miniscule risk (taking account of both the probability and the magnitude of a bad outcome), then the product or activity should not be banned or regulated (including through labels) if it promises significant benefits. Third, if a product creates a small (but not trivial) risk of catastrophe, there is a strong argument for banning or regulating it (including through labels) if the benefits are modest. Some of the most difficult cases arise when a product or activity has significant benefits and the bad outcome is potentially catastrophic and its probability is difficult or impossible to specify (creating a situation of "uncertainty," rather than risk)[60] *or* the harms associated with the bad outcome cannot be identified (creating a situation of "ignorance").[61] In such difficult cases, it is not simple to balance the two sides of the ledger, and there is a real argument for eliminating the worst-case scenario.[62]

Let us bracket the most complicated questions here and simply note that in this light, a precautionary argument for labeling GM foods (or otherwise for regulating them) depends largely on answering questions of fact. Do such foods promise modest benefits, or instead large ones? With respect to harm, are we speaking of risk, uncertainty, or ignorance? The scientific consensus appears to be risk—and that the underlying danger is very low. The consensus may or may not prove correct, but however important, its correctness raises no interesting conceptual questions for our purposes. At the same time, it is true that those who favor a kind of epistemic humility, even for scientific consensus, will be drawn to a precautionary approach.

It should be added that if GM foods really do create a potentially catastrophic risk and if a sensible version of the Precautionary Principle is therefore triggered, GM labels are hardly an obvious response. In the abstract, they seem far too weak and modest; more aggressive regulation is justified. Indeed, GM labels might do no good at all. The counterargument is that they might be able to diminish the risk, in light of certain assumptions about the likely consumer response, and so might count as one reasonable step. I have raised a question about whether the science, and gaps in scientific understanding, justify invocation of precautionary thinking here, but if they do, labeling might be a justified if partial response.

Precautions and Democracy

On one view, the Precautionary Principle is not only or even fundamentally about irreversibility, catastrophe, and decision theory. It has an insistently democratic foundation. Its goal is to assert popular control over risks that concern the public. It is about values, not facts. If members of the public are concerned about GMOs, nuclear power, or nanotechnology, then the Precautionary Principle provides them with a space in which to assert those concerns. It ensures democratic legitimation of the process of risk regulation.

For those who embrace the Precautionary Principle on this ground, efforts to speak of costs and benefits will fall on deaf ears. For those who believe that, in this domain or others, scientists are in the grip of powerful private interests, and that the system is "rigged," a precautionary approach will seem especially appealing—not least for democratic reasons. If the science is compromised and hence unreliable, it should hardly be decisive. For those who believe that popular concerns often turn out to be justified even if scientists discount them, the democratic justification for the Precautionary Principle might even turn out to be appealing on epistemic grounds.

No abstract argument can rule out the possibility that scientists are mistaken or that they have been compromised. It is true that a scientific consensus in favor of safety can be wrong; the same is the case for a scientific consensus in favor of danger. For those who favor the Precautionary Principle on democratic grounds—and believe that popular concerns about GM foods are a legitimate basis for invocation of the principle—the arguments offered here cannot be decisive. The only response is that some form of welfarism, embodied in the self-conscious efforts to catalog the human consequences of regulation, should not be trumped by baseless fear—and that cost-benefit analysis, understood as a form of applied welfarism, should not be abandoned merely because people are needlessly worried.

In numerous contexts, Congress requires or authorizes federal agencies to impose disclosure requirements. In all those contexts, executive agencies are required to catalog the benefits and costs of disclosure requirements and to demonstrate that the benefits justify the costs. As we have seen, agencies use four different approaches: estimates of willingness to pay for the relevant information; breakeven analysis; projection of end states, such as economic savings or health outcomes; and in some cases, a flat refusal to project benefits on the ground that quantification is not feasible.

Each of these approaches runs into strong objections. In principle, the right question involves willingness to pay, but in practice, agencies face formidable problems in trying to answer that question. If answers are unavailable, breakeven analysis is the very least that should be required, and it is sometimes the most that agencies can do. If it is accompanied by some account of potential outcomes, acknowledging uncertainties, breakeven analysis often will show that mandatory disclosure is justified on welfare grounds—and often that it is not.

8 The Role of Courts

In recent years, both the Supreme Court and lower courts have issued important decisions on the question whether agencies are required to engage in some form of cost-benefit analysis.[1] Some of those decisions raise difficult questions of statutory interpretation, asking whether Congress has explicitly tied the agency's hands by requiring them to regulate even if such regulation would not survive cost-benefit analysis. For example, do the words *appropriate and necessary* contemplate consideration of costs?[2] Does the word *feasible* require agencies to balance costs and benefits?[3]

Other decisions involve what is called *arbitrariness review* under the Administrative Procedure Act. That act makes it unlawful for agencies to make decisions that are "arbitrary" or "capricious." The question might be whether an agency's interpretation of the governing statute is unreasonable;[4] it might involve arbitrary policymaking as such.[5] The most general question is this: If agencies have discretion to consider costs and benefits in making regulatory choices, is it unlawful for them to refuse to do so? If so, what exactly does this obligation entail?

These questions will inevitably arise with increasing frequency in the future. In principle, a duty to engage in cost-benefit balancing could be invoked as an objection to a dazzling assortment of regulations from diverse agencies, including the Environmental Protection Agency, the Department of Labor, the Department of Transportation, the Department of Treasury, the Department of Agriculture, the Securities and Exchange Commission, the Federal Communications Commission, and the Federal Trade Commission. Whenever an agency fails to calculate costs and benefits and to show that the latter justify the former, a litigant might contend that it has acted arbitrarily. Indeed, the objection that federal agencies are acting arbitrarily when they have not engaged in cost-benefit analysis is becoming increasingly common. Importantly, that objection might be made not only by those who seek to reduce or eliminate regulation; it might be made as well by people who seek to mandate or expand regulation, on the ground that careful cost-benefit analysis so requires.

We could imagine a continuum of conclusions about how courts should respond to apparently inadequate cost-benefit analyses, reflecting judgments about two factors: (1) the appropriate intensity of judicial review and (2) the reasonableness, in principle, of agency decisions to depart from strict forms of cost-benefit analysis. It is important to separate those factors. If judicial review should be deferential, judges ought to uphold a wide range of approaches—not because all of them are genuinely sensible, but because the judicial role is properly modest and humble. This is of course an *institutional* reason to allow agencies room to select their own approach (and to specify it as they wish).

If, by contrast, departures from cost-benefit analysis are fully reasonable in principle, because important factors cannot be monetized or because that form of analysis does not deserve pride of place, then courts should uphold such departures, even if judicial review is appropriately aggressive. This is a *substantive* reason to allow such departures.

For either institutional or substantive reasons, courts might adopt a minimalist position, which is that agencies are merely required to offer plausible reasons for whatever approach they select. So long as they have done so, they are under no obligation to quantify costs or benefits or to compare them to each other. The minimalist position is that in essentially all cases, an agency might rationally decide that quantification is not helpful, possible, or worthwhile, or it might adopt a rule of decision that does not involve cost-benefit balancing at all. Nonetheless, agencies do have to justify themselves.

At the opposite pole is the maximalist position, which holds that agencies act arbitrarily if they do not (1) quantify both costs and benefits and (2) show that the benefits justify the costs, unless (3) the statute requires otherwise or (4) they can make a convincing demonstration that in the particular circumstances, quantification is not possible. The maximalist view identifies quantitative cost-benefit analysis with nonarbitrariness, at least in the sense that an agency that rejects that form of analysis bears a heavy burden of justification. On the maximalist view, cost-benefit analysis is a necessary part of rational decision-making—at least as a presumption, and at least where it is feasible in light of available information.

My goal in this chapter is to explore the relationship between cost-benefit analysis and arbitrariness review. The simplest and most modest conclusion, consistent with the minimalist position, is that whenever the governing statute authorizes an agency to quantify costs and benefits and to weigh them against each other, its failure to do so requires a nonarbitrary justification (whether the agency is acting aggressively, doing very little, or doing nothing at all). But a range of justifications may be available, including (1) the infeasibility of quantifying costs and benefits, given limitations in available information; (2) the relevance of values such as equity, dignity, and fair distribution; and (3) the existence of welfare effects that are not captured by monetized costs and benefits. Importantly, however, these justifications are not available or adequate in all circumstances, which means that even under cost-benefit minimalism, an agency's failure to engage in a degree of quantification and to show that the benefits justify the costs will sometimes leave it vulnerable under arbitrariness review—at least when the governing statute authorizes those steps.

For institutional reasons, courts should be cautious in this domain, especially in assessing agency judgments about both costs and benefits; those issues often raise highly technical issues for which judges lack specialized competence. In some domains of regulatory law, quantitative cost-benefit analysis is unusual, unsuitable, or unfamiliar, and it would be quite aggressive for courts to require it. If, for example, the Federal Communications Commission is regulating sexually explicit speech, it does not ordinary produce an account of monetized costs and monetized benefits. In this light, there is no plausible defense of the maximalist position, broadly identifying arbitrariness with a failure to quantify.

At the same time, any decision not to quantify costs and benefits or to show that the latter justify the former does require some kind of explanation (at least if the governing statute does not rule cost-benefit analysis out-of-bounds). The central reason is that agencies should be increasing social welfare, and an assessment of costs and benefits provides important information about whether regulations would achieve that goal. Of course, the judicial role is very far from primary; the cost-benefit revolution is engineered by Congress and the president, not by courts. But when a reasonable objection is made to a regulation, suggesting that it would do more harm than good, or that a different approach would have higher net benefits, courts legitimately demand some kind of justification. In some cases, that justification requires numbers.

Social Welfare and Arbitrariness

Is it even plausible to suggest that an agency's failure to engage in cost-benefit analysis might be arbitrary within the meaning of the APA? On what assumptions?

No one argues that it is arbitrary as a matter of law for agencies to decide to consider costs or for them to turn statistical lives into monetary equivalents. No one argues that it is arbitrary for an agency to reject "feasibility analysis," which would require regulation to the level of stringency beyond which it is not economically or technologically feasible. What makes cost-benefit analysis special, a kind of default position, such that any deviation potentially subjects agencies to a charge of arbitrariness?

Five points seem plain. First, an agency cannot simply refuse to take account of the "substitute risks" introduced by risk regulation.[6] Suppose, for example, that regulation of one pollutant would result in the introduction of another pollutant, which is even more dangerous. At least if the underlying statute does not require it to focus on only one pollutant, it would be arbitrary for an agency to refuse to consider that substitute risk.[7] Second, an agency may not impose costs for no benefits. If a rule would do no good at all, it is arbitrary.[8] Third, a wholesale refusal to consider costs would count as arbitrary.[9] Costs are harms, and an agency is obliged to take harms into account. Fourth, an agency may not impose very high costs for very small gains. Suppose that a regulation would cost $1 billion and deliver $1000 in monetized benefits. Unless the statute requires it to do so, the agency's decision to proceed would seem to be the very definition of arbitrary; at a minimum, it would have to explain itself. Fifth, it is arbitrary not to proceed with a regulation whose benefits are far in excess of costs, or to adopt a modest regulatory intervention when a more aggressive one would have much higher net benefits.

These points are straightforward, but they do not support the maximalist position, which imposes a presumptive duty both to quantify benefits and costs and to demonstrate that the benefits justify the costs. Indeed, that position might seem quite puzzling. The APA was enacted in 1946, as a way of disciplining the regulatory state, and cost-benefit analysis has become entrenched within the executive branch of the federal government only since the 1980s. Congress knows how to require cost-benefit balancing, and it sometimes does exactly that. In the arc of administrative law, cost-benefit analysis is a relatively recent practice; as we have seen, it remains controversial.

No one suggests that apparent best practices within the executive branch must be followed by all administrative agencies, subject to a risk of judicial invalidation on arbitrariness grounds. The more modest claim is that agencies should attempt to produce more good than harm—and if the agency has not quantified the consequences or if the quantified benefits are lower than the quantified costs, then it is reasonable to question whether it is doing that. And while I am emphasizing cases in which the costs exceed the benefits, it is also important to say that when the benefits exceed the costs, and an agency fails to proceed, there is also a serious problem.

Suppose that an agency proceeds with an automobile safety regulation without specifying the safety benefits or the relevant costs. If the regulation is challenged on the ground that the benefits might be minimal and the costs quite high, there is a strong objection on arbitrariness grounds, for a simple reason: the agency has not adequately explained itself. If a rule would impose $900 million in costs and deliver $10 million in benefits, there would appear to be a serious problem. Why, exactly, would the agency proceed in the face of such numbers? And if the benefits of a regulation or a particular approach would be $900 million, and the costs merely $10 million, an agency's failure to proceed would face the same kind of objection.

Any account of arbitrariness review must, of course, be attuned to the weaknesses and strengths of the federal judiciary. If courts are unable to understand the highly technical issues involved and if agencies are already performing well, judicial intervention would be a blunder. The problem would be compounded if, in practice, judicial policy preferences turned out to play a significant role in judicial decisions about whether agencies had made unreasonable calculations. And of course it is inevitable that judicial review will increase delay and contribute to the "ossification" of the rulemaking process, potentially postponing lifesaving initiatives. In short, a judgment about the value of judicial scrutiny depends on an inquiry into the costs of decisions and the costs of errors. Such scrutiny will necessarily increase decision costs. Whether it will increase error costs depends on assessments of the likelihood of agency error and the likelihood of judicial correction.

Many of these questions raise empirical issues; they cannot be resolved in the abstract. Because cost-benefit analysis often requires assessment of technical questions for which courts lack much competence, it does make sense to say that the judicial role should be deferential. Suppose, for example, that the question is the appropriate discount rate for benefits that will be enjoyed in the distant future or the appropriate monetary valuation of a statistical life or the risks posed by particulate matter. These are not questions for which judges are well-trained. If we emphasize that resolution of some apparently technical questions requires judgments of policy and principle, then the argument for intense judicial scrutiny becomes weaker still.

Distrust of agency decisions can produce countervailing considerations. If agencies are systematically biased or if serious errors of analysis are likely, then arbitrariness review might be heightened. But even if we think that such errors are rare—perhaps because of usually reliable processes within the executive branch—it might nonetheless make sense to say that courts should require some kind of justification for a blanket refusal to assess costs and benefits at all or for a failure to make a minimally plausible demonstration that the benefits justify the costs.

Endorsement of a position of this kind need not suggest enthusiasm for anything like careful judicial scrutiny of the particular judgments that go into cost-benefit analysis. In fact, it is compatible with the view that there should be no scrutiny of such judgments at all. To be sure, it would be possible to argue in favor of some such scrutiny while insisting that it should be highly deferential.

Two Leading Decisions

The number of decisions that scrutinize agency failure to engage in cost-benefit analysis or to give adequate consideration to it is large and growing. For the future, two such decisions are especially important. The first, from the Supreme Court itself, strongly suggests that a failure to consider costs at all is per se arbitrary. The second, from the DC Circuit, suggests far more controversially that it might be arbitrary for an agency to fail to quantify costs and benefits (if it is feasible to do so) or to fail to demonstrate that the benefits justify the costs.

Decision 1: Mercury

In *Michigan v. EPA*, an important decision involving mercury regulation, all nine members of the Supreme Court seemed to converge on a simple principle: under the APA, it is arbitrary for an agency to refuse to consider costs.[10] By itself, that principle seems quite modest, but it is far less so than it might appear. At a minimum, it implicitly requires agencies to weigh costs against benefits, at least in some sense; it is not possible to "consider" costs without engaging in such weighing. With that implicit requirement, the court may also have required agencies to make some effort to quantify costs, at least if it is feasible to do so. Is it possible to "consider" costs without knowing what they are? To be sure, the court did not embrace the maximalist position, but its holding can easily be read to make trouble for any agency that fails to show that the benefits of a regulation justify the costs.

The case itself involved not the APA, but a provision of the Clean Air Act that requires the EPA to list hazardous pollutants, for later regulation, if it is "appropriate and necessary" to do so.[11] EPA contended that it had the authority to base its listing decision only on considerations of public health (and hence to decline to consider costs). In its view, the words *appropriate and necessary* were ambiguous, and a cost-blind interpretation was legitimate.

By a five-to-four vote, the court disagreed. It held that the "EPA strayed far beyond" the bounds of reasonableness in interpreting the statutory language "to mean that it could ignore cost when deciding whether to regulate power plants."[12] In a passage of special relevance to the topic here, the court added, "One would not say that it is even rational, never mind 'appropriate,' to impose billions of dollars in economic costs in return for a few dollars in health or environmental benefits. ... Consideration of cost reflects the understanding that reasonable regulation ordinarily requires paying attention to the advantages and the disadvantages of agency decisions."[13]

These words seem quite general and not limited to a particular provision of the Clean Air Act. In light of the context, it would not be impossible to understand them as restricted to that statute—but that would be a mistake. While rejecting the majority's particular conclusion on the ground that the EPA had actually considered costs (though at a later stage), Justice Kagan's dissent, joined by three other members of the court, was more explicit on the general point, contending: "Cost is almost always a relevant—and usually, a highly important—factor in regulation. *Unless Congress provides otherwise, an agency acts unreasonably in establishing 'a standard-setting process that ignore[s] economic considerations.'*"[14] It added that "an agency must take costs into account in some manner before imposing significant regulatory burdens." The dissenters clearly adopted a background principle that would require agencies to consider costs unless Congress prohibited them from doing so. There is every reason to think that the majority—which did, after all, invalidate the EPA's regulation—would embrace that principle as well.

At the same time, the court declined to endorse cost-benefit maximalism, and by doing so, it pointedly suggested that it might well reject such a position. In the key passage, the court said: "We need not and do not hold that the law unambiguously required the Agency, when making this preliminary estimate, to conduct a formal cost-benefit analysis in which each advantage and disadvantage is assigned a monetary value. It will be up to the Agency to decide (as always, within the limits of reasonable interpretation) how to account for cost."[15] This passage brackets the question whether the Clean Air act required a "formal cost-benefit analysis," but it is highly ambiguous. Surely it would not be sufficient for an agency simply to announce that it has "considered" costs and decided to proceed. It would have to explain that decision in some way. The court seemed to be suggesting that such an explanation could be given even if the agency does not produce "a formal cost-benefit analysis."

Even with this qualification, *Michigan v. EPA* has the great virtue of identifying the fatal weakness in a tempting objection to any effort to question an agency's failure to engage with costs and benefits. The objection would be that courts lack the authority to impose procedural requirements beyond those in the APA,[16] and cost-benefit analysis is a procedural requirement not found in the APA, which thus cannot be imposed by courts. The problem with the objection is that under the APA, an arbitrary decision is unlawful. If an agency ignores costs or imposes a risk that is greater than the risk that it is reducing, it would seem to be acting arbitrarily. The fact that courts cannot add procedural requirements is irrelevant. At the same time, it must be acknowledged that *Michigan v. EPA* was a narrow ruling, and it hardly embraced cost-benefit maximalism.

Decision 2: Proxy Access

By contrast, the United States Court of Appeals for the District of Columbia Circuit appears to have held that if an agency is statutorily authorized to consider costs and benefits, it is under an obligation (1) to quantify both and (2) to make some kind of comparison, at least if these steps are feasible.[17] In its controversial decision in the *Business Roundtable* case, the court emphasized the importance of quantification. In the court's words: "Although the Commission acknowledged that companies may expend resources to oppose shareholder nominees, it did nothing to estimate and quantify the costs it expected companies to incur; nor did it claim estimating those costs was not possible, for empirical evidence about expenditures in traditional proxy contests was readily available. Because the agency failed to 'make tough choices about which of the competing estimates is most plausible, [or] to hazard a guess as to which is correct,' we believe it neglected its statutory obligation to assess the economic consequences of its rule."[18]

As the passage reveals, the decision involved the complex question of "proxy access" in corporate-shareholder voting: Must proxy materials sent to shareholder-voters by publicly traded firms include nominees of the shareholders, or may they be confined to the slate of nominees designated by the incumbent directors? In a 2009 rulemaking, the SEC decided to require shareholder proxy access. It accompanied its decision with a lengthy cost-benefit analysis that considered (as required by statute) its effects on "efficiency, competition, and capital formation."[19] Some elements of its analysis were not quantified.

The DC Circuit invalidated the regulation on numerous grounds, most of which fell into one of two general categories. The first was that the agency was required either to provide a quantitative cost-benefit analysis or to explain why doing so would not be feasible. The second was that the evidence failed to support the commission's conclusion that the rule's benefits would outweigh its costs.[20] These holdings seem to support a much broader proposition, which is that SEC regulations are at serious risk of invalidation unless they are accompanied by a clear demonstration that the quantified benefits justify the quantitative costs.[21]

For the court, one problem is that on its face, the underlying statute imposes no such requirement. True, the SEC must consider the effects of a regulation on "efficiency, competition, and capital formation." But that requirement does not, by itself, mandate a formal analysis of benefits or a comparison between costs and benefits. Indeed, it is not entirely clear that the agency must provide a quantitative analysis of costs to show the requisite consideration. Perhaps the agency could consider the costs in purely qualitative terms.

In the face of these objections, the best justification for the court's approach would take the following form: To consider the effects of a rule on "efficiency, competition, and capital formation," the commission must go beyond vague, general conclusions. If the available evidence permits quantification, it would be arbitrary not to quantify. The obligation to consider those effects requires a serious effort, consistent with what the evidence allows, and a serious effort requires numbers. It would also be arbitrary—within the meaning of the APA—for the agency to proceed if the effects on "efficiency, competition, and capital formation" were adverse and significant, at least if they were not justified by compensating quantified benefits. It would follow that, if a rule has net costs (or no net benefits) or if the commission cannot show that a rule will have quantified benefits (if relevant evidence is available), the court should invalidate that rule as arbitrary.

Thus understood, *Business Roundtable* can be taken to have offered a plausible reading of the interaction between the governing statute and the APA. The ruling would not, however, be based purely on the APA; the explicit requirement to consider effects on "efficiency, competition, and capital formation" is critical. Moreover, the court acknowledged that quantification might not be possible—and hence can be taken to give the commission an escape route in cases of ignorance or uncertainty. But because the court devoted a great deal of space to explaining its view that the commission had acted arbitrarily, it did issue a warning for any agency that fails to compare costs and benefits—at least if it is authorized to do so.

The broadest reading of *Business Roundtable*, going well beyond its particular context and in evident tension with relevant dicta in *Michigan v. EPA*, is that in order to avoid a serious charge of arbitrariness, an agency is obliged to quantify both costs and benefits and to show that the former justify the latter. To be sure, quantification is not necessary if it is impossible. But if quantification is impossible, are agencies necessarily permitted to proceed? Always? If the costs of regulation are very high and the benefits unquantifiable, are the agencies authorized to go forward? *Business Roundtable* does not answer these questions.

Simple

With *Michigan* and *Business Roundtable* as background, two types of cases are simple. If Congress expressly forbids an agency to consider costs, or requires it to regulate to the point of feasibility without balancing benefits and costs, then the APA's prohibition on arbitrariness is irrelevant. And if an agency is required to consider benefits and costs or lawfully elects to do so, then its judgments may not be senseless or unreasonable.

Suppose that a statute prohibits agencies from considering costs and requires them to proceed whenever there is a finding of significant harm. In issuing ambient air quality standards under the Clean Air Act, the EPA is essentially constrained in that way; it must issue standards "requisite to protect the public health," with an "adequate margin of safety."[22] In setting occupational safety and health standards involving toxic substances and harmful physical agents, the Department of Labor must regulate significant risks "to the extent feasible," without balancing costs and benefits.[23] If the agencies fail to engage in quantified cost-benefit analysis under the relevant statutes, an arbitrariness challenge could not possibly succeed. True, the EPA might be vulnerable if it does not show that a standard is "requisite to protect the public health," and OSHA must show that the regulated risk is "significant." But neither agency is permitted to weigh costs against benefits.

The general point is that arbitrariness review takes place against the backdrop of relevant statutes. If a statute says that costs are irrelevant or that they can be considered only in a specific way, the APA's ban on arbitrariness has no independent force (so long as the agency has complied with such directives).

What we see, then, is that any decision not to consider costs must come from the national legislature; it cannot be made by an agency acting on its own. In this respect, the arbitrariness review makes a clear statement: Congress must itself prohibit consideration of costs, and it must do so in explicit terms. In other words, only Congress has the authority to allow an agency to disregard costs altogether.[24]

Funny Numbers

Now suppose that an agency is authorized or required to consider costs and benefits, and that the agency does so, but that it also makes unexplained and apparently arbitrary choices. Examples might include

- failing to discount either costs or benefits;
- failing to apply the same discount rates to benefits as to costs;
- double-counting certain costs or benefits;
- ignoring and thus entirely failing to take account of important costs or benefits;
- making apparently irrational judgments about the effects of a regulations, such as the number of premature deaths to be prevented; or
- monetizing certain benefits, such as a statistical life, a reduction in morbidity, or the social cost of carbon, in an unexplained or apparently irrational way.

In all of these cases, an agency would be at a risk of losing a court case on arbitrariness grounds. To be sure, the judiciary should defer to the expertise of the regulating authority. The house of cost-benefit analysis has many rooms, and as we have seen, a choice among competing approaches typically raises difficult technical issues for which courts lack competence. The endorsement of cost-benefit analysis within the executive branch reflects an institutional judgment as well as a substantive one: Officials within that branch have the personnel and the capacity to engage those technical issues, which often involve both science and economics.

Because courts are in a very different position, a high degree of deference is warranted. Within the broad bounds of reason, an agency might make a large number of discretionary choices. But agencies consist of human beings, who may exceed those bounds. The prohibition on arbitrariness imposes some constraints on its choices. If an agency discounted costs but not benefits, it would have to explain itself. If an agency used $1 million or $30 million as the value of a statistical life, it would face a heavy burden of justification. To offer a real-world example: In 2017, the Environmental Protection Agency under President Donald Trump proposed to depart from the previous decision to use the "global" figure for the social cost of carbon (approximately $40, consisting of the damage done to the world from a ton of carbon emissions in the United States) in favor of the domestic figure (between $1 and $6, representing the damage done only in the United States). That decision may or may not be justifiable. But it was not justified. No explanation was given. That is the height of arbitrariness, and it should be invalidated in court.

Alternatives

Consistent with the maximalist position, it might be suggested that *an agency acts arbitrarily whenever it fails to explain, with quantitative cost-benefit analysis, why it has not chosen a less burdensome alternative.* That position is far too strong, but it is important to see exactly why.

Consider the decision by the Department of Transportation how best to improve rear visibility so as to reduce the incidence of backover crashes, discussed in chapter 4. There are three alternatives, each of which is explicitly mentioned in the governing statute: (1) mandating installation of cameras, which is the most expensive and also the most effective approach; (2) requiring side-view mirrors to be larger, which is the least expensive and least effective approach; and (3) requiring installation of sonar, which ranks between cameras and mirrors in terms of both cost and effectiveness.

Suppose that the agency chooses cameras. If it says nothing about mirrors and sonar, it has acted arbitrarily, But does it have to quantify the costs and benefits of the three approaches? The statute does not explicitly make cost-benefit analysis the rule of decision, and though it refers to the three alternatives, it does not require the agency to choose the least burdensome approach.

To make the case as easy as possible for DOT, assume that it explains that mirrors would do essentially nothing about the problem and that its judgment to that effect survives rationality review, but that it has not quantified the effects of relying on mirrors. Would it be arbitrary for it to fail to do so? That would be an implausible conclusion. If the agency has rationally concluded that mirrors would be ineffective— that it would impose significant costs for essentially no benefits—it is hardly irrational for it to reject the option of mirrors. No quantification is necessary.

The strongest counterargument would be that without numbers, it is not possible to know which approach has highest net benefits (or lowest net costs), and a nonarbitrary judgment that mirrors would be "ineffective" does not provide sufficient information. As a matter of policy, that position is not unreasonable. But as a reading of the arbitrariness requirement, it is unacceptably aggressive, because it is hardly arbitrary for an agency to conclude that it should not choose an ineffective means of satisfying a statutory requirement (supposing that the judgment of ineffectiveness is itself reasonable).

Now suppose that DOT chooses cameras over sensors, concluding that cameras would be "significantly more effective" and that "the additional expense is well justified." Is that level of abstraction sufficient to survive rationality review? A challenger might well ask: What, concretely, do these claims mean? On what are they based? The agency should be required to do more than announce its conclusions. It has to explain them. It is not implausible to think that it must support its claims with numbers—ranges, if not point estimates—unless it can explain why it has failed to do so. The question is what such an explanation might look like; I now turn to that question.

Refusing to Quantify

We now turn to the most difficult issues. An agency refuses to quantify (some or all) costs and benefits, and a litigant objects that its refusal to do so is arbitrary. When is that objection convincing?

Suppose that the agency declines to quantify certain benefits and costs on the ground that it is not feasible to do so. Let us begin with cases in which the agency claims that it lacks enough evidence or knowledge to justify anything like a specification of benefits, even before it begins the task of attempting to monetize them. The EPA might say, for example, that in light of the limits of existing information, it cannot quantify the benefits, in terms of numbers of certain kinds of cancers reduced, of more stringent regulation of arsenic in drinking water.[25] Scientists cannot give a point estimate, nor do they have confidence in any kind of range. Is that a problem?

Under arbitrariness review, the initial question is simple: Is the agency's explanation unreasonable? Because agencies have technical expertise, a challenger would face a heavy burden here. If the agency has adequately explained its failure to quantify, the issue would seem to be at an end. As the DC Circuit said in 2015 in *Inv. Co. Inst. v. Commodity Futures Trading Commission*: "The appellants further complain that CFTC failed to put a precise number on the benefit of data collection in preventing future financial crises. But the law does not require agencies to measure the immeasurable. CFTC's discussion of unquantifiable benefits fulfills its statutory obligation to consider and evaluate potential costs and benefits."[26]

If this principle holds for a statute that requires consideration of costs and benefits, it certainly holds under arbitrariness review more generally. An instructive, brief treatment of the issue can be found in *Federal Communications Commission v. Fox Television Stations, Inc*,[27] in which broadcasters objected to the government's effort to restrict the use of obscenity on television during times when children might be watching:

There are some propositions for which scant empirical evidence can be marshaled, and the harmful effect of broadcast profanity on children is one of them. One cannot demand a multiyear controlled study, in which some children are intentionally exposed to indecent broadcasts (and insulated from all other indecency), and others are shielded from all indecency. It is one thing to set aside agency action under the Administrative Procedure Act because of failure to adduce empirical data that can readily be obtained. It is something else to insist upon obtaining the unobtainable. Here it suffices to know that children mimic the behavior they observe—or at least the behavior that is presented to them as normal and appropriate. Programming replete with one-word indecent expletives will tend to produce children who use (at least) one-word indecent expletives. Congress has made the determination that indecent material is harmful to children, and has left enforcement of the ban to the Commission. If enforcement had to be supported by empirical data, the ban would effectively be a nullity.

The court's words here are plausibly invoked in many cases in which a litigant objects that an agency has failed to quantify the benefits of regulation. That failure is not arbitrary if an agency can rationally explain it—as it may well be able to do in light of the knowledge problem.

Acting amid Uncertainty: Simple Cases

Suppose that the agency has rationally concluded that certain benefits are unquantifiable and has nonetheless, or therefore, decided to proceed. That decision raises a separate question: Is it arbitrary to proceed when certain benefits cannot be measured?

The simple cases arise when an agency rationally says (1) that the quantifiable benefits of a new regulation exceed the quantifiable costs, but also (2) that there are other, unquantifiable benefits that should be taken into account. As we have seen, it might explain that (2) on the ground that scientists cannot specify their magnitude in light of limits in existing knowledge. There is nothing arbitrary here. First, the failure to specify unquantifiable benefits might be the height of reasonableness; under imaginable assumptions, specification, rather than the opposite, would be arbitrary. Second, the quantifiable benefits exceed the quantifiable costs, and so the agency's decision to proceed is not itself arbitrary.

Acting amid Uncertainty: Predictive Judgments without Numbers

Sometimes agencies make predictive judgments about the likely effects of their actions, speaking in qualitative terms without quantifying either costs or benefits. For example, the FCC might adopt a regulation to protect children from exposure to obscene words on television; the Department of Justice might require new steps to make buildings accessible to those who use wheelchairs; the Equal Employment Opportunity Commission might ban discrimination on the basis of sexual orientation; the Federal Trade Commission might require energy-efficiency labels for appliances. In all these cases, and many more, cost-benefit analysis might be possible, but it might seem to strain existing knowledge and be an awkward fit with the relevant statutes and regulations.

Note preliminarily that under existing executive orders, a full-scale Regulatory Impact Analysis, with a detailed account of costs and benefits, is required only for regulations with an annual economic impact of at least $100 million. To be sure, benefits must always "justify" costs, but for regulations with modest economic effects, a comprehensive analysis is not required. These ideas have no standing in court, but they suggest an important point, which is that the argument for a detailed catalog of costs and benefits is greatly weakened when the economic impact is not large. One reason is that in such cases, the social need for such a catalog is reduced, and so too are the social benefits. Cost-benefit analysis itself has both costs and benefits, and the costs of analysis might exceed the benefits.

In some cases, moreover, it is hardly arbitrary for agencies to make predictive judgments based not on empirical evidence and numbers, but on reasonable qualitative assumptions about likely outcomes. The easiest cases arise when evidence is unavailable. True, predictive judgments might be turned into projections of costs and benefits, but it would be extravagant to say that numbers are always necessary to avoid a charge of arbitrariness.

If the FCC takes steps to strengthen or weaken existing restrictions on obscenity, it might well be *helpful* to quantify costs, but the benefits might be thought to defy quantification, and a more qualitative approach is hardly arbitrary. If an agency adopts new regulations to reduce discrimination on the basis of disability or sexual orientation, a quantitative cost-benefit analysis might well be valuable, but it would be exceedingly difficult to argue that a failure to provide one is arbitrary under the APA. An agency can adequately explain itself without such an analysis.

The same conclusion might well apply when an agency imposes a disclosure requirement to promote informed choices. To be sure, the agency must say *something* to explain its decision, and a cost-benefit analysis can provide that explanation. In imaginable circumstances—involving, say, an evidently expensive mandate of highly questionable value to consumers—such an analysis might be necessary in order to rebut the charge of arbitrariness. But it would be implausible to say that whenever a statute requires or authorizes an agency to mandate disclosure, a quantitative analysis of costs and benefits is required by the APA.

The larger point here is that the range of agency action is exceptionally wide, and agencies can reasonably decide that quantitative analyses are not well-suited to all contexts. When the stakes are relatively low, such an analysis might not be necessary. When an agency is making reasonable predictive judgments, such an analysis might also be unnecessary—and it might not be feasible.

Of course, the underlying statute matters a great deal. Within the constraints that it contains, much depends on the costs of decisions and the costs of errors. If a litigant makes a plausible argument that an agency has acted arbitrarily, imposing serious burdens for no gain, its best defense might involve a catalog of costs and benefits. And if a litigant argues that the agency has acted arbitrarily in failing to offer such a catalog, a great deal depends on the costs and benefits of doing exactly that.

In some cases, the costs of a quantitative analysis would exceed the benefits—or so an agency might nonarbitrarily conclude. But in other cases, reliable numbers are available, and the benefits of cost-benefit analysis will so obviously exceed the costs that the agency's approach will indeed be arbitrary. Let's now explore why that might be so.

Acting amid Uncertainty: Hard Cases

Some of the hardest problems arise when the agency agrees to consider costs, acknowledging that it is arbitrary not to do so, but *chooses to proceed even though the quantifiable benefits of its action are far lower than the quantifiable costs.* By itself, that choice would be arbitrary unless it is explained. A mere statement of the agency's intentions and preferences is not sufficient. If the agency lacks evidence, it might nonetheless be able to show that it has made a reasonable predictive judgment, consistent with the underlying statute; if evidence is unavailable, or if it is not feasible to collect it, there is nothing unreasonable about that. But imposition of costs far in excess of benefits requires some kind of justification.

We have seen that one of the most promising approaches here involves breakeven analysis. The simplest way for an agency to explain its decision to proceed, in the face of (1) quantified costs that exceed quantified benefits and (2) unquantifiable benefits, is to engage in that form of analysis.

In chapter 4, I referred to the rear-visibility regulation, for which DOT acknowledged a shortfall of about $200 million: the monetized costs were between $546 million and $620 million, and the monetized benefits around $265 million and $396 million.[28] In explaining its decision to proceed, the agency referred to a range of (what it saw as) unquantifiable values, including equity (the lives of small children were at risk), parental anguish (in some cases, parents were responsible for the deaths of their own children), and increased ease of driving. Let's simply stipulate that these values were indeed unquantifiable.

Was the agency's identification of the relevant values sufficient to survive arbitrariness review? There is a good argument that it was, at least in light of the fact that the monetary shortfall, while significant, was not egregious. Without running afoul of the proscription on arbitrariness, an agency could make a plausible judgment that the list of factors was sufficient to make up that shortfall. But without a great deal of difficulty, it could have undertaken a more formal analysis.

For example, the department properly referred to the increased ease and simplification of driving. Suppose that for each driver, the relevant improvement is valued at merely thirty dollars, taken as a reasonable lower bound. Suppose too that the regulation would apply to sixty thousand cars that would otherwise lack cameras. If so, it would produce $180 million in additional benefits. At that point, the monetized benefits become very close to the monetized costs.

The department might have added that some work suggests that parents value a young child's life at $18 million[29]—a number that would add $45 million to its existing benefits figure. At that point, the benefits and costs are essentially equivalent. Indeed, that $18 million figure captures the *parents'* valuation of children's lives, not *children's* valuation of their lives. It would have been an unusual step, but the department might have undertaken a sensitivity analysis with values, for a statistical child's life, of $18 million and $27 million—with the latter adding $90 million, leaving a shortfall of $110 million. Recall finally that we are speaking here of parents who not only (only!) would lose their children, but also would be directly responsible for that loss. How much would it be worth to reduce the risk of that eventuality?

With an analysis of this kind, the department's decision to proceed seems entirely reasonable—not because of a mere list of what intuition suggests are unquantifiable benefits, but because once we speak of lower bounds and expected ranges, the arbitrariness objection starts to lose its force. It would be excessive to say that in cases of this kind an agency would be required to engage in breakeven analysis to avoid invalidation on arbitrariness grounds. But we could imagine much harder cases, in which some such analysis would be indispensable.

Simple though it is, the example is easily generalizable. At least in the face of significant costs, exceeding quantifiable benefits, it may not be enough for an agency to announce that some benefits of the regulation are not quantifiable—unless Congress has directed the agency to proceed. But if the agency has made a nonarbitrary judgment that the benefits are not quantifiable, the agency would be on firm ground if it engaged in a reasonable breakeven analysis. If the agency failed to engage in any such analysis and simply listed one or more unquantifiable benefits, it might not be acting arbitrarily—but in some cases, the answer might not be clear. As the costs grow, it becomes harder to say that such a list is sufficient to justify agency action in the face of an arbitrariness challenge.

Suppose, for example, that an agency has imposed a cost of $600 million with a regulation that will reduce the risk of a financial crisis by some unquantifiable amount. To survive a claim of arbitrariness, it would be best for the agency to engage in some kind of breakeven analysis, which is eminently doable. But in light of the sheer magnitude of a financial crisis, a court should not require breakeven analysis as a precondition for validation.

Equity, Dignity, and Fair Distribution

The agency might say that even though monetized costs exceed monetized benefits, considerations of *equity*, *dignity*, or *fair distribution* justify its action. It might contend that those considerations cannot be monetized, but that they nonetheless matter. Suppose, for example, that an agency is adopting a regulation to make buildings accessible to people who use wheelchairs. Imagine that the monetized costs of the regulation are $600 million and that the monetized benefits are $300 million. Imagine that the agency nonetheless proceeds, arguing that the purpose of the regulation is to make buildings accessible, and the fact that monetized costs exceed monetized benefits is neither here nor there. Is that arbitrary?

The initial question involves the underlying statute. Let us simply stipulate that the agency has discretion to proceed or not to proceed, and how aggressively to proceed, and that it is authorized to take costs and benefits into account in making those decisions. At first glance, it is hard to say that the agency has acted arbitrarily. The Americans with Disabilities Act, for example, does not state that cost-benefit analysis is the rule of decision. Indeed, there is a plausible argument that even if costs and benefits are relevant, the agency could not lawfully interpret it to embrace that decision rule. If the agency wishes to give significant weight to wheelchair accessibility, without turning it into some monetary equivalent, it is hardly acting arbitrarily.

The strongest response would be that considerations of equity, dignity, or fair distribution cannot possibly be priceless. With a regulation of this kind, the agency is implicitly deciding that wheelchair accessibility has a value, or at least a reasonable lower bound. Perhaps the relevant valuation is sensible; perhaps it is not. At the very least, that question can be asked as a result of arbitrariness review. To make the issue as stark as possible, suppose that the implicit valuation, for annual access by a person who uses a wheelchair, is $10 million. Many agencies value a human life at $9 million. Can a year of wheelchair accessibility be worth as much as a human life?

With an actual regulation, the Department of Justice engaged in breakeven analysis. Its calculation was that if either society or people who use wheelchairs were willing to pay a very small amount per bathroom visit—for one part of the regulation, in the vicinity of five cents,[30] and for another part, in the vicinity of $2.20—then the regulation would be worthwhile.[31] It asked what wheelchairs users would have to be willing to pay for the relevant benefits[32] and what society would have to be willing to pay to provide them[33] for the relevant requirements to have a net present value of zero. It concluded that the relevant amounts could be very small and nonetheless achieve the breakeven or threshold point.

There is nothing at all arbitrary about proceeding in this way. But was the agency legally obliged to justify itself through this relatively elaborate route? Would it have been arbitrary, within the meaning of the APA, if the agency had referred more broadly to considerations of equity and dignity and argued that a shortfall of several hundred million dollars should not be seen as prohibitive? Almost certainly not. Breakeven analysis is helpful, but the APA's ban on arbitrariness does not require agencies to engage in it.

Here as well, the analysis is generalizable. When the monetized costs and benefits are not wildly out of line, invocation of fairness and dignity can tip the balance, even if the agency's analysis is not at all quantitative. If the agency wants to be maximally secure, it would engage in some form of breakeven analysis, but that should not be required.

The idea of equity overlaps with that of fair distribution, and we could easily imagine a regulatory decision that brings distributional justice to the foreground. Suppose that an OSHA regulation imposes a total cost of $200 million and that it prevents fifteen premature deaths. (For simplification, assume that the regulation has no benefits other than prevention of premature mortalities.) If a life is valued at $9 million, the regulation has net costs of $65 million. The agency might argue that the benefit is enjoyed by workers, who are relatively disadvantaged, and that the cost will be borne by consumers, who are relatively well off. The agency might add that protection of worker safety is the primary purpose of the Occupational Safety and Health Act and that, at least so long as the net costs stay within reasonable bounds, it will act in a way that fits with that primary purpose. An argument of this kind would be controversial. But it is hardly arbitrary.

Here yet again, the argument is easily generalized. If an agency is conferring benefits on one group and imposing costs on another, it might well be acting lawfully, even if the monetized costs exceed the monetized benefits. To be sure, it might be arbitrary for the agency to say *nothing* about the magnitude of the benefits and the costs. But under statutes that are designed to help specified groups—say, victims of discrimination or rape, or people who have long lacked health insurance—it is hardly arbitrary for agencies to emphasize the importance of distributional considerations.

In Sum

I have covered a great deal of material in this chapter, and a brief summary might be helpful. In the face of a plausible objection that agencies have not adequately justified themselves, that they are imposing significant costs for modest benefits, or that they should go forward with regulation or regulate more aggressively, agencies must explain their failure to engage in some form of quantified cost-benefit analysis, showing that benefits do in fact justify the costs. Unless a statute says otherwise, a refusal to offer some such analysis, and to explain their decision by reference to it, requires some nonarbitrary justification under the APA. I have explored five possible justifications here:

(1) Some statutes forbid consideration of costs or ban agencies from making cost-benefit analysis the rule of decision; compliance with such statutes is hardly arbitrary.

(2) In some cases, agencies can explain their decisions without resort to numbers, because qualitative explanations turn out to be sufficient and perfectly reasonable (consider FCC decisions with respect to allowing obscenity on broadcast television). Such explanations might be especially appropriate where the stakes are low.

(3) In some cases, it might not be feasible to quantify costs and benefits; limits in existing evidence might make any such effort an exercise in speculation. Where quantification is not possible, it is not arbitrary to refuse to quantify—though the question remains whether it is arbitrary for an agency to proceed. Breakeven analysis might well show that no arbitrariness involved, but in most cases, such analysis is not mandatory; as in the case of the rear visibility rule, a qualitative analysis might turn out be sufficient.

(4) Values such as dignity, equity, and fairness might be relevant, and they might prove difficult or impossible to quantify (consider a regulation eliminating the entry ban, in the United States, on people who are HIV-positive). Or an agency might be attempting to promote distributive goals; consider statutes protecting mine safety or forbidding discrimination on the basis of race, sex, or disability. Even in such cases, however, some numbers might turn out to be mandatory, for example, to show that a regulation would actually produce substantial benefits. But a full-blown cost-benefit justification would not be required (and might even be inconsistent with the underlying statutory goal).

(5) A regulation might produce welfare effects that are not adequately captured by monetized or monetizable costs and benefits. The master concept is welfare, and cost-benefit analysis is the most administrable way to capture welfare. When agencies reasonably contend that it proves inadequate, reviewing courts should step aside. In a wide range of cases, justifications of this kind should protect agencies against an objection from arbitrariness. At the same time, justifications must be offered. In some cases, they will not be available.

The largest conclusions are straightforward. A central goal of administrative agencies is to promote social welfare, suitably defined. It should be unnecessary to underline the importance of that goal. Of course the judicial role is far from primary. Within the bounds of law, the principal line of defense against regulation that reduces social welfare consists of processes within the executive branch, which are specifically designed to promote analytical discipline in the interest of promoting social welfare. But those processes are not always sufficient. When they fail, courts legitimately require agencies to justify their choices. In some cases, a nonarbitrary justification requires numbers.

9 Privacy and National Security

Consider two views:

1. *The world has become an unprecedentedly dangerous place.* Terrorist threats are omnipresent. As the 9/11 attacks reveal, numerous people are prepared to engage in terrorism, and they sometimes succeed. In particular, they want to kill Americans. The first obligation of public officials is to keep the citizenry safe. To do that, the best methods may well involve widespread surveillance, both domestically and abroad. If the result is to save lives, it is worth it. Even when the probability of harm is low, and even if government is operating in the midst of grave uncertainty, it is appropriate to do whatever must be done, and whatever technology allows, to prevent deaths and to protect the nation—even, or perhaps especially, from worst-case scenarios.

2. *Americans face unprecedented threats from their own government.* In the aftermath of the 9/11 attacks, the United States has seen the rise of a massive and (at least until recently) mostly secret security apparatus, involving the collection of vast quantities of data involving the communications of ordinary people. Personal privacy is now at serious risk, and the same is true of free speech. "Trust us" is never an adequate response to citizens' legitimate concerns. We need to create aggressive safeguards to protect civil liberties, not only now, but also for periods in which government is in especially bad hands—and to create precautions against the evident dangers, including worst-case scenarios.

For vividness and ease of exposition, and without ascribing particular views to any particular person, we can describe the first position as *Cheneyism*, in honor of former vice president Dick Cheney. Consider his suggestion that "sooner or later, there's going to be another attack and they'll have deadlier weapons than ever before, that we've got to consider the possibility of a nuclear device or biological agent. ... And when you consider somebody smuggling a nuclear device into the United States, it becomes very important to gather intelligence on your enemies and stop that attack before it ever gets launched."[1] There is a catastrophic worst-case scenario here, in the form of a nuclear device in the hands of terrorists in the United States. (President Donald Trump seems to agree with Cheney.)

Also for vividness and ease of exposition, and again without ascribing particular views to any particular person, we can describe the second position as *Snowdenism*, in honor of former National Security Agency contractor Edward Snowden. Consider his suggestion that "if we want to live in open and liberal societies, we need to have safe spaces where we can experiment with new thoughts, new ideas, and [where] we can discover what it is we really think and what we really believe in without being judged. If we can't have the privacy of our bedrooms, if we can't have the privacy of our notes on our computer, if we can't have the privacy of our electronic diaries, we can't have privacy at all."[2] There is a catastrophic worst-case scenario here, in the form of a situation in which "we can't have privacy at all." (Some politicians on the political left, and some on the political right, seem to agree with Snowden.)

Both Cheneyism and Snowdenism reflect enthusiasm for aggressive precautions against risks, though they display radically different perspectives on what we have to fear most. My principal goal here is to reject the two approaches and to link them with a standard, but unhelpful, approach to risks in general. I will sketch a behavioral explanation of why that unhelpful approach has such widespread appeal, perhaps especially in the domain of national security. I will suggest that to avoid narrow viewscreens, a far better approach focuses on risk management, with a particular focus on cost-benefit analysis. One of the many advantages of a cost-benefit analysis is that it reduces (without eliminating) the twin dangers of selective attention and motivated reasoning.

In the face of high levels of uncertainty, however, cost-benefit analysis faces especially serious challenges, above all because we may not know enough to specify either costs or benefits. (Recall the knowledge problem.) I will suggest that it is possible to respond to that uncertainty with four ideas: breakeven analysis; the avoidance of gratuitous costs (economic or otherwise); a prohibition on the invocation of certain illicit grounds; and maximin, which requires attention to the worst of the worst-case scenarios. I shall explore how these ideas might help us get beyond Cheneyism and Snowdenism.

Precautions and Paralysis

In chapter 7, we saw that in environmental policy, many people accept the Precautionary Principle. In the abstract, the principle has evident appeal. A clear demonstration of imminent or eventual harm is hardly necessary to justify precautions. But there is a serious, even devastating problem with the Precautionary Principle, at least in its crudest forms: risks are on all sides of social situations, and efforts to reduce risks can themselves create risks. For this reason, the Precautionary Principle forbids the very steps that it requires. If a nation takes aggressive steps against genetic modification of food, it might deprive people, including poor people, of food that is low in cost and high in nutrition. Precautions themselves can create risks of significant health or environmental damage to others or to future generations. (If precautions are very expensive, they create such risks for just that reason.) It follows that the very steps mandated by the Precautionary Principle violate the Precautionary Principle (at least if it is not refined).

The point is general. Increases in costs can create risks, including potentially catastrophic ones. If a nation adopts a health or safety regulation that costs $1 billion, or even $500 million, there is some danger that it will have significant adverse effects (perhaps through increasing costs to consumers, perhaps through creating job losses, perhaps by causing companies to choose to do business in other nations) that will have harmful, cascade-like consequences. Some straws end up breaking the camel's back, and through processes that are ill-understood, a single-shot intervention can disrupt whole systems, potentially producing catastrophes. The point is that few precautions lack downside risks: if we are concerned to build a "margin of safety" into all decisions, any such margins must apply to precautions too. Worst-case thinking can be quite dangerous.

For this reason, the Precautionary Principle turns out to be incoherent, even paralyzing, because it forbids the very measures that it requires. Precautions are mandated by the principle, but precautions create risks, so they simultaneously offend the principle. None of this means, of course, that nations should not be concerned about genetic modification of food or that they should demand a certainty of harm, or even a probability of harm, before undertaking regulation. If an activity creates a 1 percent (or less) risk of producing catastrophic environmental damage, then it is worthwhile to expend significant resources to eliminate that risk, even if our only focus is on expected value. People buy insurance against low-probability harms, and sensibly so. We might refine the Precautionary Principle by narrowing its domain—for example, with a catastrophic harm Precautionary Principle, or an irreversible harm Precautionary Principle, that would create margins of safety, or impose precautions, against risks of especially grave harm, or against risks that cannot readily be reversed, once they have come to fruition. Nothing I have said here rules out those possibilities, especially if we take the knowledge problem into account.

The only point is that reasonable regulators must consider both sides of the equation. They must engage in some form of risk management and try to consider whether the costs of precautions are worth the benefits, acknowledging that both of those concepts need to be specified, and that there may be much that they do not know.

The Appeal of Precautions

These points raise a genuine puzzle: Why do reasonable people accept forms of the Precautionary Principle that do not make much sense? The answers bear directly on environmental policy, but, as we shall see, they account for the appeal of Cheneyism and Snowdenism as well. The most general point is that the Precautionary Principle seems appealing and workable because and when people use narrow viewscreens, focusing on a subset of the risks at stake rather than the whole.

Narrow viewscreens can produce *motivated reasoning*. Suppose that we are focused above all on risks associated with terrorism. If so, we might be motivated to discount, and to treat as trivial, the privacy and liberty risks said to be associated with certain measures designed to reduce the risks of terrorism. Or suppose that we are focused above all on privacy and liberty. If so, we might be motivated to discount, and to treat as trivial, the risks said to be associated with certain measures designed to protect against risks to privacy and liberty. In my view, both forms of motivated reasoning play a significant role (and perhaps especially the latter).

Three other factors seem especially important. We have encountered the first: the availability heuristic. Mortality risks that are familiar, like those associated with nuclear power, will be seen as more serious than mortality risks that are less familiar, like those associated with heat during the summer.[3] Similarly, recent events will have a greater impact than earlier ones. This point helps explain much risk-related behavior, including decisions to take or to urge precautions. In the aftermath of an earthquake, insurance for earthquakes rises sharply—but it declines steadily from that point, as vivid memories recede.[4] Whether people will buy insurance for natural disasters is greatly affected by recent experiences.[5] If floods have not occurred in the immediate past, people who live on flood plains are far less likely to purchase insurance.[6] In the words of Amos Tversky and Daniel Kahneman, "A class whose instances are easily retrieved will appear more numerous than a class of equal frequency whose instances are less retrievable."[7]

The central point is that for those who embrace the Precautionary Principle, some risks are cognitively available, and others are not. Because the focus is on the former, the principle seems far more coherent than it is. Suppose, for example, that the Precautionary Principle has appeal in the context of nuclear power. The appeal might have a great deal to do with highly salient incidents in which the risks associated with nuclear power came to fruition, or close to it—as in the case of Three Mile Island and Fukushima. Or suppose that the principle seems to suggest the importance of a new initiative to reduce the risk of train accidents. It would not be surprising if those who are motivated by the principle are alert to a recent train accident, appearing to justify precautions.

The second factor involves *loss aversion*.[8] Behavioral scientists have emphasized that people much dislike losses from the status quo. In fact, they dislike losses about twice as much as they like corresponding gains. The Precautionary Principle often seems coherent only because losses, or particular losses, are salient, whereas foregone gains, or other kinds of gains, are not. In the context of genetically modified food, for example, the environmental risks seem, to many, to be salient and "on-screen," because they are self-evidently losses, whereas the various costs of regulation might not be, because they prevent potential gains. In the context of privacy, loss aversion can be especially important, as people strongly resist a loss of privacy that they have come to expect. (The idea of *reasonable expectation of privacy* may, in fact, encode some form of loss aversion.)

The third factor, and perhaps the most important, involves *probability neglect*.[9] The largest point is that if a bad outcome is emotionally gripping, people might well be inclined to eliminate it, even if it has a low probability of coming to fruition. The emotionally gripping outcome crowds out an assessment of the question of probability. In fact, both Cheneyism and Snowdenism seem to derive a significant amount of their attraction from probability neglect.

Suppose that you are asked how much you would pay to eliminate a small risk of a gruesome death from cancer, a terrorist attack, or a fatality risk to a small child. You might well focus on the tragic outcome, and not so much on the question of probability. A great deal of evidence confirms the phenomenon of probability neglect. The Precautionary Principle often has appeal and seems sensible because some subset of risks seems emotionally gripping; the bad outcomes associated with those risks serve to crowd out other considerations.

Consider in this regard the finding that when people are asked how much they will pay for flight insurance for losses resulting from "terrorism," they will pay more than if they are asked how much they will pay for flight insurance for losses from all causes.[10] The evident explanation for this peculiar result, fitting with a form of Cheneyism, is that the word *terrorism* evokes vivid images of disaster, thus crowding out probability judgments. Note also that when people discuss a low-probability risk, their concern rises even if the discussion consists mostly of apparently trustworthy assurances that the likelihood of harm really is infinitesmal.[11] One reason may well be that the assurances focus their minds on the risk; neglecting probability, they end up even more scared. If you are made to think about the risk of terrorism, you are unlikely to become more relaxed, even if an informed person explains that the danger is quite low.

Cheneyism

Some people embrace a version of the Precautionary Principle that no one rejects, which grows out of the self-evident idea that it is exceedingly important to counteract serious threats to the nation, including terrorist attacks, even if the risk of a successful attack in any given year is pretty small. Vice President Cheney himself offered the core of the principle, stating, "We have to deal with this new type of threat in a way we haven't yet defined. ... With a low-probability, high-impact event like this ... if there's a one percent chance that Pakistani scientists are helping al Qaeda build or develop a nuclear weapon, we have to treat it as a certainty in terms of our response."[12]

In terms of standard decision theory, of course, it is preposterous to treat a 1 percent risk the same way as a certainty. People should not, and ordinarily do not, live their lives that way. A 1 percent risk of dying in the next two years is very different from certain death in that period. But as the stakes grow higher, the expected value of a 1 percent risk becomes higher as well, and a precautionary approach to a 1 percent risk of catastrophe, trying to counteract that risk, has a great deal of appeal.

For purposes of illustration, let's focus on the question of surveillance. Even if some kinds of surveillance sweep up an immense amount of material, including much that has no interest from the standpoint of national security, surely it is better to be safe than sorry. It is tempting to emphasize the great difficulty of ruling out the possibility that if the intelligence community obtains as much information as technology permits, it will find some information that is ultimately helpful for national security purposes. "Helpful" here is not mere abstraction; it may mean "saves lives" or "prevents catastrophes."

Perhaps surveillance could prevent another 9/11; perhaps some forms of surveillance have not proved indispensable in the recent past, but perhaps they could prove indispensable in the future. A precautionary measure in ordinary life—say, purchase of safety equipment for a car—is not valueless because it has not proved necessary over the initial years of ownership. It might well be worthwhile if it avoids just one incident at some point during the life of the vehicle.

This defense of widespread surveillance could be elaborated in different ways, emphasizing diverse consequences from a successful terrorist attack. In the worst cases, numerous lives could be lost. Whenever such an attack occurs, it also has a series of proliferating costs, economic and otherwise. And if a future attack occurs, it might well lead to a demand for further restrictions on civil liberties—meaning that aggressive steps, designed to protect against attacks and objectionable from the standpoint of civil liberties in the eyes of some, might ultimately be justified or even necessary *as a means of protecting civil liberties*. With these points in view, it seems plausible to argue that at least in the context of national security, a Precautionary Principle makes a great deal of sense.

In light of that point, it is similarly tempting to think: If national security officials *can* obtain information, they *should* obtain information. This thought is especially tempting to those whose mission is to protect the nation from harm. If your job is to reduce the risk of terrorist attacks—and if you will be responsible, at least in part, for any such attacks if they occur—you might well want every available tool to increase the likelihood that no attacks will occur on your watch. That attitude might even seem indispensable to successful performance of your most important task.

Here as elsewhere, however, the problem is that multiple risks are involved. The point may be simplest to see when the question involves standard war-making. Any effort to use military force—against, say, a nation that appears to endanger us—will itself create obvious risks, including risks to life and limb. Perhaps our use of force will necessarily and immediately endanger civilians. Perhaps it will predictably lead to some kind of counterattack. What is required is a balance of risks, including probabilistic ones, rather than abstract invocation of the idea of precaution.

The same point holds true for widespread surveillance, which creates multiple risks of its own. Of these, perhaps the most obvious involve personal privacy. If government holds a great deal of information, there is at least a risk of abuse—perhaps now or soon, but if not, potentially in the future. We could imagine a range of possible fears and threats. Perhaps public officials are learning, or would learn, about interactions or relationships for which people have a reasonable expectation of privacy. Perhaps people could be threatened or punished for their political commitments or their religion. Perhaps their conversations, or relevant "metadata," could be released to the public, thus endangering their ability to keep their private lives private. Perhaps officials will see such conversations, or such metadata, producing a degree of intrusion into the private domain.

There is also a risk to civil liberties, including freedom of speech. If government acquires massive data about who is calling whom, there might well be (and perhaps there now is) a chilling effect on free discussion, on journalists and on journalists' sources. How many sources would be comfortable speaking to journalists, if they knew that a suspicious or unfriendly government, or any government at all, might be listening? Extensive forms of surveillance also create risks to commercial and economic interests and to relationships with foreign nations. How good is it for Apple or Google if people all over the world know that their communications, on relevant products, can be made visible to the United States government? How easy is it to retain friendly relations between (say) the United States and Germany, if it turns out that the United States has decided to spy on the communications of Germany's chancellor?

Each of these risks could be elaborated in great detail. For now, we need not undertake the relevant elaboration; the underlying risks have received a great deal of attention and have helped animate proposals for reform. The central point is that a form of Cheneyism, focused reasonably but solely on risks associated with terrorism, artificially truncates an appropriately wide viewscreen.

Snowdenism

Emphasizing an important subset of risks, some people embrace a *Privacy Precautionary Principle*. In their view, the risk to personal privacy requires political reforms that reduce the risk that an incompetent or ill-motivated government might now or at some future time jeopardize personal privacy. In one form, associated with Snowdenism, the objection is that some invasions of privacy have already occurred and are unacceptable in a free society. In another form, also associated with Snowdenism, the claim is that more egregious invasions are possible or likely unless corrective steps are taken.

An evident source of the Privacy Precautionary Principle is the avail-ability heuristic: to some people, certain highly publicized cases of abuse are highly salient, not least in the United States and Europe, and they make the risk of future abuse seem far from speculative. Another under-pinning is loss aversion: people are used to certain safeguards against invasion into what they see as their private domain, and widespread surveillance threatens to impose significant losses on core interests in freedom, dignity, and civic respect. A final underpinning is probabil-ity neglect: it is easy to imagine (and in the view of some to identify) privacy violations of an extreme or intolerable sort, and because those violations call up strong emotions, the very possibility that they will occur stirs strong emotions.

At the same time—and to return to my general theme—a Privacy Precautionary Principle, taken by itself and for all that it is worth, would not make a great deal of sense, if only because it would give rise to potentially serious national security risks. The problem is that if our only or central goal is to eliminate any and all risks to privacy, we would abandon forms of surveillance that might turn out to save lives. Safeguards for privacy are exceedingly important, of course, but at the conceptual level, the question remains: Why should a nation adopt a form of precautionary thinking in the context of privacy while repudi-ating it in the context of national security, or vice versa?

This question suggests that the relevant questions are best under-stood as involving a form of risk management. As in the environmental context, so too in the context of national security: risks of many kinds are on both sides of the ledger, and the task is to manage the full set, not to focus on one or few. But the risks need to be identified and speci-fied, and in the context of national security, that effort creates serious challenges. This is the knowledge problem, and it produces formidable problems for sensible risk management in this context.

Expected Values and Worst-Case Scenarios

Ideally, we would be able to identify a range of possible outcomes, to assign probabilities to each, and to come up with some kind of com-mon metric by which to make sensible comparisons. If we did that, we would be engaging in cost-benefit analysis.

We have seen that one of the hardest challenges for that form of analysis is that many of the variables at stake can be difficult or perhaps even impossible to monetize. In the context of national security, the challenge of quantification is especially daunting. Suppose that the relevant risk is a terrorist attack. In advance, it might be exceedingly difficult to quantify the costs of such an attack. The difficulty is serious even before we try to monetize. What is the likely effect of a successful attack? How many lives are at risk? Ten? Two hundred? Three thousand? More? Even if the number is at the low end of the scale, we have seen that any terrorist attack has proliferating costs, some of them involving life itself—as, for example, when people decide to drive rather than fly.[13]

Of course, assessment of the expected value of precautions must also explore their likely effect in reducing risks. If some initiative (such as surveillance) is undertaken, what is the reduction in the probability of a successful terrorist attack? Officials might not be able to come up with anything like a good answer to that question. In this respect, the domain of national security overlaps with that of financial regulation, where identification of the benefits of regulatory safeguards can also be daunting.

There are second-order effects as well as first-order effects: What kinds of social consequences follow from a successful terrorist attack? Do they include long-term economic costs? Do they include intrusions on privacy and liberty? If so, how should these be counted in the risk-management calculation? Should a civil libertarian favor national safeguards that appear to threaten civil liberties on the ground that, if they are successful, those very safeguards will help preserve civil liberties against further intrusions? These questions might prove difficult to answer when policymakers are assessing particular programs.

Breakeven Analysis

Even if such questions lack clear answers, officials may not be entirely at sea. In chapter 6, we noted that within the federal government, it is standard to speak of breakeven analysis. At least in theory, breakeven analysis can play a role in the context of national security as well. In some cases, it might make things pretty easy. With plausible assumptions about the potential cost of a terrorist attack and the likely contribution of a measure designed to ensure that it will not happen, we might have clarity about whether the measure is justified.

Let us consider a stylized example. Suppose that the cost of a terrorist attack, if it were to occur, is at least $200 billion, and suppose that the measure in question would reduce the probability of its occurrence by 10 percent. (Nothing turns on these particular numbers, which are introduced simply for purposes of analysis.) Suppose too that the measure in question would consist of security precautions at airports or certain forms of surveillance. We might ask: Is the cost of an invasion of privacy in excess of $20 billion? There is no purely arithmetic answer to that question, but the question itself might turn out to be helpful, at least if we know something about the nature of the risk to privacy. Advocates of the measure will ask a legitimate question: Is it plausible to think that the risk to privacy is worth $20 billion? Maybe it just isn't.

True, this is an artificial example, in which we have some solid numbers with which to work. In Hard Cases, breakeven analysis runs into particular trouble, at least if we indulge two reasonable assumptions: (1) a great deal of important information is often missing and (2) moral valuations will play an inescapable role. When hard-to-quantify costs are on both sides of the ledger—as they are in the contexts under discussion—then breakeven analysis becomes especially hard to undertake. If so, its chief advantage is that it may promote transparency about the issues involved.

Avoid Gratuitous Costs

Diverse people should be willing to converge on a simple principle: avoid gratuitous costs. In the environmental context, that seemingly self-evident principle turns out to have real bite. Suppose, for example, that on reflection, certain environmental risks turn out to be trivial. It makes sense to say that government should not regulate those risks, at least if regulation itself imposes costs. The principle is also important in the context of national security: Suppose that some forms of surveillance produce no benefits, or only modest benefits. Suppose that their only function is to pick up information that cannot plausibly contribute to the prevention of terrorist attacks. If so, there would seem to be no reason that they should be continued.

The principle does not only inform the scope of surveillance activities. It should also inform the design of relevant institutions. For example, the President's Review Group recommended that metadata should be held not by the government itself, but by the phone companies, with access by the government only when justified by a judicially approved warrant. We can understand this recommendation as an outcome of the no-gratuitous-costs principle: on optimistic (but not unrealistic) assumptions, it would deprive the government of exactly nothing that it is important for the government to have, while also providing a layer of protection against risks to privacy and free speech. Even if the government does not "hold" the metadata, it can obtain it on a showing of need—and indeed, if time requires (e.g., under emergency conditions), it need not obtain judicial authorization in advance. Under these assumptions, the review group's recommendation flows directly from the no-gratuitous-cost principle.

That principle is a sensible way to provide a layer of privacy protection without threatening national security. Consider a much more controversial question: Can the principle be used to *scale back* some kinds of apparent privacy protection, on the ground that they do no real good, in terms of privacy, but also impose some costs (in the form of national security risks)? However uncomfortable, the question deserves attention. We can easily imagine cases in which privacy protections (say, to ensure that national security organizations cannot monitor certain web-browsing habits) do not really help avoid misuse or abuse, but make it harder for government to discover and stop people who are genuinely dangerous. Some safeguards for privacy, though comforting, fail to help anyone. If so, they should be reassessed.

Avoid Illicit Grounds

If the purpose of surveillance is to protect national security, then some grounds for surveillance, and some uses of surveillance, are automatically off-limits. They do not count in the balance at all. This is an exceedingly important idea, because it captures and takes directly on board some of the most plausible judgments behind a Privacy Precautionary

Principle. More specifically, it addresses several concerns that motivate that principle.

The major categories are straightforward. Surveillance cannot legitimately be used to punish people because of their political views or their religious convictions. Under current conditions, surveillance that is designed to reduce risks to national security should not be designed to protect against criminal activity that raises no national security issue. If the underlying activity involves unlawful gambling or tax evasion, there are established routes by which government may obtain relevant information. It is generally agreed that surveillance should not be designed to give a commercial advantage to American firms. In these and other respects, the interest in national security—which is what motivates surveillance in this context—also limits and disciplines the permissible grounds for surveillance. No sensible form of Cheneyism should reject those limits.

To be sure, we could imagine more difficult cases. Suppose, not implausibly, that a certain set of political views or identifiable religious convictions are closely associated with a desire to do harm to the United States and its allies. If people are members of the Islamic State of Iraq and the Levant (ISIL), then the United States is entitled to focus on them by virtue of that fact. But the reason involves national security, not politics or religion as such. We can imagine cases that might test the clarity of that line, but the basic principle should not be obscure.

Avoid the Worst of the Worst Cases

Decision theorists sometimes distinguish between situations of *risk*, in which probabilities can be assigned to various outcomes, and situations of *uncertainty*, in which no such probabilities can be assigned. In the domain of national security, we can imagine instances in which analysts cannot specify a usefully narrow range of probabilities and in which the extent of the harm from bad outcomes is also not susceptible to anything like precise prediction. Here again, the analogy to financial regulation is plausible: analysts might be able to identify only an unhelpfully wide range of bad outcomes, and they might not be able to say a great deal about the contribution of a regulation to prevention of such outcomes.

In situations of uncertainty, when existing knowledge does not permit regulators to assign probabilities to outcomes, it is standard to follow the maximin principle: Choose the policy with the best worst-case outcome.[14] Suppose that the worst case associated with one policy involves a successful terrorist attack on the United States, with consequently significant loss of life. Suppose that the worst case associated with another policy involves a serious threat to privacy, in the form (say) of widespread official reading of private metadata, leading to official invasion of the private sphere. Suppose finally that we cannot say much about the probability that one or another worst case will occur.

In a case of that kind, there is a good argument for Cheneyism, and a much weaker one for Snowdenism. The reason is that the worst case associated with a successful terrorist attack is so much worse than the worst case associated with a breach of personal privacy.

Of course, this case is artificial along multiple dimensions. We might be speaking of *bounded uncertainty*; in a given period, the probability of a successful terrorist attack might not be between 0 and 100 percent, but between 0 and 30 percent (though we might not be able to say much about where it falls within that range). We might be able to say that if a terrorist attack occurs, very bad outcomes would have a cost between $X and $Y, where $X is (say) $100 billion, and where $Y is (say) $950 billion. (These numbers are merely illustrative.) Although the contribution of a particular initiative might not be susceptible to precise specification, policymakers might have an idea of a sensible range.

Moreover, maximin is most useful in cases when the outcomes can easily be rendered commensurable. Suppose that a policymaker has two options, which would lead to different worst-case scenarios: (1) a loss of $500 million or (2) a loss of $900 million. The option that leads to the lower worst-case loss is better (and it is clear which is lower). Or suppose that with option 1, the worst-case scenario involves a loss of one thousand lives, whereas with option 2, the worst-case scenario would lose six thousand lives (no ambiguity there). The issue is more difficult when the outcomes are not easily made commensurable. Suppose that a policymaker has two options, with different worst-case scenarios: (1) a loss of $600 million and two hundred lives and (2) a loss of $900 million and 150 lives. Are the 50 lives saved from (2) worth the

$300 million cost? The answer depends on the value of a statistical life. The government now values a statistical life at about $9 million, so the answer is yes.

Far harder cases are imaginable. In the context at hand, suppose that with one approach, the worst-case scenario is a loss of significant numbers of lives, whereas with another, the worst-case scenario is a massive intrusion into personal privacy. For progress to be made, both of these would have to be specified. How many lives? One thousand? Five thousand? Forty thousand? More? And what kind of intrusion counts as massive? Issues of valuation cannot be avoided here. Official reading of (say) private metadata is far more alarming to some people than to others.

On one view, a certain degree of vulnerability, with respect to private metadata, does not involve anything like the worst-case scenarios associated with successful terrorist attacks. That view might be accompanied by a judgment that the risk of vulnerability, with respect to private metadata, can be sufficiently contained. On another view, a cavalier approach to personal privacy threatens both liberty and self-government themselves, so the worst-case scenario is very bad indeed (and cannot be ruled out).

Disagreements of this kind cannot be resolved by arithmetic. A reference to maximin will not do the trick. Perhaps the best that can be done is to attempt to identify safeguards, with respect to privacy, that plausibly reduce the risks associated with worst-case scenarios while also allowing officials to do what must be done with respect to protecting national security. In the abstract, it might well seem more difficult to achieve that goal than it is in practice.

Wide Viewscreens

In ordinary life, people take precautions, and sensibly so; insurance policies are often an excellent idea. The Precautionary Principle is animated by the reasonable idea that it is prudent to act even when it is far from certain that the underlying danger will come to fruition. The problem is that action can create dangers of its own. In the environmental context, the Precautionary Principle runs into self-evident trouble when efforts to reduce some environmental risks give rise to other environmental risks. It is also problematic when those efforts create risks that have nothing to do with the environment. A wide viewscreen, rather than a narrow one, is indispensable in the regulatory domain.

In the area of national security, it may be especially tempting for public officials to adopt some kind of Precautionary Principle, not least because they are confronted with a dazzling array of low-probability risks. It would be both irresponsible and dangerous to ignore those risks. At the same time, some precautions create risks of their own, and they must be considered in an overall balance. Cheneyism, as I have understood it here, runs afoul of the need for wide viewscreens. The same point certainly holds for those who embrace Snowdenism, which I have understood as an insistence on a Precautionary Principle for privacy and civil liberties.

To the extent feasible, the best approach to risk management involves cost-benefit balancing. The challenge is that in some domains, both costs and benefits are exceedingly hard to quantify, much less to monetize. I have argued for four ideas that can help. First, officials should consider the use of breakeven analysis. Second, they should not impose essentially gratuitous costs (including risks). Third, they should ensure that illicit grounds are not being invoked to intrude on privacy, liberty, or anything else. Fourth, they should take steps to prevent the worst of the worst-case scenarios. There are no algorithms here, but a form of risk management embodying those ideas can help avoid some of the pathologies of both Cheneyism and Snowdenism: Precautionary Principles of the most blinkered or myopic sorts.

Imagine that a coal company is emitting harmful pollutants: particulate matter, greenhouse gases, ozone. Imagine too that if public officials direct it to reduce its emissions, it will face high costs, perhaps in the tens of millions of dollars. Imagine finally that the benefits of emissions reductions would be felt mostly in the future, in the form of reductions in premature mortality in a decade or more and a small (but far from zero) reduction in climate change. Imagine finally that the monetized benefits of emissions reductions, with the appropriate discount rate, would dwarf the costs. On those assumptions, is there any doubt that regulation would be a good idea, even though the principal benefits would not be enjoyed for several years? (This is not meant to be a difficult question. There is no such doubt.)

Now suppose that the Department of Homeland Security and the Federal Aviation Administration are considering a new policy to reduce the risk of successful terrorist attacks at airports. They are contemplating the use of a new security scanner that will (according to experts) prove more effective in detecting potential weapons, including small or novel kinds that terrorists might use in the future. The economic cost of the new scanner is high—at least $2 million for each one. Federal officials concede that they cannot say, with confidence, that the new scanner will save lives; they cannot even say that it is more likely than not to do so. But they believe that it will reduce the risk of a successful terrorist attack. Would it be a mistake to mandate the scanner? (This is meant to be a difficult question. The answer is not obvious. But mandating the scanner would not be a clear mistake.)

The two cases just given are standard. Federal regulators often act without the slightest hesitation, even though the benefits of their action will not be immediate; indeed, such benefits might occur many years in the future (as in the case of climate change). Federal regulators also act without much hesitation when reasonable people think that the chance of producing any benefits at all is under 50 percent. Consider, for example, regulations designed to reduce the risk of a nuclear power accident (improbable but potentially catastrophic) or another financial crisis—for example, by increasing capital and liquidity requirements. Of course, regulators will not impose costs for no benefits. Instead, they will think about the expected value of regulatory requirements. If a mandate will have a 1 in x chance of producing $500 million in benefits, it might be worth proceeding even if x is pretty big—and if the potential benefits are (say) $5 billion, a chance of 1 in 20 would justify a quite costly regulatory mandate.

The most general point is that in deciding whether to proceed, regulators need not be much moved by learning that the benefits would not be imminent, or even that they are not likely to occur at all. The question is the *expected value of proceeding*. A lack of imminence suggests that the discount rate (based on the judgment that future costs and benefits should be "discounted" to present value) will greatly matter; of course, a low probability of obtaining benefits must be recognized, and it will drive the expected value way down. But these are points about the magnitude of the benefits, which may nonetheless be high, or at least high enough to justify proceeding.

We have seen that in the regulatory context, some people reject cost-benefit balancing in favor of some kind of precautionary principle, calling for regulation even when it cannot be said, with anything like certainty, that precautions actually will eliminate harm. No nation has become a precautionary state, but there are good arguments for taking regulatory steps to reduce low-probability risks of harm, especially if those steps are not especially costly.

We have also seen that, especially to those who favor cost-benefit balancing, the precautionary principle is highly controversial, in part because it seems to require steps that impose risks of their own—and thus violate the precautionary principle. For that reason, the precautionary principle is self-defeating, and cost-benefit analysis is a preferable approach. Some people endorse a more limited idea, the *catastrophic harm precautionary principle*, which supports regulatory restrictions in cases in which catastrophic harm cannot be ruled out. The basic claim here is that even if a harm is unlikely to occur, and even if it will not occur imminently, sensible regulators might be willing to proceed; consider the risks posed by nuclear power. In the regulatory context, no one seriously questions that general proposition.

The Costs and Benefits of Speech

Is speech different? How?

For purposes of analysis, I am going to use a broadly welfarist framework, suggesting that we should focus on the real-world consequences of various approaches.[1] If, for example, an approach to free speech would seriously harm people's capacity to learn about values or facts, it would be exceedingly hard to defend. (Think of dictatorships.) If an approach to free speech would allow significant numbers of people to be killed, it would have a big strike against it. (Think of free speech absolutism.) It should be readily acknowledged that welfarism raises many questions and doubts. For one thing, we need to specify whether we are speaking of some form of utilitarianism or of something more capacious.[2] Perhaps more fundamentally, we need to know *what kinds of welfare losses count*. Suppose that certain forms of speech make people sad or mad. May they be regulated for that reason? The standard forms of welfarism must count sadness and anger as hedonic losses, but a system of free speech could not stand as such if it did so as well. Speech often makes people sad or mad—criticisms of the status quo certainly can—and it must not be regulable for that reason. (I am not going to count sadness and anger as losses here.)

For those who reject welfarism, and think that, for example, a deontological approach to speech emphasizing the importance of individual rights would be preferable, my focus will seem quite misplaced. Notwithstanding this point, I believe that a broadly welfarist approach to free speech has considerable appeal and that we can make considerable progress on the underlying issues without running into murky philosophical waters. The proof, of course, lies in the pudding.

At least in principle, current thinking about costs and benefits would seem to apply to speech no less than to conduct. Suppose that we had a perfect technology for making predictions about the probability that certain causes, including speech, will produce certain effects. Suppose that the technology demonstrates that a specified kind of speech—promoting, say, terrorism—is more likely than not to produce serious harm in the form of successful attacks, resulting in a specified (and large) number of deaths—not in a month, but in two years. Or suppose that a speech is not exactly likely to produce harm and that the likelihood that the speech will result in harm is just 1 in 5—but that if the harm occurs, it will be very grave. In such cases, it would seem odd to say that regulation is off-limits.

A full evaluation would require attention to the benefits of the speech, not only its costs. With respect to the assessment of benefits, there are special challenges perhaps especially for speech that combats a tyrannical or unjust status quo and that promotes, purposefully or otherwise, violence as a form of resistance. But we could easily imagine cases in which the benefits of speech that has a high expected cost would also be relatively low—so that the outcome of cost-benefit analysis is not at all favorable to protecting such speech.

In fact, it is not necessary to use our imaginations. Terrorist organizations are engaged in incitement and recruitment activities every day. Their initial weapon is speech. On the Internet and elsewhere, they call for acts of murder and destruction. Let us simply stipulate that however hateful, most or many of these statements cannot be said to be more likely than not to produce imminent lawless action. In such cases, there is no *clear and present danger*, as that phrase is generally understood. Instead, they create a *nonquantifiable but real risk that such action will occur at some point in the unknown future*. On standard regulatory principles, government may nonetheless be permitted to take action, depending on a full analysis of costs and benefits (acknowledging relevant uncertainties).

Those principles are hardly foreign to free speech law. Some form of cost-benefit balancing played a central role in *Dennis v. United States*, a decision that is generally treated as a dinosaur, or an object of ridicule, in constitutional law circles. The case involved an alleged conspiracy by members of the Communist Party, hoping to overthrow the US government. The court said that it was "squarely presented with the application of the 'clear and present danger' test, and must decide what that phrase imports." In that sense, it purported to apply rather than to reject that test. The court explained:

> Obviously, the words cannot mean that, before the Government may act, it must wait until the putsch is about to be executed, the plans have been laid and the signal is awaited. If Government is aware that a group aiming at its overthrow is attempting to indoctrinate its members and to commit them to a course whereby they will strike when the leaders feel the circumstances permit, action by the Government is required. ... Certainly an attempt to overthrow the Government by force, even though doomed from the outset because of inadequate numbers or power of the revolutionists, is a sufficient evil for Congress to prevent. The damage which such attempts create both physically and politically to a nation makes it impossible to measure the validity in terms of the probability of success, or the immediacy of a successful attempt.[3]

At that point, the court referred to Judge Learned Hand's formulation from the lower court, a form of cost-benefit balancing in accordance with which "in each case, [courts] must ask whether the gravity of the 'evil,' discounted by its improbability, justifies such invasion of free speech as is necessary to avoid the danger." The court adopted this standard as its own, on the ground that it "takes into consideration those factors which we deem relevant, and relates their significances. More we cannot expect from words."

Not coincidentally, Hand's free speech formula is similar to the famous Hand formula for negligence, celebrated in (and helping spur) the economic analysis of law. Hand's negligence standard calls for cost-benefit analysis:

> Since there are occasions when every vessel will break from her moorings, and since, if she does, she becomes a menace to those about her; the owner's duty, as in other similar situations, to provide against resulting injuries is a function of three variables: (1) The probability that she will break away; (2) the gravity of the resulting injury, if she does; (3) the burden of adequate precautions. Possibly it serves to bring this notion into relief to state it in algebraic terms: if the probability be called P; the injury, L; and the burden, B; liability depends upon whether B is less than L multiplied by P: i.e., whether $B < PL$.[4]

For speech, Hand was singing the song of contemporary American regulators—and in *Dennis*, the court embraced the idea as a rendering of the clear and present danger test. But today, almost no one likes that idea. Why not?

"More Speech, Not Enforced Silence"

In their great free speech opinions, written long before *Dennis*, Oliver Wendell Holmes Jr. and Louis Brandeis rejected cost-benefit balancing. Brandeis offered the most elaborate explanation. In his view, "Only an emergency can justify suppression."[5] That conclusion undergirded his own understanding of the clear and present danger test, which (contrary to *Dennis* and Hand) required a showing of imminence. In his account, "No danger flowing from speech can be deemed clear and present unless the incidence of the evil apprehended is so imminent that it may befall before there is opportunity for full discussion. If there be time to expose through discussion the falsehood and fallacies, to avert the evil by the processes of education, the remedy to be applied is more speech, not enforced silence."[6] As he put it, that is "the command of the Constitution," and it "must be the rule if authority is to be reconciled with freedom."

Some of this is mere rhetoric on Brandeis' part. There are plenty of ways to reconcile authority with freedom, and the clear and present danger test is merely one. The *Dennis* approach may or may not be underprotective of speech, but it is surely an effort at reconciling authority and freedom. Perhaps it is not the best one. At one point, Hand himself offered a radically different route, one with great contemporary relevance in light of the rise of terrorism. In his view, the free speech principle does not protect explicit or direct incitement to violence, even if no harm was imminent.[7]

If you are merely agitating for change, the government cannot proceed against you, but if you are expressly inciting people to commit murder, you are no longer protected by the Constitution. What matters is what you are saying, not whether it will have bad effects. Hand greatly preferred his approach to the clear and present danger test, which he thought squishy and susceptible to biased assessments by federal judges. As he wrote:

I am not wholly in love with Holmes' test and the reason is this. Once you admit that the matter is one of degree, while you may put it where it genuinely belongs, you obviously make it a matter of administration, i.e. you give it to Tomdickandharry, D.J., so much latitude ... that the jig is at once up. Besides their Ineffabilities, the Nine Elder Statesmen have not shown themselves wholly immune from the "herd instinct" and what seems "immediate and direct" today may seem very remote next year even though the circumstances surrounding the utterance be unchanged.[8]

Cost-benefit analysis has been criticized on similar grounds, though modern economic understandings can greatly reduce the problem. By contrast, Hand defended his exemption of incitement as a "qualitative formula, hard, conventional, difficult to evade."[9] Hand's test would allow punishment of a great deal of terrorist speech, because it qualifies as incitement insofar as it calls for violence. (Note that expressing and calling for hatred of Americans, as such, would not be punishable.)

Whether or not it is right to exclude incitement as Hand understood it, Brandeis' version of the clear and present danger test cannot simply be read off the Constitution, and we cannot see the *Dennis* approach as necessarily or inherently incompatible with it. To be sure, the first amendment protects "the freedom of speech," but you can embrace that form of freedom while agreeing or even insisting that on a certain showing of harm, regulation or subsequent punishment is acceptable. Brandeis' judgment on behalf of his understanding of the Constitution's command depends on an argument of his own. The Constitution does not speak clearly on the point.

Of course, Brandeis does offer an argument, and it is an exceedingly famous one to boot. The argument is essentially a defense of the imminence requirement: If there is time to avert the evil through discussion, then the remedy is not forced silence, but *counterspeech*. Instead of censoring speech or threatening to punish it, government should attempt to rebut it. If people defend overthrow of the government or claim that women should be subordinate to men or attack racial minority groups, their arguments should be rebutted. For reasons elaborated by John Stuart Mill,[10] that process of rebuttal has numerous advantages; it corrects error, opens possibilities, sharpens thought even when it does not change it, undoes complacency, and helps societies to move in the direction of truth.

These are appealing ideas—but on reflection, they are a bit of a mess, certainly as a defense of the clear and present danger test in genuinely Hard Cases. Suppose that a speaker is saying something that is 40 percent likely to result in the death of one hundred children—not imminently, but in the next two years. By emphasizing the potential value of discussion, Brandeis is fighting the hypothetical. He is assuming or stipulating that because there is no emergency, speech can provide the remedy. Maybe so, but that is simply a way of denying the predicate of the question, which seems to deserve a real answer.

The regulatory analogy is helpful here. It is true that with respect to Brandeis' central concerns, speech is unique; for, say, pollution, the harm that regulators seek to address is unlikely to be addressable (merely) through discussion, if only because we are not dealing with speech. To stop environmental harm, we need action as well. To tighten the analogy, that harm might well be addressable though some other means, short of regulating the underlying conduct. If the harm is premature mortality or climate change, a less than imminent harm might well turn out to be preventable at some point before it occurs.

For climate change in particular, adaptation or some unforeseen technological fix might prevent the harm in, say, 2040. That possibility raises a fair question, often offered by those who would be regulated: Why should we impose expensive precautions today? Whenever the issue involves health and safety, it is possible to think that interim steps will prevent the feared harms from coming to fruition. Would it not be better to delay costly measures until tomorrow or the day after?

Actually, no. To be sure, some people make that argument in the context of climate change, but it is not convincing. The best reason, of course, is suggested in *Dennis* itself: If we do not act now, it might turn out to be too late in the future. An ounce of prevention might well be worth a pound of cure. Regulators should certainly consider the possibility that the harm can be averted through other means, but there is no reason to foreclose regulatory action merely because of that possibility. As always, it is part of the analysis; if the probability of averting the harm is 50 percent, the benefits should be discounted accordingly, taking into consideration the costs of the steps that avert the harm.

A complete analysis would consider the full set of costs and benefits, with reference to the appropriate discount rate and estimates of all relevant probabilities—but (and this is the central point) it would hardly lead to Brandeis' approach. The upshot that the imminence requirement is difficult indeed to defend, unless it is a rough-and-ready way to instantiate the idea that the harm must be likely. Brandeis might be thinking that if the harm is not imminent, it is simply too speculative to say that it is likely and that nonimminent harms are unlikely to occur so long as discussion is available. But purely as a matter of logic, that cannot be true.

So much for the imminence requirement. What about the idea that harms must be *likely*? We could imagine a free speech regime that requires a showing of likelihood but that says nothing at all about imminence: a likelihood ten years hence is the same as a likelihood tomorrow. But as in the regulatory context, this is a puzzling view. A small risk of catastrophe deserves more attention than a large risk of modest harm; at least as a first approximation, expected value is what matters. What is so magical about a probability of more than 50 percent? Why should that be the threshold?

At its origin, the idea of a "clear" danger almost certainly meant something far more modest, now lost to history. When Holmes first announced the clear and present danger test, he did not intend anything especially speech-protective.[11] After all, he upheld a conviction of someone for speech that was not especially dangerous. When he used the word *clear*, he might well have meant not *more likely than not*, but something more akin to *real rather than fanciful*. In that view, the word *clear* was intended to clarify the word *danger* in a modest way, by signaling the simple fact that the government must be able to point to one. That would bring free speech law closely into line with the modern approach to regulation in general. In that context, fanciful risks also cannot be regulated, because regulation would fail cost-benefit balancing.

As a matter of current understanding, however, this point is moot. In *Brandenburg v. Ohio*,[12] the court read *clear* to mean *likely*. That interpretation has been unchallenged for decades. What I am suggesting thus far is that the unchallenged interpretation seems very hard to defend, because cost-benefit balancing is better. Indeed, the difficulty of defending it becomes only clearer when we expand the viewscreen. In regulation, the expected value of the harm is only one part of the picture; the benefit of the underlying activity matters as well. We might be dealing with socially beneficial activity, and it might cost, say, $900 million to regulate it; or we might be dealing with activity from which society does not much benefit, and it might cost $1 million to regulate it. It much matters with which we are dealing.

Shouldn't the same be true for speech? Once we start thinking in terms of both benefits and costs, we will be refining the framework in *Dennis* in a way that makes that framework compatible with regulatory approaches more broadly. In the cost-benefit state, why would that be a mistake?

Defending Likelihood and Imminence

I now turn to three possible defenses of the clear and present danger test, taking them in ascending order of persuasiveness. The first is that in light of the insuperable difficulties of quantification, cost-benefit analysis is not feasible in this domain. The second points to the pervasive risk of institutional bias, arguing that the clear and present danger test is designed to counteract that bias. In that view, the test is what cost-benefit analysis calls for, because it responds to the danger of inaccurate case-by-case assessments. The third and most convincing justification is that in the real world, the cases for which the clear and present danger test fails did not exist in the last half of the twentieth century—or at least could not easily be identified if they did exist. If the second and the third justifications are put together, the clear and present danger test looks pretty good.

A reasonable conclusion is that the clear and present danger test is hard to defend in principle or in the abstract. The difference from the more general regulatory context is that it is challenging to identify real-world situations in which speech should be regulated because it produces nonimminent, low-probability harms. Because of the rise of terrorism, however, the first half of the twenty-first century might be different from the second half of the twentieth on that count.

Challenges of Quantification

In the world of regulation, it is often possible to quantify both costs and benefits, or at least to make good approximations. The whole exercise is far more challenging for speech, and in some ways it is neither feasible nor attractive. Suppose that a speaker is calling for violent acts to resist what he sees as oppression. Suppose that the acts would result in some number of deaths. We might enlist the usual number of the value of a statistical life ($9 million), and multiply that times the number of lives at risk, discounted by the probability that the bad outcome will occur. But there are multiple uncertainties here: How many lives are at risk? What is the probability? Perhaps analysts can produce lower or upper bounds, which might make the analysis more tractable, but the guesswork here is substantial.

Valuation of the benefits of speech is even more difficult. We would hardly want to rest content with asking speakers how much they would be willing to pay to retain their right to say what they want (or how much they would demand to give up that right). Even if the answers to such questions are in some sense relevant (and that is hardly clear), the value of speech is not fully captured by its value to speakers; the audience matters as well, and it is probably what matters most. Speech is for listeners even more than speakers. For listeners, willingness to pay creates its own problems. To assess the value of speech, would it make sense to ask (nationally representative?) people how much they would be willing to pay to hear certain speeches? To ensure that certain speakers are allowed to speak? In a nation that values freedom, those are terrible questions. One reason is that speech is supposed to affect people's values and preferences. Those values and preferences are endogenous to what people hear. Economic analysis of willingness to pay does not adequately capture what matters.

Here is a way to sharpen the point. The costs of regulation usually involve economic burdens on producers and consumers (and perhaps workers); consider environmental and food-safety regulations. By contrast, the costs of free speech restrictions involve some loss to speakers and to those who would benefit from hearing what they have to say. How can that loss be valued? Economists have an array of tools, focused on willingness to pay, but those tools do not appear sufficiently well-suited to the context. Freedom of speech is not a commodity in the standard economic sense. The value of your freedom of speech is not captured by how much you would be willing to pay to retain it (or be willing to accept to give it up). That form of freedom is central to the creation of preferences, beliefs, and values, which is why it cannot be traded on markets.

For these reasons, the usual approach to valuing costs and benefits seems to fail in this context. But what is the implication of that conclusion? *Dennis* did not purport to use economic analysis of any formal kind; it did not rely on willingness to pay; it endorsed something far looser and more intuitive, designed to specify or soften the clear and present danger test in circumstances in which the danger was neither clear nor present. The basic idea is that if speech has some nontrivial probability of causing or contributing to catastrophic or egregious harm, government is not powerless to prevent it.

We can take this idea as a form of rough-and-ready cost-benefit analysis or as a version of the catastrophic harm precautionary principle. The basic point is that the difficulty of quantifying costs and benefits is neither a convincing objection to the *Dennis* approach nor an adequate defense of the clear and present danger test.

Institutional Bias

An alternative view is that the clear and present danger test is an excellent response to a pervasive institutional risk, which is that the government's own assessments will be systematically skewed, above all because its own self-interest is so often at stake. When invoking a risk of harm and speaking of danger and costs, public officials are often trying to insulate themselves from criticism. Their real concerns are about protecting their own power and legitimacy, rather than protecting the society from serious harm. At the very least, they confound the interest in their own authority, and in maintaining it, with a concern about stability, peace, and violence.

In authoritarian nations, the point is clear. Even in the United States, history speaks volumes.[13] Public officials have often argued, and often apparently believed, that restrictions on speech were necessary to avoid serious harm, certainly in connection with war and national security threats but also outside of those contexts. In retrospect, their arguments look implausible; it seems clear that they were seeking to censor or punish ideas and perspectives with which they disagreed. At the time, however, their claims were highly credible. In the heat of the moment, it is all too easy to convince the public and even oneself that suppression of speech is necessary to avoid harm, even if that is entirely false. In recent years, it is easy to think of examples, whether they come from Russia, China, Cuba, or Turkey. On this view, citizens in authoritarian nations desperately need the protection of the clear and present danger test, or something close to it—and citizens in democracies do as well.

Suppose, for example, that some protesters, objecting to what they see as racist violence by the police, are demonstrating noisily in a large city, or that other protesters, skeptical of what they see as an overreaching national government, are vigorously objecting to recent legislation. Public officials might complain about a risk of violence, but their actual goal (whether conscious or not) might be to insulate themselves or their friends from criticism. (It would not be the first time.) Their interest in precautions and their assessment of costs and benefits will be systematically self-serving—an unreliable and even dangerous basis for authorizing action. Any precautionary principle, with respect to the harms stemming from speech, would put democracy itself at immediate and severe risk.

Cost-benefit analysis might seem much better, but it suffers from precisely the same vice, which is that it enables untrustworthy officials to invoke a seemingly neutral and abstractly appealing standard in defense of outcomes that violate that very standard. On welfarist grounds and in principle, the clear and present danger test might not be close to perfect; for reasons we have explored, it protects speech too much. But in the real world, it is incalculably preferable to what would emerge from open-ended balancing by unreliable balancers. In short, it counteracts the risk of biased, self-serving judgments by those who would be charged with assessing the costs and benefits. We are better off with the clear and present danger test because it prevents censorship and suppression that would come from self-interested cost-benefit balancers.

In the regulatory context, a similar argument is not unfamiliar. A standard claim, especially within the business community, is that government regulators typically overstate the benefits and understate the costs of what they do. Whether or not that is true, the proper response, if it is indeed true, is to put in place institutional safeguards that correct mistaken judgments. We might, for example, allow assessment by some kind of independent entity within the executive branch, or insist on judicial review of the agency's analysis. As in the context of regulation in general, so in the free speech context: the most natural response to institutional bias is not to depart from cost-benefit analysis, but to create safeguards to make sure that it is fairly conducted. Federal judges need not defer to whatever legislative and executive officials think; they could force them to meet a (high) burden of proof. With this approach, some version of the *Dennis* test would be firmly in place, but with strong judicial efforts to reduce the risk of bias. Other institutional safeguards might be put in place to reduce that risk, in the form of independent analysts within the legislative or executive branches, whose job would be to monitor the assessment of both costs and benefits.

The upshot is that the risk of institutional bias is entirely real—but the more direct corrective is not to jump from a cost-benefit test to a clear and present danger test, but to increase the likelihood that the proper test will be properly applied. The institutional defense of the clear and present danger test is forceful but incomplete. It identifies the right ailment, but it does not offer the most obvious cure. The most that can be said is that if the right cure is unavailable, the test might be a second best—but the institutional defense cannot, on its own, produce a full-scale defense of the test.

As It Happens

Here is a final argument on behalf of the clear and present danger test. In my view, it is basically convincing—or at least it has been convincing for most of the time in which the test has held sway. The problem is that it depends on empirical assumptions that will not always hold and that may not hold today.

The central claim is that in the world in which we live, the cases that confound the clear and present danger test exist rarely or not at all. *Dennis* might be right in principle, but the speech that it allows government to ban causes no harm at all in practice. To paraphrase Oliver Wendell Holmes Jr.: the life of the law is experience, not logic. I have pointed to situations in which harm is neither likely nor imminent, and when speech causes an uncertain risk of harm in a distant future. But the stubborn fact is that in such cases, the costs of allowing the speech have turned out to be low (in reality), and those costs could be and generally have been avoided or minimized without restricting speech—as, for example, by taking strong steps (and not unduly costly ones) to avert violence.

Suppose, for example, that a number of people call for violent acts in circumstances in which the clear and present danger test is not satisfied: to overthrow the government, to kill police officers, to have some kind of revolution. If such calls in fact end up producing violent acts that could not be prevented through means that do not involve regulating speech, then the argument for speech regulation would be difficult to avoid; the clear and present danger test would be responsible for tragedy. But (the argument goes) there are essentially no such cases.

On this count, the regulatory context is altogether different. It is easy to find cases in which regulation is important or even critical to prevent harms even if they would not occur imminently. It is reasonable to think that in the context of climate change and financial stability, numerous actions have been justified and desirable even if the harms were not "likely." A clear and present danger test would be crazy for regulation in general; it would impose high net costs. Simply as a practical matter, the same cannot be said in the context of speech. That is, in a nutshell, the central defense of the clear and present danger test.

We would need a lot of detail to know for sure, but for the decades in which the clear and present danger test has held sway, this defense seems convincing. Defenders of *Dennis* would be hard-pressed to point to situations in which their preferred approach would have prevented serious harm. There is no need for a cost-benefit test, because the clear and present danger test imposed no costs—and avoided unjustified censorship.

To be sure, we could easily imagine a nation facing a high degree of volatility and serious risks of speech-induced violence, in which the argument for the *Dennis* approach would be quite strong. From the standpoint of the British, would that be the situation in the American colonies in the years immediately preceding the American Revolution? In an era of international terrorism, the argument for something like *Dennis* is unquestionably stronger. Would-be murderers are trying to recruit people to engage in murderous actions. Perhaps the clear and present danger test is ill-suited to that situation, because it does not allow regulation of speech until it is too late.

I cannot press that point in detail here, but with this sketch of the best arguments for the clear and present danger test, we can see that under imaginable assumptions, it would have unacceptably high costs. If the risk of institutional bias could be reduced and if the test would allow horrifying acts to occur, then *Dennis* would be better. It is hard to say that the clear and present danger test has caused much mischief over the last fifty years. But it is not implausible to say that it will cause mischief over the next fifty. In the context of terrorism, whether that possibility justifies something more like *Dennis* or perhaps something akin to Hand's incitement test is not entirely clear.

Principles and Contexts

It would make no sense to say that the regulatory choices of the Environmental Protection Agency, the Department of Transportation, and the Department of Health and Human Services should be based on the clear and present danger test. Reasonable people have contended that cost-benefit analysis fails to take sufficient precautions against risks; it is hard to argue that such balancing generally produces excessive regulation (even if it might do so in particular cases).

In principle, some form of cost-benefit balancing might well seem preferable to the clear and present danger test in the context of speech as well. A natural objection involves valuation: What, exactly, are the costs and the benefits of speech that, say, calls for political revolution? That is an excellent question, but at least in some cases, it is unnecessary to resolve difficult questions about valuation to say that the balance comes out unfavorably to speech, even though no danger is clear and present.

The best justifications for the clear and present danger test point to institutional biases and to the possibility that the cases that confound that test, and make it seem unreasonable, are not likely to arise in the real world. Public officials will sometimes find a danger even when there is no such thing; their own desire for self-insulation can pervert their judgments. In any case, *Dennis*, allowing censorship of speech that creates a small risk of a not imminent but catastrophic harm, may respond to a nonexistent risk. In principle, a cost-benefit test might be a good idea, at least if we could trust those who administer it. But in practice, the clear and present danger test has not caused serious problems, at least in most democracies.

In the United States for the period between 1960 and 2001, that conclusion seems right. It might also be right in the United States and Europe today—but that is hardly self-evident. The clear and present danger test is not a test for all seasons. In imaginable times and places, it rests on doubtful assumptions. Even in the face of international terrorism, it would be reckless to say that we would be better off without it. But it is not reckless to say that that is a perfectly fair question to ask.

Conclusion: Best-Laid Plans

Writers of fiction report that their stories take unanticipated directions—that their characters seem to have wills of their own, producing plot developments that they could not possibly have expected. Sometimes the hero falls for the wrong woman; sometimes he turns out to be a killer. Writers of nonfiction say something similar. They begin with an argument in which they have considerable confidence, but as they develop it, they learn that it is not quite right, that it needs to be redirected, or even that it is fundamentally wrong. What they produce is very different from what they planned. No less than cost-benefit analysts, writers end up being surprised.

Celebrating

When I began this book, I expected it to be an enthusiastic and essentially unambivalent celebration of the cost-benefit revolution. My plan was to establish that careful attention to costs and benefits is unfathomably better than reliance on intuitions, on political processes, on rights-based thinking, and above all on any kind of expressivism. I hoped also to show that political disagreements could often be quieted, or in any case begin to be made to look silly, once we quantify and focus on costs and benefits. For those with firm political commitments, it might not be hard to answer the question of whether to regulate some air pollutant or to take new steps to increase worker safety. But if air pollution regulation would have only modest health benefits and costs billions of dollars, it would not be a good idea, even to the most committed environmentalists. And if a worker safety regulation would cost relatively little and prevent three hundred premature deaths annually, the argument in opposition would seem stupid or vicious, even to those who think that regulation is a dirty word.

When I was in the Obama administration, two air pollution regulations received a great deal of attention in a short period. One of them involved ozone; the other involved mercury. Environmental groups enthusiastically supported both of them. Business organizations vigorously opposed both of them. In my view, they were fundamentally different. The ozone regulation would produce far lower benefits in terms of public health; if you wanted to reduce premature deaths, the mercury regulation was a lot better. Both regulations were very expensive, but the mercury regulation would cost about $9.5 billion annually, about half of the cost of the ozone regulation. It followed that the ozone regulation was (in my view) hard to defend, because the net benefits would be in the vicinity of zero, whereas the mercury regulation was hard to oppose, because the net benefits would be in the tens of billions of dollars.

The two regulations were spectacularly different, but my strong impression was that to the environmental community, they were essentially the same. And many environmentalists thought it bizarre and inexplicable that the Obama administration (and yours truly) rejected the ozone regulation and supported the mercury regulation. So far as I could tell, the prevailing explanation was that the administration was somehow playing politics. Nothing could be further from the truth. Among the scientists and the economists, the ozone rule was a loser. The mercury rule was a winner.

I do not mean to pick on environmental groups. Business organizations, and those who oppose regulation, often think in the same way. They tend to see environmental regulations as falling in two categories: very burdensome and not very burdensome. The ozone and mercury regulations fell in the former category, and so they were both bad. When government is working well, high-level officials focus on both benefits and costs, and they do not neglect either. They insist on attending to the magnitude of relevant effects, with lots of numbers.

These are points about the importance of a technocratic conception of democracy. I would add that celebration of the cost-benefit revolution, and insistence on attending to numbers, have long seemed especially important in periods in which the left, or something like it, is in charge of some part of the government. In such periods, there is a serious risk that certain kinds of regulatory interventions—worker safety, food safety, the environment—will have the wind at their backs. High-level officials will see these issues in "we vs. they" terms, as if regulations work a kind of transfer from the bad guys (the corporations) to the good guys (the people).

They don't. One problem, of course, is that the real victims of aggressive regulations may be workers (who lose benefits or even jobs), consumers (who pay more for goods, or who may lose access to some goods altogether), or small enterprises (for whom regulation may serve as a stiff tax or even a barrier to entry).

Consider a small example, which haunts me to this day: Under the Montreal Protocol, which is designed to protect the ozone layer, the nations of the world must phase out the use of chloroflourocarbons (CFCs). Some asthma inhalers use CFCs, so to comply with its obligations under the Montreal Protocol, the United States phased out several of them. Of those, at least one inhaler, called MaxAir, had (as I recall) about 250,000 intensely loyal users, many of whom claimed that no other delivery system worked nearly as well for them.

Asthma inhalers contribute very little to the destruction of the ozone layer. On cost-benefit grounds, a ban on MaxAir would be exceedingly hard to defend. (The same might be said for other inhalers.) In my position in the White House, I fought successfully for an extension of time before the ban would come into effect—but I did not fight hard, or hard enough, to stop the ban altogether. True, it would not have been easy to win that fight, because no one else in government seemed to care about the issue, and because some lawyers thought that the Montreal Protocol required the ban. But I am a lawyer too, and I think they were wrong.

The Food and Drug Administration wanted to ban all asthma inhalers that emitted CFCs, and so did the Environmental Protection Agency, and so did the Department of State. In my view, none of them cared nearly enough about asthma sufferers who were used to and depended on particular inhalers. Cost-benefit analysis would have made those people count. In that way, it gives voice to the voiceless. With respect to some inhalers, the ban was dumb, and it was cruel.

A big advantage of cost-benefit analysis is that it reduces the number of such stories. In a left-of-center government, it is a crucial safeguard. But it also has an important role in a right-of-center administration, inclined to be cautious about or even dismissive of regulatory interventions. A demonstration that a safety regulation would save dozens or hundreds of lives every year and cost very little should get people's attention. I have been told that in Republican administrations, cost-benefit analysis has been a spur to regulatory interventions about which high-level officials would otherwise be skeptical.

As I write, Donald Trump is serving as president, and he says that he wants to scale back the regulatory state in a big way. Some of the time, his administration seems to focus on costs, which is great, but not so much on benefits, which is not so great. As we have seen, one of his major initiatives is the "one in, two out" rule, which means that if an agency wants to issue a new regulation, it has to eliminate two others. In the abstract, of course, it sounds like a gimmick, and it's a pretty silly idea. The real question is whether regulations, new or old, are justified. That requires a careful analysis of their costs and their benefits.

For some agencies, the right approach might be "zero in, ten out," because there's no justification for anything new and a lot have to go. For other agencies, the right approach could be "ten in, zero out," because all ten have benefits well exceeding costs, and there's really nothing to eliminate. It follows that the right approach is not "one in, two out" but a careful check on issuing new rules, with the help of cost-benefit analysis—accompanied by an insistence on issuing those rules if the benefits justify the costs and an ambitious program to scrutinize rules on the books to see if they should be scrapped. No administration needs to use a gimmick to make progress on those fronts.

For the Trump administration, the real test is whether agencies will be allowed to go forward with expensive regulations that would deliver benefits that justify that expense. (Recall the mercury rule.) If the cost-benefit revolution is fully in place, it will work to ensure that right-of-center administrations engage in regulatory activity when the numbers suggest that they ought to do so. Under Presidents Reagan, George H. W. Bush, and George W. Bush, precisely that happened—not enough for some people, perhaps, but a lot.

If the Trump administration fails the test, that is a terrible stain, and testimony to the crucial importance of seeing cost-benefit analysis as a spur and a prod, not merely a check and a veto. One way to celebrate the revolution would be for Congress to entrench it, by enacting the requirements of existing executive orders. At the same time, Congress should give affected people a legal right to go to court to require regulations to be issued when the benefits unambiguously justify the costs. It should give voice to the voiceless. If an agency refuses to act even in such circumstances, it should have a duty to explain itself—and if its explanation is not good enough, it should be required to provide the necessary protection.

Beyond Celebrating

Economists like to say that "the perfect is the enemy of the good." John Dewey responded that "the better is often the enemy of the still better." After a while, celebrations get dull. There's too much work to be done. For now, and for the future, the most interesting questions are the limits of the cost-benefit revolution and where we go from here.

A general point involves the immense importance of institutions. One of Reagan's best ideas was to create the Office of Information and Regulatory Affairs, an institution with both power and responsibility. In principle, it has effective veto authority. But in some administrations, its power is diminished, and the more political offices have the upper hand. The Office of the Vice President might have a loud voice on some issues; the same is true of the Domestic Policy Council (a White House office that is often highly attuned to politics). OIRA's ability to ensure careful attention to science and economics inevitably depends on personalities. I was privileged to have a long-standing friendship with President Obama, and he was himself strongly committed to cost-benefit balancing, which strengthened my hand. But for some questions in some administrations, the real questions are seen as insistently political ("What is in the President's political interest now?"), and OIRA's role becomes secondary. It has a seat at the table, but no more than that. When political pressures are intense, references to costs and benefits might seem a bit fussy—even naive.

In this light, there are occasional calls for reliance on a new and more independent institution, created by either Congress or the president, with the authority to check the numbers and to give them public visibility. Call it the Office of Regulatory Accountability, operating apart from the Executive Office of the President, and assured, by tradition or law, a degree of immunity from the White House. True, no president is likely to love that idea; it takes control away from the commander-in-chief. And any OIRA is likely to be skeptical; it will fear that the supposedly independent entity might be either politicized or technically clueless.

Nonetheless, I think that the suggestion is a good one. At least for rules with costs above a certain magnitude—say, $500 million—it makes sense to combine public comment with regular resort to an institution that can produce some kind of reality check. Such an institution should have a high degree of immunity from political winds, and it should be staffed by people who know what they are doing. It should also have the authority to investigate inaction as well as action. It should be authorized to propose rules, to the relevant agency and the American public, that would have high net benefits. As I have emphasized, excessive regulation is bad, but insufficient regulation can be a big problem as well.

Welfare, and Dancing

In terms of the future, I have pressed two points above all. The first, and the most important in principle, is that cost-benefit analysis is only a proxy for welfare effects and therefore cannot give us the complete picture of what we need to know in order to improve welfare. Consider three examples:

1. If a regulation creates serious job losses, it will have a significant negative impact on people's well-being, even if cost-benefit analysis does not recognize or capture that fact. People who lose their jobs suffer serious harm, both economic and psychological. At the moment, cost-benefit analysis ignores that harm. Perhaps it should be amended so that it takes that harm into account. Perhaps regulators should accompany cost-benefit analysis with an analysis of unemployment effects.

2. If a workplace safety regulation imposes $900 million in annual costs on millions of consumers and delivers $700 million in annual benefits (including, say, avoidance of fifty annual deaths), it seems unjustified on cost-benefit grounds, but the welfare losses might be dwarfed by the welfare gains. In cases of this kind, the monetary figures might give us the wrong answer, even if we are focused on the actual effects on people's well-being.

3. It is tempting to rest content with the proposition that a cost of $1 billion is simply and always a cost of $1 billion. But in welfare terms, there might a big difference between a situation in which that cost is imposed on a relatively small number of people and a case in which 250 million people must spend four dollars each. Might it not be true that in the latter case, the welfare loss is small, even once it is aggregated? I am not sure how to answer that question. What is clear is that we need to learn far more about welfare itself.

Cost-benefit analysis is far better than what preceded it, but if we focus more directly on welfare, what is coming will be better still.

The second point involves the knowledge problem. Many people think that agencies regularly cook the numbers, but I have not so argued, and I do not believe that it is true. (Sure, it must happen on occasion. But I never saw it—not even once.) At the same time, agencies certainly make mistakes. Sometimes they overestimate costs; sometimes they underestimate them. Sometimes benefits turn out to be much larger than they expect; sometimes they turn out to be smaller. Cost-benefit analyses are predictions, and sometimes they turn out to be wrong.

Equally important, unintended consequences are common. The world is like a spider's web, or the human body: if you pull on one part, you might get reactions in places you didn't expect. Circumstances may change, leading to far higher or far lower net costs. New technology might develop; prices might spike or fall. Or the world might turn out to be different, in important ways, from how regulators imagined it, leading to consequences that no one, or not enough people, foresaw.

Consider an example with which I was involved: The Affordable Care Act promotes and subsidizes the use of electronic medical records. The admirable idea was that by incentivizing such use, life would end up being easier and better for both doctors and patients. With electronic medical records, it should be very easy to find out a patient's medical history and to track progress and retrogression over time. Whether or not the program has been an overall success, many doctors complain that it has caused them to spend significantly less time with their patients—and significantly more time entering information into a computer. I was involved in many discussions of the issue in government, and no one raised that problem.

I have suggested several strategies for addressing the knowledge problem. First, agencies need to obtain public comment, because members of the public will often have valuable or even indispensable information. Second, retrospective review, with careful attention to costs and benefits, has generated substantial savings; in the future, it should be far more systematic and far more technocratic. One of the benefits of retrospective analysis is that if agencies engage in it, they can use what they learn to make more accurate prospective analyses. Third, agencies should take far more advantage of randomized controlled trials.

Of the strategies I have outlined, the most exciting and intriguing by far is to track actual outcomes in real time (or close to it). The idea of measure-and-react is a terrific model for businesses and political campaigns; it directly addresses the crudeness of before-the-fact prognostications. For some regulatory issues, something like measure-and-react is feasible; consider highway safety, for which we can see outcomes in real time. (Were there crashes last week? How many?) For other issues, it is not, because certain effects develop over extended periods of time; consider increases in heart disease and cancer.

There is every reason to expect that over time, measure-and-react approaches will become more feasible. Even when they are not feasible because of the nature of the problem, at least we should be able to measure, fairly quickly, important variables, including cost (what were they last month?) and proxies for long-term effects (are we seeing significant increases in ambient air quality?). Modern technologies will offer astonishing opportunities for using measure-and-react to overcome the knowledge problem.

As it has developed since the early 1980s, cost-benefit analysis has made governments work much better than they did before—at least when that analysis has been done properly and when the highest-level officials insisted on acting in accordance with it. In terms of saving money and saving lives, the cost-benefit revolution has produced immeasurable improvements. It has stopped bad things, spurred good things, and turned good things into better things. But the revolution remains unfinished. In the fullness of time, it may well turn out to be a transition to something far better, focused more directly on the measurement of human welfare and enlisting unimaginably ambitious strategies to capture and improve the real-world effects of public-sector initiatives.

There will be dancing at that revolution, and I'm coming.

Acknowledgments

Thanks go first to Emily Taber, editor extraordinaire, who helped at every stage and whose wisdom and sharpness made this book a lot better. Two anonymous reviewers offered a host of objections and criticisms; I have tried to respond to them, and though I am sure that I have not done so adequately, the argument is greatly improved as a result of their comments. Sarah Chalfant, my agent, was a great help throughout.

Eric Posner, a terrific colleague and collaborator, has greatly informed my thinking on these topics. I am grateful to him in general and in particular for allowing me to use joint work as chapter 6 here. Of the numerous colleagues whose work, comments, and conversations have provided indispensable help, I single out Matthew Adler, Richard Posner, the late Edna Ullmann-Margalit, Adrian Vermeule, W. Kip Viscusi, and Duncan Watts. The Program on Behavioral Economics and Public Policy at Harvard Law School provided support. Madeleine Joseph provided exceptional research assistance.

I have drawn here on a series of essays that should be seen as initial drafts of chapters of this book. They have also been substantially revised, but I am grateful to the following publications for permission and for superb editorial work: for chapter 2, *Is Cost-Benefit a Foreign Language?*, Journal of Experimental Psychology (2018); for chapter 3, *The Value of A Statistical Life; Some Clarifications and Puzzles*, 42 J. of Cost-Benefit Analysis 237 (2013); for chapter 4, *Cost-Benefit Analysis, Who's Your Daddy?*, 7 J. Cost-Benefit Analysis 107 (2016); for chapter 6, *Moral Commitments and Cost-Benefit Analysis*, 103 Virginia L. Review 1809 (2017), with Eric Posner; for chapter 7, *On Mandatory Labeling*, 165 U. Pa. L. Rev. 1043 (2017); for chapter 8, *Cost-Benefit Analysis and Arbitrariness Review*, 41 Harv. Env. L. Rev. 1 (2017); for chapter 9, *Beyond Cheneyism and Snowdenism*, 83 U. Chi. L. Rev. 271 (2016); and for chapter 10, *Does the Clear and Present Danger Test Survive Cost-Benefit Analysis?*, 104 Cornell L. Rev. (2018).

Notes

1 The Triumph of the Technocrats

1. Exec. Order No. 12291, § 3, 3 C.F.R. 127 (1981), reprinted in 5 U.S.C. § 601 (2012), https://www.archives.gov/federal-register/codification/executive-order/12291.html.

2. Id.

3. See Alan B. Morrison, *OMB Interference with Agency Rulemaking: The Wrong Way to Write a Regulation*, 99 Harv. L. Rev. 5 (1986).

4. See David L. Weimer, *Behavioral Economics for Cost-Benefit Analysis* 6 (2017).

5. Exec. Order No. 12866, 3 C.F.R. 638 (1993), reprinted as amended in 5 U.S.C. § 601 (2012), https://www.archives.gov/files/federal-register/executive-orders/pdf/12866.pdf.

6. Id.

7. Exec. Order No. 13563 § 1, 3 C.F.R. 215, 215-16 (2012), reprinted in 5 U.S.C. § 601 (2012), https://obamawhitehouse.archives.gov/the-press-office/2011/01/18/executive-order-13563-improving-regulation-and-regulatory-review.

8. See Matthew D. Adler and Eric A. Posner, *New Foundations of Cost-Benefit Analysis* (2006); Cass R. Sunstein, *Valuing Life* (2015).

9. See Online Guide to Ethics and Moral Philosophy, Excerpts from Jeremy Bentham (2002), http://caae.phil.cmu.edu/cavalier/80130/part1/sect4/PofU.html.

2 A Foreign Language

1. See Paul Slovic, *The Perception of Risk* (2000).

2. See Roger G. Noll and James E. Krier, *Some Implications of Cognitive Psychology for Risk Regulation*, 19 J. Legal Stud. 747, 749–760 (1990). In this and following paragraphs, I draw on Cass R. Sunstein, *Cognition and Cost-Benefit Analysis*, 29 J. Legal Stud. 1059 (2000).

3. See Amos Tversky and Daniel Kahneman, *Judgment under Uncertainty: Heuristics and Biases*, in Judgment under Uncertainty: Heuristics and Biases 3, 11 (Daniel Kahneman, Paul Slovic, and Amos Tversky eds., 1982), describing the availability heuristic.

4. Jonathan Baron, *Thinking and Deciding* 218 (2d ed. 1994).

5. See David Hirshleifer, *The Blind Leading the Blind: Social Influence, Fads, and Informational Cascades*, in The New Economics of Human Behavior 188 (Mariano Tommasi and Kathyrn Ierulli eds., 1995); Timur Kuran and Cass R. Sunstein, *Availability Cascades and Risk Regulation*, 51 Stan. L. Rev. 683, 720 (1999).

6. See Dietrich Dorner, *The Logic of Failure* (1993).

7. For an overview, see Sayuri Hayakawa et al., *Using a Foreign Language Changes Our Choices*, Trends Cogn. Sci. (forthcoming 2017).

8. Summaries can be found in Daniel Kahneman, *Thinking, Fast and Slow* (2011). For a superb collection, see *Perspectives on Framing* (Gideon Keren ed., 2011).

9. See Boaz Keysar et al., *The Foreign-Language Effect: Thinking in a Foreign Tongue Reduces Decision Biases*, 23 Psych. Science 661 (2012).

10. See Amos Tversky and Daniel Kahneman, *The Framing of Decisions and the Psychology of Choice*, 211 Science 453 (1981).

11. See Keysar et al., supra note 9.

12. Albert Costa et al., *"Piensa" Twice: On the Foreign Language Effect in Decision Making*, 130 Cognition 236 (2014), https://www.ncbi.nlm.nih.gov/pubmed/24334107.

3   Willingness to Pay and the Value of Life

1. See Louis Kaplow and Steven Shavell, *Why the Legal System Is Less Efficient than the Income Tax in Redistributing Wealth*, 23 J. Legal Stud. 667 (1994).

2. The literature appears to begin with Richard Thaler and Sherwin Rosen, *The Value of Saving a Life: Evidence from the Labor Market* (1976), http://www.nber.org/chapters/c3964.pdf.

3. See, e.g., W. Kip Viscusi and Joseph Aldy, *The Value of a Statistical Life*, 27 J. Risk & Uncertainty 5 (2003); W. Kip Viscusi, *The Heterogeneity of the Value of a Statistical Life*, 40 J. Risk & Uncertainty 1 (2010), noting a median value of $7 million to $8 million.

4. For examples in an important and unusually interesting setting, see Sean Hannon Williams, *Statistical Children*, 30 Yale J. Reg. 63 (2013).

5. Peter Diamond and Jerry Hausman, *Contingent Valuation: Is Some Number Better than No Number?*, 8 J. Econ. Persp. 45 (1994).

6. Memorandum from Polly Trottenberg, Under Sec'y for Policy, and Robert S. Rivkin, General Counsel, to Secretarial Officers and Modal Administrators (February 28, 2013), https://www.transportation.gov/sites/dot.dev/files/docs/VSL%20Guidance_2013.pdf.

7. See, generally, Russell Korobkin, *The Endowment Effect and Legal Analysis*, 97 Nw. U. L. Rev. 1227 (2003), which explains the so-called endowment effect, by which individuals often demand more to relinquish an item (WTA) than they would pay to obtain that same item (WTP).

8. See Thomas Kniesner et al., *Willingness to Accept Equals Willingness to Pay for Labor Market Estimates of the Value of Statistical Life* (2013), http://papers.ssrn.com/sol3/papers.cfm?abstract_id=2221038.

9. For varying perspectives, see, e.g., John Bronsteen et al., *Well-Being Analysis versus Cost-Benefit Analysis*, 62 Duke L. J. 1603 (2013); Peter Dorman, *Markets and Mortality* (1996); Peter Dorman and Paul Hagstrom, *Wage Compensation for Dangerous Work Revisited*, 52 Indus. & Lab. Rel. Rev. 116 (1998); Orley Ashenfelter and Michael Greenstone, *Using Mandated Speed Limits to Measure the Value of a Statistical Life* (2002), http://www.nber.org/papers/w9094.

10. On definitional questions, see Matthew D. Adler, *Happiness Surveys and Public Policy: What's the Use?*, 62 Duke L. J. 1509 (2013); Carol Graham, *An Economist's Perspective on Well-Being Analysis and Cost-Benefit Analysis*, 62 Duke L. J. 1691 (2013).

11. John Stuart Mill, *On Liberty* 8 (Kathy Casey ed., 2002) (1859).

12. See Ronald Dworkin, *Sovereign Virtue* (2002). For a tentative suggestion that autonomy might be a heuristic for welfare, see Cass R. Sunstein, *The Storrs Lectures: Behavioral Economics and Paternalism*, 113 Yale L. J. 1826 (2013).

13. There is a question of whether a "cancer premium" is justified by the existing literature. For an affirmative answer, see US Environmental Protection Agency, Valuing Mortality Risk Reductions for Environmental Policy: A White Paper (review draft, 2010), prepared by the National Center for Environmental Economics for consultation with the Science Advisory Board—Environmental Economics Advisory Committee. For an ambivalent view, see C. L. Kling et al., Review of 'Valuing Mortality Risk Reductions for Environmental Policy: A White Paper' (December 10, 2010), memorandum to Lisa P. Jackson, EPA Administrator, from the EPA Science Advisory Board and Environmental Economics Advisory Committee, EPA-SAB-11-011 (2011).

14. For different perspectives, see Sean Hannon Williams, *Statistical Children*, 30 Yale J. Reg. 63 (2013); Joanne Leung and Jagadish Guna, *Value of Statistical Life: Adults versus Children*, 38 Accident Illness and Prevention 1208 (2006).

15. Joseph Aldy and W. Kip Viscusi, *Age Differences in the Value of Statistical Life*, 1 Review of Environmental Economics and Policy 241 (2007). See also C. L. Kling et

al., Review of 'Valuing Mortality Risk Reductions for Environmental Policy: A White Paper' (December 10, 2010), memorandum to Lisa P. Jackson, EPA Administrator, from the EPA Science Advisory Board and Environmental Economics Advisory Committee, EPA-SAB-11-01, at 8 (2011).

16. See, e.g., Ted R. Miller, *Variations between Countries in Value of a Statistical Life*, 34 J. Transport Economics and Policy 169 (2000).

17. Price V. Fishback and Shawn Everett Kantor, *A Prelude to the Welfare State* 69, app. D at 231–238 (2000).

18. See Cass R. Sunstein, *Risk and Reason* (2002), noting that a particular proposal to increase drinking water quality would have resulted in an annual increase of thirty dollars in the water bills for most households.

19. Matthew E. Kahn, *The Beneficiaries of Clean Air Act Regulation*, 24 Reg. 34, 35–38 (2001). A different view can be found in R. J. Hedbegian, W. Gray, and C. Morgan, *Benefits and Costs from Sulfur Dioxide Trading: A Distributional Analysis*, in Acid in the Environment: Lessons Learned and Future Prospects (G. R. Visgilio and D. M. Whitelaw eds., 2007).

20. For an analysis and explanation of the idea of miswanting, see Daniel T. Gilbert and Timothy D. Wilson, *Miswanting*, in Feeling and Thinking: The Role of Affect in Social Cognition 178, 179 (Joseph P. Forgas ed., 2000). See generally Timothy D. Wilson and Daniel T. Gilbert, *Affective Forecasting*, in 35 Advances in Experimental Social Psychology 345 (Mark P. Zanna ed., 2003), analyzing people's ability to accurately predict their own feelings.

21. See Elizabeth Dunn and Michael Norton, *Happy Money* (2013).

22. See Daniel Kahneman and Carol Varey, *Notes on the Psychology of Utility*, in Interpersonal Comparisons of Utility (Jon Elster and John Roemer eds. 1991), distinguishing between experience utility and predicted utility.

23. See Jon Elster, *Sour Grapes* 109–110 (1983), defining "adaptive preferences" as what happens when "people tend to adjust their aspirations to their possibilities"; Matthew D. Adler and Eric A. Posner, *Implementing Cost-Benefit Analysis When Preferences Are Distorted*, 29 J. Legal Stud. 1105–1147 (2000), hypothesizing, for instance, that "people are not willing to pay for parks because they have adapted to a world without parks."

24. Alexis de Tocqueville, *Democracy in America* 317 (1969).

25. Kahneman and Varey, supra note 22, at 128–129.

26. Daniel J. Benjamin et al., *What Do You Think Would Make You Happier? What Do You Think You Would Choose?*, 102 Am. Econ. Rev. 2083, 2085–2086 (2012).

27. See Niklas Karlsson, George Loewenstein, and Jane McCafferty, *The Economics of Meaning*, 30 Nordic J. Pol. Econ. 61, 62 (2004); Peter A. Ubel and George Loewen-

stein, *Pain and Suffering Awards: They Shouldn't Be (Just) About Pain and Suffering*, 37 J. Legal Stud. 195, 206–207 (2008).

28. Benjamin et al., supra note 26, at 2085.

29. See Serene Khader, *Adaptive Preferences and Women's Empowerment* (2011).

30. Amartya Sen, *Rationality and Freedom* 287 (2002).

31. Id., at 289 (emphasis omitted).

32. Relevant discussion can be found in M.W. Jones-Lee, *Paternalistic Altruism and the Value of a Statistical Life*, 102 Ec. Journal 80 (1992); M. W. Jones-Lee, *Altruism and the Value of Other People's Safety*, 4 J. Risk & Uncertainty 213 (1991).

33. See Richard Arneson, *Luck Egalitarianism and Prioritarianism*, 110 Ethics 339, 343 (2000); see also Matthew D. Adler, *Future Generations: A Prioritarian View*, 77 G.W. L. Rev. 1478 (2009); Matthew D. Adler, *Well-Being and Fair Distribution* (2011).

34. W. Kip Viscusi, *The Benefits of Mortality Risk Reduction*, 62 Duke L. J. 1735 (2013).

35. See J. R. Hicks, *The Rehabilitation of Consumer Surplus*, 8 Rev. Econ. Stud. 108, 111 (1941).

36. See Adler, supra note 33.

37. See, e.g., Louis Kaplow and Steven Shavell, *Why the Legal System Is Less Efficient than the Income Tax in Redistributing Income*, 23 J. Legal Stud. 667, 667 (1994): "Redistribution through legal rules offers no advantage over redistribution through the income tax system and typically is less efficient." See also Steven Shavell, *A Note on Efficiency vs. Distributional Equity in Legal Rulemaking: Should Distributional Equity Matter Given Optimal Income Taxation?*, 71 Am. Econ. Rev. Papers & Proc. 414, 414 (1981), describing how an income tax can compensate for inefficient liability rules and redistribute income; David A. Weisbach, *Should Legal Rules Be Used to Redistribute Income?*, 70 U. Chi. L. Rev. 439, 439 (2003).

38. See Matthew D. Adler, *The Ethical Value of Risk Reduction: Utilitarianism, Prioritarianism and Cost-Benefit Analysis*, in Ethics and Risk Management 9 (Lisa Svedin ed., 2015).

39. See Dennis Cory and Lester Taylor, *On the Distributional Implications of Safe Drinking Water Standards*, 8 J. Benefit-Cost Analysis 49 (2017).

4   Welfare

1. See Jonathan Masur and Eric A. Posner, *Regulation, Unemployment, and Cost-Benefit Analysis*, 98 Va. L. Rev. 580 (2012). Masur and Posner refer to several sources, including Andrew E. Clark and Andrew J. Oswald, *Unhappiness and Unemployment*, 104

Econ. J. 648, 650–651 (1994), finding that unemployment is associated with significantly lower self-reported mental well-being; William T. Gallo et al., *The Persistence of Depressive Symptoms in Older Workers Who Experience Involuntary Job Loss: Results from the Health and Retirement Survey*, 61 J. Gerontol. B. Psychol. Sci. Soc. Sci. S221, S221 (2006), finding that older, lower net-worth workers who lose their jobs are more likely to suffer from depression than those who do not; and Knut Gerlach and Gesine Stephan, *A Paper on Unhappiness and Unemployment in Germany*, 52 Econ. Letters 325, 325 (1996), finding that unemployment reduces life satisfaction beyond what would be expected from the loss of income.

2. See Masur and Posner, supra note 1.

3. See https://www.federalregister.gov/articles/2014/04/07/2014-07469/federal-motor-vehicle-safety-standards-rear-visibility. The example is real, but the numbers definitely are not. For the actual numbers, see id.

4. Overviews can be found in Paul Dolan, *Happiness by Design* (2014); Daniel Kahneman et al., *Well-Being* (2002); and Daniel Gilbert, *Stumbling on Happiness* (2006). I am bracketing the question of whether it is best to have a subjective or objective account of welfare; certainly, subjective welfare matters, even if we adopt an objective account. Valuable discussion can be found in Matthew D. Adler, *Well-Being and Fair Distribution: Beyond Cost-Benefit Analysis* (2011).

5. See Dolan, supra note 4.

6. See id.

7. See Richard Layard, *Happiness* (2006).

8. For discussion, see Cass R. Sunstein, *Illusory Losses*, 37 J. Legal Stud. S157 (2008).

9. *Subjective Well-Being: Measuring Happiness, Suffering, and Other Dimensions of Experience* (A. A. Stone and C. Mackie eds., 2014).

10. Daniel Kahneman and Jason Riis, *Living, and Thinking about It: Two Perspectives on Life*, in The Science of Well-Being (N. Baylis et al. eds., 2005), http://www.princeton.edu/~kahneman/docs/Publications/Living_DK_JR_2005.pdf.

11. *Subjective Well-Being*, supra note 9, at 33.

12. See Kahneman and Riis, supra note 10.

13. See id. Dolan, supra note 4, argues for the priority of experienced well-being. *Subjective Well-Being*, supra note 9, concludes that multiple dimensions exist and are worth measuring. Id., at 32.

14. See *Subjective Well-Being*, supra note 9.

15. Id., at 33. See also the discussion of *eudaimonic well-being*, drawn from ideas about human flourishing, in id., at 18.

16. For various views, see Deirdre McCloskey, *Happyism*, New Republic (2012), http://www.newrepublic.com/article/politics/magazine/103952/happyism-deirdre -mccloskey-economics-happiness; Richard Layard, *Happiness* (2005); Daniel Kahneman et al., *A Survey Method for Characterizing Daily Life Experience: The Day Reconstruction Method*, Science 1776 (2004); Peter Ubel and George Loewenstein, *Pain and Suffering: It's Not (Just) about Pain and Suffering*, 37 J. Legal Stud. (2007). Adler, supra note 4, includes highly relevant discussion.

17. Aside from issues about specific studies, there is a pervasive question about whether and how people use the relevant scales. For example, do they engage in "scale recalibration?" Perhaps they think, for example, "I am a 7, on a scale of 1 to 10, considering that I need to use a wheelchair," instead of "I am a 4, on a scale of 1 to 10, because I need to use a wheelchair." For a strong argument that scale recalibration is not a serious problem, see Heather Lacey et al., *Are They Really That Happy? Exploring Scale Recalibration in Estimates of Well-Being*, 27 Health Psychology 669 (2008).

18. See McCloskey, supra note 16.

19. See Cass R. Sunstein, *Who Knows If You're Happy?*, NY Review of Books (2014), http://www.nybooks.com/articles/archives/2014/dec/04/who-knows-if-youre -happy/.

20. See John Stuart Mill, *Bentham*, in Utilitarianism and Other Essays 132 (Alan Ryan ed., 1987).

21. See Daniel Benjamin et al., *Beyond Happiness and Satisfaction: Toward Well-Being Indices Based on Stated Preference*, 104 Am. Econ. Rev. 2698 (2014).

22. Id.

23. See John Bronsteen, Christopher Buccafusco, and Jonathan S. Masur, *Well-Being Analysis vs. Cost-Benefit Analysis*, 62 Duke L. J. 1603, 1670–1679 (2013), discussing VSL's limitations and possible alternative measures.

24. Nattavudh Powdthavee and Bernard van den Berg, *Putting Different Price Tags on the Same Health Condition: Re-evaluating the Well-Being Valuation Approach*, 30 J. Health Econ. 1032, 1038 tbl.3 (2011).

25. Id., at 1644.

26. See Raj Chetty, *Behavioral Economics and Public Policy: A Pragmatic Perspective*, Am. Econ. Rev. 25 (Papers and Proceedings) (2015).

5 The Knowledge Problem

1. See Friedrich Hayek, *The Uses of Knowledge in Society*, 35 Am. Econ. Rev. 519 (1945).

2. Hayek, supra note 1.

3. Duncan Watts, *Everything Is Obvious* (2011); Jim Manzi, *Uncontrolled: The Surprising Payoff of Trial-and-Error for Business, Politics, and Society* (2012); Michael Greenstone, *Toward a Culture of Persistent Regulatory Experimentation and Evaluation*, in New Perspectives on Regulation 113, 113 (David Moss and John Cisterno eds., 2009). A relevant discussion, involving quasi-experimental techniques in an especially important area, is found in Francesca Dominici et al., *Particulate Matter Matters*, 244 Science 257 (2014). It is true that randomized controlled experiments have been subject to some concerns. See Angus Deaton, *Instruments of Development* (2009), http://www.nber.org/papers/w14690.

4. See Daniel Ernst, *Toqueville's Nightmare* (2013), for a valuable discussion of the background.

5. The classic discussion is James Landis, *The Administrative Process* (1935).

6. Exec. Order No. 13563, http://www.gpo.gov/fdsys/pkg/FR-2011-01-21/pdf/2011-1385.pdf.

7. Winston Harrington, Grading Estimates of the Benefits and Costs of Federal Regulation (Res. for the Future, Paper No. 06-39, 2006), http://papers.ssrn.com/sol3/papers.cfm?abstract_id=937357.

8. Winston Harrington et al., *On the Accuracy of Regulatory Cost Estimates*, 19 J. Pol'y Analysis and Mgmt. 297 (2000).

9. See Office of Management and Budget, *Validating Regulatory Analysis: 2005 Report to Congress on the Costs and Benefits of Federal Regulations and Unfunded Mandates on State, Local, and Tribal Entities* 41–46 (2005), http://www.whitehouse.gov/sites/default/files/omb/assets/omb/inforeg/2005_cb/final_2005_cb_report.pdf. This report collects studies comparing ex ante and ex post analyses of regulations' costs and benefits, including examples in which cost and benefit estimates were off by more than a factor of ten.

10. Exec. Order No. 13610, 3 C.F.R. 258 (2012), reprinted in 5 U.S.C. § 601 at 820–821 (2012).

11. See generally Abhijit Banerjee amd Esther Duflo, *Poor Economics* (2011).

12. Charlotte L. Brace et al., *Analysis of the Literature: The Use of Mobile Phones while Driving* (2007), http://www.nsc.org/news_resources/Resources/Documents/Analysis%20of%20the%20Literature,%20The%20Use%20of%20Mobile%20Phones%20While%20Driving.pdf.

13. Saurabh Bhargava and Vikram S. Pathania, *Driving under the (Cellular) Influence*, 5 Am. Econ. J.: Econ. Policy 92, http://pubs.aeaweb.org/doi/pdfplus/10.1257/pol.5.3.92.

14. See David Halpern, *Inside the Nudge Unit* (2015).

15. See Duncan Watts, *Everything Is Obvious* (2010).

6   Moral Commitments

1. Conflict Minerals, 77 Fed. Reg. 56,274, 56,277–278 (September 12, 2012) (codified at 17 C.F.R. pts. 240 and 249b).

2. 16 U.S.C. § 1385 (2012).

3. Id.

4. Sydney E. Scott et al., *Evidence for Absolute Moral Opposition to Genetically Modified Food in the United States*, 11 Perspectives on Psychol. Sci. 315, 316 (2016).

5. National Bioengineered Food Disclosure Standard, Pub. L. No. 114-216 (2016) (codified at 7 U.S.C. § 1621 *et seq.* (2016)).

6. On some of the challenges and potential solutions in an especially difficult context, see Sean Hannon Williams, *Statistical Children*, 30 Yale J. Reg. 63 (2013).

7. See Ohio v. United States Dep't of the Interior, 880 F.2d 432 (DC Cir 1989).

8. The EPA so concluded in issuing the regulation at issue in *Entergy Corp v. Riverkeeper, Inc.*, 556 U.S. 208 (2009).

9. Frank Ackerman and Elizabeth A. Stanton, Comments on Regulation of Cooling Water Intake Structures at Existing Facilities (August 8, 2011), http://frankackerman .com/publications/costbenefit/Regulation_Cooling_Water.pdf.

10. *Ohio*, 880 F.2d, at 462–64.

11. See John Quiggin, *Existence Value and the Contingent Valuation Method*, 37 Australian Econ. Papers 312 (1998), http://onlinelibrary.wiley.com/doi/10.1111/1467-8454.00022/abstract.

12. For skeptical views, see Jerry Hausman, *Contingent Valuation: From Dubious to Hopeless*, 26 J. Econ. Persp. 43 (2012); Daniel Kahmeman and Jack Knetsch, *Valuing Public Goods*, 22 J. Envtl. Econ. & Mgmt. 57 (1992).

13. United States Dep't of Justice, Regulatory Impact Assessment for Prison Rape Elimination Act Final Rule (May 17, 2012), http://www.ojp.usdoj.gov/programs/pdfs/prea_ria.pdf.

14. See Conflict Minerals, 77 Fed. Reg. 56,274, 56,277–56,278 (September 12, 2012) (codified at 17 C.F.R. pts. 240 and 249b).

15. See Richard Brandt, *A Theory of the Good and the Right* (1998).

7   On Mandatory Labeling

1. See Howard Beales et al., *The Efficient Regulation of Consumer Information*, 24 J. L. & Econ. 491, 502 (1981).

2. Oren Bar-Gill and Oliver Board, *Product-Use Information and the Limits of Voluntary Disclosure*, 14 Am. L. & Econ. Rev. 235, 237 (2012).

3. For a summary from the FDA itself, see Gluten and Food Labeling, US Food & Drug Administration, http://www.fda.gov/Food/GuidanceRegulation/GuidanceDoc umentsRegulatoryInformation/Allergens/ucm367654.htm.

4. See Daniel Kahneman, *Attention and Effort* (1973); Sendhil Mullainathan and Eldar Shafir, *Scarcity* (2013).

5. One example is Revisions and Additions to Motor Vehicle Fuel Economy Label, 76 Fed. Reg. 39,478, 39,517 (proposed July 6, 2011) (to be codified at 40 C.F.R. pts. 85, 86, 600; 49 C.F.R. pt. 575) [hereinafter Fuel Economy Labels Rule]. In short, "The primary benefits associated with this rule are associated with improved consumer decision making resulting from improved presentation of information. At this time, EPA and NHTSA do not have data to quantify these impacts."

6. See Hunt Allcott and Judd B. Kessler, *The Welfare Effects of Nudges: A Case Study of Energy Use Social Comparisons* 2 (Nat'l Bureau of Econ. Research, Working Paper No. 21,671, 2015), http://www.nber.org/papers/w21671(https://perma.cc/9MD3-8QX2), noting that nudges "can affect behavior without changing prices or choice sets."

7. See Maria L. Loureiro et al., *Do Consumers Value Nutritional Labels?*, 33 Eur. Rev. Agric. Econ. 249, 263 (2006), finding that "on average, consumers are willing to pay close to 11 per cent above the initial price to obtain cookies with nutritional label-ling"; see also id., at 249: "Consistent with prior expectations, our results also indi-cate a difference between the [willingness-to-pay] of individuals suffering from diet-related health problems (estimated mean 13 per cent) and those who do not suffer any diet-related health problems (estimated mean 9 per cent)."

8. See Required Warnings for Cigarette Packages and Advertisements, 76 Fed. Reg. 36,628, 36,719 (proposed June 22, 2011) (to be codified at 21 C.F.R. pt. 1141), http:// www.fda.gov/downloads/TobaccoProducts/Labeling/RulesRegulationsGuidance/ UCM339834.pdf (https://perma.cc/UY5U-JJEE), noting the longer lifespans, fewer cancers and diseases, and increased property and monetary values of nonsmokers; Improve Tracking of Workplace Injuries and Illnesses, 81 Fed. Reg. 29,624, 29,628 (proposed May 12, 2016) (to be codified at 29 C.F.R. pts. 1904, 1902) [hereinafter OSHA Reporting Requirement Rule], requiring that employees have access to OSHA logs; and Revisions and Additions to Motor Vehicle Fuel Economy Label, 76 Fed. Reg. 39,478, 39,517 (proposed July 6, 2011) (to be codified at 40 C.F.R. pts. 85, 86, 600; 49 C.F.R. pt. 575): "The agencies believe that informed choice is an end in itself, even if it is hard to quantify; the agencies also believe that the new labels will

provide significant benefits for consumers, including economic benefits, though these benefits cannot be quantified at this time." See also Calorie Label Rule Impact Analysis, US Food & Drug Admin., FDA-2011-F-0172, Food Labeling: Nutrition Labeling of Standard Menu Items in Restaurants and Similar Retail Food Establishments 11 (2014), at 11: "The final rule may also assist consumers by making the long-term health consequences of consumer food choices more salient and by providing contextual cues of food consumption."

9. Food Safety: Frequently Asked Questions on Genetically Modified Foods, World Health Org., http://www.who.int/foodsafety/areas_work/food-technology/faq-genetically-modified-food/en/(https://perma.cc/JF9F-6Q6C).

10. R. Michael Roberts, *Genetically Modified Organisms for Agricultural Food Production: The Extent of the Art and the State of the Science*, in Labeling Genetically Modified Food 10–11 (Paul Weirich ed., 2007).

11. See id., at 11–12, providing a brief overview of the process of creating GMOs.

12. See Hans De Steur et al., *Status and Market Potential of Transgenic Biofortified Crops*, 33 Nature Biotechnology 25, 25–26 (2015), describing "Golden Rice," which is fortified with vitamin A and was able to "expand the range of micronutrient strategies available to malnourished populations"; and L. L. Wolfenbarger and P. R. Phifer, *The Ecological Risks and Benefits of Genetically Engineered Plants*, 290 Sci. 2088, 2091 (2000), discussing sustainability of crops that have "insecticidal properties, viral resistance, or herbicide tolerance."

13. Jorge Fernandez-Cornejo et al., US Dep't of Agric., No. 162, Genetically Engineered Crops in the United States 2 (2014), https://www.ers.usda.gov/webdocs/publications/err162/43668_err162.pdf (https://perma.cc/H7H5-W4B4).

14. Id.

15. See *About Genetically Engineered Foods*, Ctr. for Food Safety, http://www.centerforfoodsafety.org/issues/311/ge-foods/about-ge-foods (https://perma.cc/H7PK-FDYL): "It has been estimated that upwards of 75% of processed foods on supermarket shelves—from soda to soup, crackers to condiments—contain genetically engineered ingredients."

16. See Peter Celec et al., *Biological and Biomedical Aspects of Genetically Modified Food*, 59 Biomedicine & Pharmacotherapy 531, 532–533 (2005), discussing the potential for genes to "improve[] flavor characteristics," "increase nutritional status of the foods," and confer higher food qualities, such as "shelf-life, taste, nutritional value."

17. See Andrew Pollack, *U.S.D.A. Approves Modified Potato. Next Up: French Fry Fans*, N.Y. Times (November 7, 2014), http://www.nytimes.com/2014/11/08/business/genetically-modified-potato-from-simplot-approved-by-usda.html (https://perma.cc/46FK-TXF8): "The potato's DNA has been altered so that less of a chemical

called acrylamide, which is suspected of causing cancer in people, is produced when the potato is fried. The new potato also resists bruising."

18. See Xudong Ye et al., *Engineering the Provitamin A (ß-Carotene) Biosynthetic Pathway into (Carotenoid-Free) Rice Endosperm*, 287 Science 303 (2000), discussing how genetically engineered rice can combat vitamin A deficiency; see also Robert E. Black et al., *Maternal and Child Undernutrition and Overweight in Low-Income and Middle-Income Countries*, 382 Lancet 427, 433 (2013), finding Vitamin A deficiencies to be responsible for 157,000 deaths of those aged five years and younger in 2011.

19. See Martina Newell-McGloughlin, *Nutritionally Improved Agricultural Crops*, 147 Plant Physiology 939, 940 tbl.I (2008), http://www.plantphysiol.org/content/147/3/939.full-text.pdf, listing canola, maize, and soybeans as crops with high "Lys." Newell-McGloughlin provides an overview of techniques for and products of GM nutritional supplementing—with carbohydrates, fiber, vitamins, and more—as well as for reduced antinutrients, allergens, and toxins.

20. See Barry J. Lamphear et al., *Expression of the Sweet Protein Brazzein in Maize for Production of a New Commercial Sweetener*, 3 Plant Biotechnology J. 103, 109 (2005), reporting on "the use of a maize expression system for the economical production of the intensely sweet protein, brazzein, for both low- and high-intensity sweetener markets."

21. See Hortense W. Dodo et al., *Alleviating Peanut Allergy Using Genetic Engineering: The Silencing of the Immunodominant Allergen Ara h 2 Leads to Its Significant Reduction and a Decrease in Peanut Allergenicity*, 6 Plant Biotechnology J. 135, 140 (2007), reporting that the study produced "a significant reduction in the level of Ara h 2, the most immunodominant peanut allergen"; see also Steven Novella, *CRISPR and a Hypoallergenic Peanut*, Neurologica Blog (October 8, 2015), http://theness.com/neurologicablog/index.php/crispr-and-a-hypoallergenic-peanut/ (https://perma.cc/RRJ3-S9KB): "In 2005 a study was published showing that it is possible to silence the gene for the Ara H2 protein, the primary allergenic protein in peanuts. A 2008 follow up by the same team showed decreased allergenicity of the altered peanut."

22. See Celine A. Hayden et al., *Oral Delivery of Wafers Made from HBsAg-expressing Maize Germ Induces Long-term Immunological Systemic and Mucosal Responses*, 33 Vaccine 2881, 2885 (2015), reporting that there was "evidence for long-term efficacy … [and] safety of oral administration of the wafers"; see also Celine A. Hayden et al., *Production of Highly Concentrated, Heat-Stable Hepatitis B Surface Antigen in Maize*, Plant Biotechnology J. 979, 984 (2012), reporting the results of further studies; and Celine A. Hayden et al., *Bioencapsulation of the Hepatitis B Surface Antigen and Its Use as an Effective Oral Immunogen*, 30 Vaccine 2937, 2940–2942 (2012).

23. See Fred H. Degnan, Biotechnology and the Food Label, in *Labeling Genetically Modified Food*, supra note 10, at 17, 17, discussing "the FDA's science-backed conclusion that, as a general rule, there is nothing inherently unsafe or mysterious about

food biotechnology." For a more recent overview, see US Food & Drug Admin., Guidance for Industry: Voluntary Labeling Indicating Whether Foods Have or Have Not Been Derived from Genetically Engineered Plants (November 2015), http://www .fda.gov/Food/GuidanceRegulation/GuidanceDocumentsRegulatoryInformation/ LabelingNutrition/ucm059098.htm (https://perma.cc/YY79-H86J) [hereinafter Voluntary GMO Labeling Guidance].

24. Am. Ass'n for the Advancement of Sci., Statement by the AAAS Board of Directors on Labeling of Genetically Modified Foods (2012), http://www.aaas.org/sites/ default/files/AAAS_GM_statement.pdf (https://perma.cc/J7E4-NBDE).

25. See Nat'l Acads. of Sci., Eng'g, & Med., *Genetically Engineered Crops: Experiences and Prospects* 10 (2016) [hereinafter Genetically Engineered Crops Report].

26. Id., at xvii.

27. Id., at 10; see also Labeling of Foods Derived from Genetically Engineered Plants, US Food & Drug Admin., http://www.fda.gov/Food/IngredientsPackagingLabeling/ GEPlants/ucm346858.htm (https://perma.cc/B4RC-LP7R): "The agency is not aware of any information showing that foods derived from genetically engineered plants, as a class, differ from other foods in any meaningful or uniform way. These foods also don't present different or greater safety concerns than their non-genetically engineered counterparts."

28. Genetically Engineered Crops Report, supra note 25, at 10.

29. Am. Ass'n for the Advancement of Sci., Statement by the AAAS Board of Directors on Labeling of Genetically Modified Foods (October 20, 2012), http://www.aaas .org/sites/default/files/AAAS_GM_statement.pdf (https://perma.cc/3FFK-7QQG).

30. Ioannis Economidis, Danuta Cichocka, and Jens Högel, *A Decade of EU-Funded GMO Research (2001–2010)*, in European Comm'n, A Decade of EU-Funded GMO Research (2001–2010) 15–17 (2010), https://ec.europa.eu/research/biosociety/pdf/ a_decade_of_eu-funded_gmo_research.pdf (https://perma.cc/RL8J-AAFK).

31. See Genetically Engineered Crops Report, supra note 25, at 8: "Overall, the committee found no conclusive evidence of cause-and-effect relationships between GE crops and environmental problems."

32. See id., stating that studies of monarch populations "have not shown that suppression of milkweed by glyphosate is the cause of monarch decline."

33. See Council on Sci. & Pub. Health, *Labeling of Bioengineered Foods* 2 (2012): "Bioengineered foods have been consumed for close to 20 years, and during that time, no overt consequences on human health have been reported and/or substantiated in the peer-reviewed literature."

34. Nassim Nicholas Taleb et al., *The Precautionary Principle (with Application to the Genetic Modification of Organisms)* 10 (Extreme Risk Initiative—NYU Sch. of

Eng'g Working Paper Series, 2014), http://www.fooledbyrandomness.com/pp2.pdf (https://perma.cc/66NY-972V).

35. See, e.g., Emily Glass, *The Environmental Impact of GMOs, One Green Planet* (August 2, 2013), http://www.onegreenplanet.org/animalsandnature/the-environmental-impact-of-gmos/ (https://perma.cc/K23Z-Y7YD): "GMOs may be toxic to non-target organisms, [including] bees and butterflies. ... There is potential for GMO's [*sic*] ... to become invasive species in delicate, natural ecosystems ... Biodiversity ... is put at risk by GMOS." For a deeper look into the risks posed by GMOs to biodiversity, see World Conservation Union, *Current Knowledge of the Impacts of Genetically Modified Organisms on Biodiversity and Human Health* 22–31 (2007), https://cmsdata.iucn.org/downloads/ip_gmo_09_2007_1_.pdf (https://perma.cc/YH5P-UEJP), which discusses habitat change, pollution, invasive alien species, and risk management; and Heather Landry, *Challenging Evolution: How GMOs Can Influence Genetic Diversity*, Harv. U.: Sci. News (August 10, 2015), http://sitn.hms.harvard.edu/flash/2015/challenging-evolution-how-gmos-can-influence-genetic-diversity/ (https://perma.cc/6J5R-WV7N), which notes, "Although there is little evidence that GMOs have impacted genetic diversity in today's environment, scientists and ecologists are very aware of the potential influence that GMOs have on biodiversity."

36. See Sarah L. Bates et al., *Insect Resistance Management in GM Crops: Past, Present and Future*, 23 Nature Biotechnology 57, 58 (2005), discussing mandated monitoring of GMO resistance.

37. See World Conservation Union, supra note 35, at 7: "Proponents for GM claim ... production can be enhanced while indirectly reducing environmental impacts, for example, through less use of pesticides or fertilizers."

38. Scott et al., *Evidence for Absolute Moral Opposition to Genetically Modified Food in the United States*, 11 Persp. on Psychol. Sci. 316, 317 (2016).

39. See Cass R. Sunstein, *Do People Like Nudges?*, 68 Admin. L. Rev. 177, 191 tbl.3 (2016).

40. See Why Label It? Just Label It, http://www.justlabelit.org/right-to-know-center/right-to-know/ (http://perma.cc/44BA-M3CP): "While our reasons for wanting to know what's in our food may vary, what unifies us is the belief that it's our right."

41. See Sunstein, supra note 39, at 189, finding "strong majority support (73 percent) for a mandatory warning label on products that have unusually high levels of salt." Similar findings have been made in Europe. See Lucia A. Reisch and Cass R. Sunstein, *Do Europeans Like Nudges?*, 11 Judgment & Decision Making 310, 316 fig.2 (2016), showing 69–90 percent support for government-mandated labels for foods containing high levels of salt across different European countries.

42. See Scott et al., supra note 38, at 316–317, studying "the roles of disgust and moral absolutism in Americans' attitudes toward genetically modified food."

43. Id.

44. See Paul Rozin and April E. Fallon, *A Perspective on Disgust*, 94 Psychol. Rev. 23, 23 (1987): "Like other basic emotions, disgust has a characteristic facial expression. … an appropriate action (distancing of the self from an offensive object), a distinctive physiological manifestation (nausea), and a characteristic feeling state (revulsion)."

45. See Jonathan Baron and Sarah Leshner, *How Serious Are Expressions of Protected Values?*, 6 J. Experimental Psychol.: Applied 183, 192 (2000), noting that individuals "will accept actions that violate [their protected values] if the probability or amount of the harm is small relative to the probability and magnitude of benefit."

46. See Memorandum from Andrew Dyke and Robert Whelan, ECONorthwest, to Consumers Union 1 (September 12, 2014), https://consumersunion.org/wp-content/uploads/2014/09/GMO_labeling_cost_findings_Exe_Summ.pdf, finding that the median estimated cost of mandatory labeling is $2.30 per person per year.

47. Taleb et al., supra note 34. Note that Taleb et al. defend the Precautionary Principle "in extreme situations: when the potential harm is systemic (rather than localized) and the consequences can involve total irreversible ruin, such as the extinction of human beings or all life on the planet."

48. *Lessons from Wingspread*, in Protecting Public Health and the Environment: Implementing the Precautionary Principle, app. A at 353–354 (Carolyn Raffensperger and Joel A. Tickner eds., 1999) (quoting the Wingspread Statement on the Precautionary Principle). The Wingspread Declaration was issued by a group of international scientists, government officials, lawyers, labor activists, and grassroots environmental activists following a meeting at Wingspread in Racine, Wisconsin to discuss the Precautionary Principle. See id., at 349.

49. Quoted in Bjorn Lomborg, *The Skeptical Environmentalist* 347 (2001).

50. See id., at 348.

51. For a valuable and subtle discussion, see Daniel Steel, *Risk and the Precautionary Principle* (2014). Of course, we could imagine varieties of Cheneyism and Snowdenism that take many different forms. They might, for example, suggest that the danger is real and present, and not conjectural or probabilistic. Even in those forms, however, the analysis here is essentially unaffected. As the interest in national security or in privacy protection begins to focus on the full range of variables at stake—including expected outcomes and probabilities—it begins to converge on the risk-management approach that I mean to endorse.

52. See Kenneth Arrow and Anthony Fischer, *Environmental Preservation, Uncertainty and Irreversibility*, 88 Q. J. Economics 312, 313–314 (1974).

53. Id., at 319.

54. See Anthony C. Fisher, *Uncertainty, Irreversibility, and the Timing of Climate Policy* 9 (2001), http://are.berkeley.edu/courses/IAS175/Spring2006/pdfs/Fisher.pdf.

55. I use the word *uncertain* to refer to both risk and uncertainty. *Risk* exists when it is possible to assign probabilities to various outcomes; *uncertainty* exists when no probabilities can be assigned. For the seminal discussion, which has prompted a heated debate, see Frank H. Knight, *Risk, Uncertainty, and Profit* (1933). For a nontechnical overview, see Jon Elster, *Explaining Technical Change* 185–207 (1983).

56. Margaret Rosso Grossman, European Community Legislation for Traceability and Labeling of Genetically Modified, Crops, Food, and Feed, in *Labeling Genetically Modified Food*, supra note 10, at 36.

57. See Indur M. Goklany, *The Precautionary Principle: A Critical Appraisal of Environmental Risk Assessment* 7 (2001), observing that a "one-sided application of the Precautionary Principle itself provides no guidance ... in situations where an action ... could simultaneously lead to uncertain benefits and uncertain harms" [internal citation omitted]; Cass R. Sunstein, *Laws of Fear: Beyond the Precautionary Principle* 14 (2005), concluding that "the Precautionary Principle in its strongest forms is that it is incoherent" because "it purports to give guidance, but it fails to do so."

58. See *The Precautionary Principle*, supra note 57, at 1, collecting the "histories of a selection of hazards" and how the Precautionary Principle was applied to them to "try[] to reduce current and future risks"; Nabil I. Al-Najjar, *A Bayesian Framework for the Precautionary Principle*, 44 J. Legal Stud. S337, S361 (2016), concluding that the Precautionary Principle is a means of correcting human and societal biases; see also Caroline E. Foster, *Science and the Precautionary Principle in International Courts and Tribunals* 20 (2013), at 20, arguing that the Precautionary Principle has allowed "states to take action in response to the early warnings signs of [serious environmental] threats."

59. For an especially good discussion of this point, see generally Al-Najjar, supra note 58. Also valuable is Daniel Steel, *Philosophy and the Precautionary Principle: Science, Evidence, and Environmental Policy* (2014).

60. See Frank H. Knight, *Risk, Uncertainty, and Profit* 19–20 (1985) (1921), distinguishing measurable uncertainties, or "'risk' proper," from unknowable uncertainties, called *uncertainty*; Paul Davidson, *Is Probability Theory Relevant for Uncertainty? A Post Keynesian Perspective*, 5 J. Econ. Persp. 129, 129–131 (1991), describing the difference between true uncertainty and risk; Cass R. Sunstein, *Irreversible and Catastrophic*, 91 Cornell L. Rev. 841, 848 (2006), noting that for risk, "probabilities can be assigned to various outcomes," whereas for uncertainty, "no such probabilities can be assigned." For a technical treatment of the possible rationality of maximin, see generally Kenneth J. Arrow and Leonid Hurwicz, *An Optimality Criterion for Decision-Making under Ignorance*, in Uncertainty and Expectations in Economics: Essays in Honor of G. L. S. Shackle 1 (C. F. Carter and J. L. Ford eds., 1972). For a

nontechnical overview, see Jon Elster, *Explaining Technical Change*, app. 1 at 185–207 (1983).

61. See *The Precautionary Principle*, supra note 57, at 217 tbl.17.1, defining *ignorance* as "'unknown' impacts and therefore 'unknown' probabilities."

62. For a discussion of maximin, see John Rawls, *A Theory of Justice* 152–157 (1971). For information about complications of "acting as if the worst will happen," see Elster, supra note 60, app. 1 at 203–204. See also Adrian Vermeule, *Rationally Arbitrary Decisions in Administrative Law*, 44 J. Legal Stud. S475, S478 (2015): "In the face of uncertainty a rational decision maker may set the α-value—the parameter that captures pessimism or optimism—anywhere within a range defined by the worst-case and best-case scenarios." Relevant discussion also can be found in Martin L. Weitzman, *Fat-Tailed Uncertainty in the Economics of Catastrophic Climate Change*, 5 Rev. Envtl. Econ. & Pol'y 275, 276 (2011), which discusses "structural uncertainties in the economics of extreme climate change."

8 The Role of Courts

1. *Michigan v. EPA*, 135 S. Ct. 2699 (2015); *Business Roundtable v. SEC*, 647 F3d 1144 (D.C. Cir. 2011); *Nat'l Ass'n of Home Builders v. EPA*, 682 F.3d 1032, 1040 (D.C. Cir. 2012); *Corrosion Proof Fittings v. EPA*, 947 F.2d 1201 (5th Cir. 1991); *Center for Biological Diversity v. NHTSA*, 538 F.3d 1172 (DC Cir 2008); *Indus. & Fin. Mkts Ass'n v. CFTC*, 67 F. Supp. 3d 373 (D.D.C. 2014). Thirty-eight recent cases are examined in Caroline Cecot and W. Kip Viscusi, *Judicial Review of Agency Benefit-Cost Analysis*, 22 Geo. Mason L. Rev. 575 (2015).

2. *Michigan v. EPA*, 135 S. Ct. 2699 (2015).

3. *American Textile Mfrs. Inst. v. Donovan*, 452 U.S. 490 (1981). There, the court wrote: "Thus, § 6(b)(5) directs the Secretary to issue the standard that 'most adequately assures … that no employee will suffer material impairment of health,' limited only by the extent to which this is 'capable of being done.' In effect, then, as the Court of Appeals held, Congress itself defined the basic relationship between costs and benefits by placing the 'benefit' of worker health above all other considerations save those making attainment of this 'benefit' unachievable. Any standard based on a balancing of costs and benefits by the Secretary that strikes a different balance than that struck by Congress would be inconsistent with the command set forth in § 6(b)(5). Thus, cost-benefit analysis by OSHA is not required by the statute, because feasibility analysis is." Id., at 509.

4. See *Chevron U.S.A., Inc. v. Natural Resources Defense Council, Inc.*, 467 U.S. 837 (1984).

5. Because they do not raise different issues, I shall treat the two the same, referring in general to arbitrariness review.

6. *Corrosion Proof Fittings v. EPA*, 947 F.2d 1201 (5th Cir. 1991).

7. See *Am. Trucking Ass'ns v. EPA*, 175 F.3d 1027, 1051–1053 (D.C. Cir. 1999); *CEI v. NHTSA*, 956 F.2d 321 (D.C. Cir. 1992); see also *American Water Works Ass'n. v. EPA*, 40 F.3d 1266 (D.C. Cir. 1994). To be sure, some risks, said to follow from risk regulation, have a sufficiently complex causal connection to that regulation that agencies are not required to consider them. For example, air-pollution regulation might increase unemployment, and unemployment increases risks (for those who are unemployed); but no case holds that it is arbitrary for agencies to decline to consider those risks.

8. *Chemical Manufacturers Assn. v. EPA*, 217 F.3d 861 (D.C. Cir. 2000).

9. See *Michigan v. EPA*, 135 S. Ct. 2699 (2015).

10. *Michigan v. EPA*, 135 S. Ct. 2699 (2015).

11. Id., at 2704–2705.

12. Id., at 2707.

13. Id.

14. Id., at 2716–2717 (Kagan, J., dissenting; emphasis added). The dissent rejected the majority's conclusion in large part because the EPA had considered costs at a later stage in its processes, when it was deciding on the appropriate level of stringency. Id., at 2719–2721.

15. Id. at 2711.

16. See *Vermont Yankee Nuclear Power Corp. v. NRDC*, 435 U.S. 518 (1978).

17. *Business Roundtable v. SEC*, 647 F.3d 1144 (D.C. Cir. 2011).

18. *Business Roundtable*, 647 F.3d at 1150 (citations omitted) (quoting Pub. Citizen v. Fed. Motor Carrier Safety Admin., 374 F.3d 1209, 1221 (D.C. Cir. 2004)).

19. Id., at 1146, noting that this analysis was required by "Section 3(f) of the Exchange Act and Section 2(c) of the Investment Company Act of 1940, codified at 15 U.S.C. §§ 78c(f) and 80a-2(c), respectively."

20. See *Business Roundtable*, 647 F.3d, at 1149, rebuking the agency for "neglect[ing] to support its predictive judgments"; id., at 1151, criticizing the agency's use of "mixed empirical evidence" (quotation marks omitted).

21. Id., at 1148–49.

22. See 42 U.S.C. §7409(b)(1); *Whitman v. Am. Trucking Ass'ns, Inc.*, 531 U.S. 457 (2001).

23. 29 U.S.C. § 655(b)(5); *Indus. Union Dep't v. Am. Petroleum Inst.* (the Benzene Case), 448 U.S. 607 (1980).

24. For related discussion, see Cass R. Sunstein, *Cost-Benefit Default Principles*, 99 Mich. L. Rev. 1651 (2001).

25. See 66 Fed. Reg. 6976, 7009 (January 22, 2001).

26. *Inv. Co. Inst. v. Commodity Futures Trading Comm'n*, 720 F.3d 370, 372–375 (D.C. Cir. 2013).

27. 556 U.S. 502, 519–520 (2009).

28. Federal Motor Vehicle Safety Standards; Rear Visibility, 79 Fed. Reg. 19,178, 19,178–19,179 (April 7, 2014).

29. See Sean Williams, *Statistical Children*, 30 Yale J. Reg. 63 (2013), http://papers .ssrn.com/sol3/papers.cfm?abstract_id=2176463.

30. "We estimate that people with the relevant disabilities will use a newly accessible single-user toilet room with an out-swinging door approximately 677 million times per year. Dividing the $32.6 million annual cost by the 677 million annual uses, we conclude that for the costs and benefits to break even in this context, people with the relevant disabilities will have to value safety, independence, and the avoidance of stigma and humiliation at just under 5 cents per use." Dep't of Justice: Disability Rights Section of the Civil Rights Division, Final Regulatory Impact Analysis of the Final Revised Regulations Implementing Titles II and III of the ADA, Including Revised ADA Standards for Accessible Design 143 (2010), http://www.ada .gov/regs2010/RIA_2010regs/DOJ%20ADA%CC20Final%20RIA.pdf.

31. "We estimate that people with the relevant disabilities will use a newly accessible single-user toilet room with an in-swinging door approximately 8.7 million times per year. Dividing the $19.14 million annual cost by the 8.7 million annual uses, we conclude that for the costs and benefits to break even in this context, people with the relevant disabilities will have to value safety, independence, and the avoidance of stigma and humiliation at approximately $2.20 per use." Id.

32. "Under this methodology, for three of these four requirements, persons with disabilities need place a value of less than 1 cent on the benefits of avoided humiliation and/or improved safety (or any other non-monetized benefits) on each visit to facilities with elements affected by these requirements in order to make each requirements' respective NPVs equal zero." Id., at 146.

33. "The second threshold estimate, by contrast, calculates the average monetary value each American (on a per capita basis) would need to place annually (over a fifteen year period) on the 'existence' of improved accessibility for persons with disabilities (or the 'insurance' of improved accessibility for their own potential use in the future) in order for the NPVs for each respective requirement to equal zero. Under this methodology, if Americans on average placed an 'existence' value and/or 'insurance' value of between 2 cents on the low end to 7 cents on the high end per requirement, then the NPVs for each of these requirements would be zero. Note that

this later calculation assumes no added value of avoided humiliation, of increase safety and increased independence." Id.

9 Privacy and National Security

1. See http://www.foxnews.com/on-air/fox-news-sunday-chris-wallace/2013/06/16/ former-vice-president-dick-cheney-talks-nsa-surveillance-program#p//v/ 2482865656001.

2. James Bamford and Tim De Chant, *Exclusive: Edward Snowden on Cyber Warfare,* PBS, January 8, 2015, http://www.pbs.org/wgbh/nova/next/military/snowden -transcript/.

3. See Eric Klinenberg, *Heat Wave* (2000).

4. Paul Slovic, *The Perception of Risk* 40 (2000).

5. Id.

6. Id.

7. Amos Tversky and Daniel Kahneman, *Judgment under Uncertainty: Heuristics and Biases,* 186 Science 1124 (1974).

8. See Eyal Zamir, *Law, Psychology, and Morality: The Role of Loss Aversion* (2014).

9. Cass R. Sunstein, *Probability Neglect,* 112 Yale L. J. 61 (2002).

10. See E. J. Johnson et al., *Framing, Probability Distortions, and Insurance Decisions,* 7 H. Risk and Uncertainty 35 (1993).

11. See A. S. Alkahami and Paul Slovic, *A Psychological Study of the Inverse Relation- ship between Perceived Risk and Perceived Benefit,* 14 Risk Analysis 1086, 1094–1094 (1994).

12. See Ron Suskind, *The One Percent Doctrine* (2007).

13. See Gerd Gigerenzer, *Dread Risk, September 11, and Fatal Traffic Accidents,* 15 Psych. Science 286 (2004).

14. See Jon Elster, *Explaining Technical Change* 185–207 (1983), for a helpful discussion.

10 Free Speech

1. On the underlying issues, see Frederick Schauer, *Free Speech: A Philosophical Inquiry* (1982).

2. See Amartya Sen, *Utilitarianism and Welfarism,* 76 J. Phil. 463 (1979).

3. 341 U.S. 494 (1951).

4. *United States v. Carroll Towing Co.*, 159 F.2d 169 (2d. Cir. 1947).

5. *Whitney v. California*, 274 U.S. 357 (1927) (Brandeis, J., concurring).

6. Id.

7. See *Masses Publishing Co. v. Patten*, 244 F. 535 (S.D.N.Y. 1917).

8. Gerald Gunther, *Learned Hand and the Origins of Modern First Amendment Doctrine—Some Fragments of History*, 27 Stan. L. Rev. 719, 770 (1975).

9. Id., at 725 (2d ed. 2010).

10. See J. S. Mill, *On Liberty* (1859).

11. See Thomas Healy, *The Great Dissent* (2013).

12. 395 U.S. 444 (1969).

13. See the powerful presentation in Geoffrey R. Stone, *Perilous Times* (2004).

Index